Crucibles

Crucibles

**HOW FORMIDABLE RITES *of* PASSAGE SHAPE
THE WORLD'S MOST ELITE ORGANIZATIONS**

James R. McNeal
J. Eric Smith

A B2 BOOK
AGATE
CHICAGO

First printed in June 2025
Printed in the United States of America

Cover design: Morgan Krehbiel
Cover image: "The Oath of the Horatii" by Jacques-Louis David, courtesy of the Toledo Museum of Art
James R. McNeal portrait: Heather Crowder Modern Portrait
J. Eric Smith portrait: Jill Kristine Photography

10 9 8 7 6 5 4 3 2 1   25 26 27 28 29

Library of Congress Cataloging-in-Publication Data

Names: McNeal, James R., author. | Smith, J. Eric, 1965- author.
Title: Crucibles : how formidable rites of passage shape the world's most elite organizations / James R. McNeal and J. Eric Smith.
Description: Chicago : B2 Books, 2025. | Includes bibliographical references and index. |
Identifiers: LCCN 2024050828 (print) | LCCN 2024050829 (ebook) | ISBN 9781572843523 (hardcover) | ISBN 9781572848979 (ebook)
Subjects: LCSH: Rites and ceremonies. | Initiation rites. | Organizational commitment.
Classification: LCC GN473 .M36 2025 (print) | LCC GN473 (ebook) | DDC 394/.4--dc23/eng/20250205
LC record available at https://lccn.loc.gov/2024050828
LC ebook record available at https://lccn.loc.gov/2024050829

B2 Books is an imprint of Agate Publishing. Agate books are available in bulk at discount prices. For more information, visit agatepublishing.com.

This book is dedicated to the memories of our proud Marine Corps fathers, Col. Charles R. Smith Jr. and Capt. Robert James McNeal, recognizing and respecting both the crucibles they endured and the crucibles they created.

TABLE OF CONTENTS

PROLOGUE:

On Being a Plebe (Part 1), Annapolis, Maryland, Summer 1982

"Training is everything. The peach was once a bitter almond; cauliflower is nothing but cabbage with a college education."
—Mark Twain

"It was written I should be loyal to the nightmare of my choice."
—Joseph Conrad

A S HIS HIGH SCHOOL CAREER wound to its close through the 1980–81 school year, Jim McNeal's plans hinged on one driving consideration: getting far from California's suburban San Fernando Valley, where his family had settled as his father pursued a career with the Federal Bureau of Investigation after he left the United States Marine Corps. It was, Jim thought, a reasonable plan for an ambitious young man with dreams of seeing the world, but as is so often the case for such ambitious young men and women with such worldly dreams, financing said academic adventures far from home was not going to be possible without full parental support. And Jim's parents were not planning to offer said support, believing, equally reasonably, that California's state-run universities would provide their smart and athletic son with a perfectly fine collegiate experience, subsidized with those precious tuition discounts available for in-state students whose parents were conscientious taxpayers in the Golden State, as they were.

As he was prepping for and then taking the innumerable standardized admissions tests and completing the complex applications that typically define the latter part of the high school experience for college-bound students, Jim elected to have his PSAT scores sent to his father's alma mater, the United States Naval Academy in Annapolis, Maryland. The school was one of the country's most selective, sure, but it was located a long way away from the Los Angeles suburbs, and it did not charge tuition in the traditional sense, so the financial arguments against Jim's studies far from home would be negated, he figured. Of course, attendance at the Naval Academy was not actually "free," as the terms of admission and graduation from Annapolis involved a minimum five-year commitment on active duty in the U.S. Navy or Marine Corps, conceivably in harm's way, after the four years of college study. But the average American seventeen-year-old does not necessarily understand the nuances of such noncash transactions for services rendered, and plus, that possible payment period and its attendant perils were years away and could be worried about when they needed to be worried about. If then. If ever.

As Jim's senior year in high school drew to its close, he had not heard anything affirmative from Annapolis about his interest in attending the Naval Academy, but he had been accepted to a couple of other schools close to home, and he needed to advise them of his intentions before May 1, 1981. He waited, hopefully, until nearly the last minute, when at last he received a message from the Academy, informing him that he had not been admitted for the upcoming year, but inviting him to attend the Naval Academy Preparatory School (NAPS) in Newport, Rhode Island, for a year instead. Should Jim complete his course of studies at NAPS, he would be admitted to the Naval Academy in the summer of 1982 as a member of Navy's Class of 1986. Jim had never heard of NAPS, but Newport was a long way from the San Fernando Valley, and it was "free" (in the same way that the Academy was "free," i.e., not really), so he felt he had received a winning offer, and he accepted its terms.

Upon arriving in Newport, Jim and his classmates were officially enlisted into the Navy as seaman recruits ("E-1s" in Department of Defense cross-service parlance). Members of Jim's class who had come to NAPS from prior active-duty enlistment in the Navy retained the ranks they had already achieved, which ranged as high as petty officer second class (E-5). The cohort underwent a three-week boot-camp program overseen by members of the Naval Academy's Class of 1982, who would be returning for their senior (midshipman first class) year at Annapolis that autumn. Once that initial drill-style training period was over, the members of Jim's NAPS cohort got down to their studies, lightly overseen by an active-duty company officer and a senior enlisted master chief petty officer. For the most part, they were left to their own devices over the course of the year (later on, Jim would remember it as being "a tad bit of *Lord of the Flies*") and treated like any other enlisted personnel within Newport's then-large Navy community, frequenting the Enlisted Club to drink cheap beer in their off hours and using their modest paychecks on the modest entertainments available to young men and women in uniform far from the home communities where most of them had been raised. While the academic regimen was challenging, but not inordinately difficult, the payoff (i.e., admission to the Naval Academy) often did not prove to be as strong a motivating factor as it might have seemed when its students first committed to NAPS. Jim's class suffered high attrition accordingly, with about 40 percent of the class not making it to their commencement in the spring of 1982.

Jim did complete the course of study, and he also managed his finances better than some of his classmates, managing to scrape together enough of his E-1 money to buy a car during his year in Newport. Upon graduating from NAPS, and with six weeks of downtime awaiting before his reporting date at Annapolis, Jim and one of his classmates embarked on a cross-country road trip home to California. Their route included a stop at the Knoxville

(Tennessee) International Energy Exposition, better known then and to posterity as the 1982 World's Fair, a festival-style celebration of international science initiatives that drew 11 million visitors over the course of its six-month run. The exciting technologies and products revealed to the public at that World's Fair included touch-screen technology, pay-at-the-pump gas station terminals, cordless telephones, and Cherry Coke.

While their paths did not cross at the time, to the best of their knowledge, while Jim McNeal was at the World's Fair, one of the other visitors to Knoxville was J. Eric Smith, a long-haired senior from White Oak High School in Jacksonville, North Carolina. White Oak had chosen the World's Fair for its Class of 1982's senior trip, ostensibly to offer its upcoming graduates with a glimpse of tomorrow's science and technology, though said graduates, with Eric as an admitted ringleader, seemed far more interested in opportunities for debauched partying on the lightly chaperoned adventure. Eric's father was a career officer in the U.S. Marine Corps and had deployed some months before the World's Fair for Beirut, Lebanon, where he was serving as the executive officer for the 32nd Marine Amphibious Unit during one of the more extremely fraught periods of that troubled nation's often-parlous history.

Eric's father's travels with the Marine Corps had resulted in Eric attending four different high schools, two in New York, one in Newport, Rhode Island (the year before Jim was there), and concluding with his senior year at White Oak. Frequent moves of that variety among active-duty families typically produce one of two types of military brats: those who disappear into the woodwork and just put their heads down and work, knowing that any connections they make are going to be ephemeral; and those who develop flamboyant personalities to stand out wherever they go, however briefly they may be there. Eric was one of the latter, a smart, creative, and highly undisciplined student who wrote provocative articles for the school newspaper and formed a country-punk band before many had thought to merge those disparate musical elements. Eric was not pioneering. He just thought he had come up with the most absurd musical concept imaginable.

Eric was also the unlikely possessor of an appointment to the United States Naval Academy as a member of the Class of 1986; his father's standing as a current active-duty officer deployed in harm's way helped in that regard, as did his grandfather's political connections in North Carolina, which greased the skids for Eric to receive one of the coveted congressional appointments to the Academy offered that year by Senator Jesse Helms. Having received his appointment in the spring of 1982, Eric essentially deemed school to be an optional pursuit for the remainder of the year, viewing it as more of a social endeavor than an academic one. Since appointments to the Naval Academy were prestigious for the high schools whose students earned them, White Oak did not much bother pressing the point of classroom attendance with Eric or his mother. He graduated just after his seventeenth birthday (having skipped a grade some years earlier in elementary school and having always been among the youngest members of his academic cohorts ever since), and, like Jim, Eric then had six weeks of downtime before heading to Annapolis. He spent most of it at the beach, happy to know that he also had a "free" college education coming up, unencumbered by any lingering familial or financial constraints.

In early July 1982, Jim flew from California to Washington, DC, for a final night of freedom with some fellow NAPS classmates at a family friend's house in Springfield, Virginia, the day before they were to report to the Naval Academy with the rest of their surviving NAPS cohort. The NAPSters were scheduled to check in at the Academy the day before the incoming high school graduates (like Eric) were to arrive, at which time the Class of 1986 would assemble for the first time to take the Oath of Office. Eric was in nearby Mount Vernon, Virginia, in early July, having driven up with his mother and sister, staying with a family they had known since Eric was in third grade, the eldest son of which was going for his own induction at the Virginia Military Institute later that same week. Early on the morning of July 7, 1982, the Smiths headed over to Annapolis for the first time to see where Eric would spend his next four years. In those simpler pre-internet days, they had few if any preconceived notions of what they would find when they got there, beyond some pretty pictures in a glossy admissions package they had received.

The first few hours after Eric arrived at the Academy were a busy blur, as he and his fellow incoming high school graduates were registered, issued uniforms and books and other military sundries, given brutal haircuts (Jim already had one), organized into little training groups (Eric was put in the 23rd Platoon of Hotel Company, while Jim was assigned to India Company's 27th Platoon), and guided to their rooms in "Mother B" (Bancroft Hall, the immense dormitory where all midshipmen live). Having arrived with the NAPS cohort, Jim had already been to his room, and had taken the time and effort to get the lay of the land of "The Yard" (as the Naval Academy's campus is known) before the entire class arrived, which turned out to be quite an advantageous position for him to be in. The Academy's officers and midshipmen first class tasked with training the incoming Class of 1986 were brisk, but polite, and despite the hustle and bustle of the day, a sense of excitement grew among the soon-to-be-minted midshipmen, along with a general feeling of confidence that, yeah, we can do this!

Later that afternoon, the Class of 1986 was awkwardly mustered for the first time into amateur-looking military formations in the Academy's centrally located Tecumseh Court, heads freshly shaven and sweating in their itchy government-issue sailor's uniforms and "Dixie cup" hats. At the appointed hour, approximately 1,400 young men and women (mainly men, as the Class of 1986 was only the seventh class in the Academy's his-

tory to include female members, who were still a small minority
of the class accordingly), raised their right hands and collectively
repeated, upon command, the following words:

*I, [name], do solemnly swear that I will support and
defend the Constitution of the United States against
all enemies, foreign and domestic; that I will bear true
faith and allegiance to the same; that I take this obligation freely, without any mental reservation or purpose of
evasion; and that I will well and faithfully discharge the
duties of the office of which I am about to enter. So help
me God.*

At that point, Jim and Eric and their classmates were officially admitted with pay and benefits to the United States Navy
as midshipmen fourth class, technically classified as "officers of
the line," though with limited authority due to their training status. From a legal and payroll standpoint, all midshipmen (the
fourth, third, second, and first class designations align with the
traditional freshmen, sophomore, junior, and senior cohorts of
a "normal" college) are ranked between the levels of warrant
officers (W-1s) and the lowest grades of chief warrant officers
(W-2s). Eric and Jim also officially became, as they completed
their Oaths, enrolled students at the Naval Academy, one of five
federally owned and operated schools tasked with training commissioned officers for the United States Armed Forces.

"Navy" (as it is colloquially known, most especially for its
collegiate sports teams) is the second oldest of the service academies, having been founded in 1845, four-plus decades after
its academic and athletic archrival, the U.S. Military Academy
at West Point, New York ("Army" to its alumni and devotees).
The Naval Academy offers a four-year collegiate program culminating in the award of accredited and highly regarded bachelor of science degrees in a variety of academic disciplines, while

also offering mandatory courses in naval arts and sciences and requiring its students to participate in a wide variety of athletics, physical readiness programs, and leadership training activities. The Academy has always stressed that traditional school studies are but one component under its purview, chartered as it is with preparing midshipmen "morally, mentally, and physically" for their expected service in the Navy or Marine Corps. (The Marine Corps, as an autonomous part of the Department of the Navy, under the Department of Defense, does not have its own service academy).

After taking the Oath and becoming "links in the chain" of Navy's long history, Jim and Eric and their classmates were given a short time to say goodbye to their families, along with instructions to be in their rooms by a set time soon thereafter. When those instructions were given, it seemed like the time granted to complete those steps would be more than adequate, so Eric dawdled a bit, giving his teary mother and too-cool teen sister time to fawn over their beloved son and brother before he set off to be a big boy with the other big girls and boys. Jim's parents did not travel to Annapolis for his induction day, planning instead to visit that autumn when Jim's father came for his twentieth class reunion. Having been briefed about what was to come during his time at NAPS, Jim wisely took his time making his way back to his room, circuitously staying outside of Mother B for as long as he possibly could, then slipping into his room in the remote Eighth Wing of Bancroft Hall to await his roommate's arrival, which did not come until nearly two hours later.

Eric, not having been briefed, waved farewell to his family, and lazily stepped back into Bancroft Hall at the nearest entry point, at which point all hell broke loose. He thought he had remembered how to get from Tecumseh Court (where the Oath had been issued) back to his room on the Fourth Deck (e.g., fifth floor, with the ground as Deck Zero) of the Sixth Wing of Mother B, but the place was truly a rat's nest maze, and there were cer-

tain stairs that "Plebes" (as midshipmen fourth class were and
are derisively known) could use, and some they could not, and
all elevators were out of the question. Complicating the journey
was the fact that Plebes had specific instructions on how they
were to move about Bancroft Hall: they must "ping" (essentially
a stiff-legged race-walk) at all times, they could only move down
the center of Bancroft Hall's corridors, they could only turn corners on silver plates embedded in the floors of those corridors
at various key junction points (shouting "Go Navy!" or "Beat
Army!" with each pivot and turn), and they had to keep their
heads forward at all times, only able to catch room numbers or
glimpses down desired corridors out of the corners of their eyes.
It made for difficult navigation for the disoriented newcomers to
the Academy's vast dormitory complex.

Even more dramatically complicating that first journey was
the fact that the formerly brisk and polite officers and midshipmen first class (most especially the latter) had suddenly transformed into a pack of howling, raging, frothing-at-the-mouth
monsters, seemingly hell-bent on thwarting the Plebes' progress,
questioning their intelligence, scrambling their brains, and even
offering incorrect directions for the swarming ranks of panicked
young people pinging about Mother B's halls. For many Plebes,
that budding sense of "I can do this" lasted about three minutes
after they stepped back into Mother B, replaced immediately by
a deeper sense of "Oh my God, what have I done?!" The Plebes
also quickly realized that the midshipmen first class who were
tasked with training their new wards seemed less interested in
helping them develop "morally, mentally, and physically," and
more interested in crushing their souls, quickly and completely.

Eric eventually made it to his room (it took him less time
than Jim's roommate's two-hour-long slog, but not by much),
and found his own new roommate already there, along with a
few sheets of paper on his assigned desk. He flopped down on
his bed, ready to take a load off and rest and recover for a bit,

but his roommate (who was another former enlisted sailor, and like Jim, had been given "good gouge," Navy slang for straight dope or inside information, on what was to come) told him that he needed to read those sheets of paper on the desk as quickly as he could because their little respite was not going to last long.

The required reading was a short essay called "A Message to Garcia," which Eric and Jim later learned was written by Elbert Hubbard in 1899. Eric started to skim it quickly: some guy named Rowan had to find some guy named Garcia, who was in some jungle somewhere because President McKinley needed to get him some message, and Rowan did not know where Garcia was, but he set out anyway and . . .

BLAAAMM!!!! The door to Eric's room was kicked open, and some howling midshipman first class demanded that he and his fellow victims assemble into squads and platoons in the sweltering main corridor of their company area. Like some macroscopic examples of Brownian motion, the Plebe members of Hotel and India Companies careened about and ricocheted off each other trying to assemble themselves into their proper molecular structures, all while pinging, and turning corners on the damned metal plates, and bracing up (i.e., keeping the chin pulled back to the neck as tightly possible), and trying to answer the barrage of questions and demands being fired at them from all sides.

Once assembled, the Plebes were interrogated about "A Message to Garcia," eventually figuring out that the message they were supposed to learn from "Garcia" was that when given an order, military personnel were just to execute it to the best of their abilities, without pestering their senior officers for information on why they were to do what they were told, or how, or when, or where. Or something like that. It was all a bit of a blur for the pitiful Plebes.

The rest of I-Day (as July 7, 1982, was known for the Class of 1986) offered more of the same. And then the Plebes finally slept. Or at least they laid in their beds and tossed and turned in the sweltering Annapolis summer heat, as Bancroft Hall was a vast non-air-conditioned space at the time, capped with a broiling copper-topped roof. And then the Plebes of '86 got up early the next day for some heinous morning calisthenics and sprints and gymnastics called "PEP," (a wry, bordering on cruel, acronym for "physical education program") overseen by a ridiculously spry and highly caffeinated septuagenarian named Heinz Lenz, who truly looked and sounded like somebody sent from central casting for a World War II German prisoner of war camp commandant movie role. And then the Plebes marched, and ran, and studied from a little book called *Reef Points*, a massive volume of "rates" (arcane and detailed Navy factoids) that Plebes were required to spout upon command, and then the Plebes got yelled at because they didn't know their rates, and then they ran, and swam, and marched, and shot things, and sailed things, and climbed things, and crawled under things, and ran, and swam, and studied, and got yelled at, over and over and over again.

The Class of 1986's Plebe Summer program, as that boot camp phase of the Academy's training was known, lasted until August 21, 1982, with one tiny little two-day reprieve for Parents Weekend, when the howling dervishes training the Plebes got brisk and polite again for a couple of days while outside witnesses were around and about. Jim's parents did not make the trip back East, so he enjoyed some private and quiet downtime. Eric's mother and sister returned for a nice weekend visit, and as the deadline to return to Bancroft Hall crept up, they were hanging out in a hotel near the Academy, monitoring the time on the hotel room clock. Alas, and in pre-cellphone days, said clock was nearly an hour slow, meaning that Eric arrived for the first post–Parents Weekend formation nearly an hour late.

Eric and Jim had both actually done okay, all things considered, through Plebe Summer's First Set (the period before Parents Weekend) and had both gotten decent performance reviews, in some large part because their upbringing in Marine

Corps households meant that they already knew a lot of the basic military rates, e.g., the names of the various ranks of the various services, how chains of command worked, and how to quickly learn and remember the names and hometowns of their company mates, which was really no harder than going to a new school regularly and having to do the same through elementary, middle, and high school. They also both had the unexpected psychological benefit of being raised by Marine Corps officers, and no one at the Naval Academy was ever going to be able to yell at them worse than their own fathers had. Tack on the fact that Jim and Eric were also both blessed with good memories for seemingly useless facts (which many of the required rates, frankly, were), and that was a recipe for success through the early travails of Plebe Summer.

But that late arrival to formation after Parents Weekend clearly rebranded Eric as "trouble!" in the eyes of the new group of midshipmen first class who helmed the Second Set, who had already seemed perversely interested in focusing on and breaking the Plebes who had done well through First Set. While Eric's "formal" punishment for missing formation was a mild (in relative terms) chewing-out and counseling session with his company officer, the "informal" responses from various midshipmen first class were far more damaging and directed, with Eric being singled out for particular harassment of both a physical (e.g., repeated "Come Around" sessions to spout rates while standing at rigid attention, occasionally while holding a heavy drill rifle) and psychological (e.g., constant reminders of the failure paired with dire promises that his Naval Academy career would be but a brief one) nature. That focused abuse took its toll: by the end of the Second Set's three-week regime, Eric had dropped down to the bottom ranking in his company, beginning what would prove to be his sub-illustrious career as a Naval Academy "shit screen," the lowest of the lowest dregs of the Class of 1986, upon which all the filth of the place eventually settled, bypassing the backs of the better-performing midshipmen. Jim dodged that bullet and maintained good-quality performance reviews through Second Set, positioning himself well as the next phase of the Naval Academy experience began to loom large on the horizon.

Plebe Summer was physically, mentally, and psychologically grueling, certainly, as the members of the Class of 1986 (and all who came before them, and all who followed) were pushed extremely hard to test their capabilities and capacities for suffering, and to evaluate whether they could function lucidly under such stress for a sustained period. But throughout that long, hot summer, the Plebes knew that ten days before Labor Day, Plebe Summer would officially end, and the remainder of the Brigade of Midshipmen would return to Annapolis. (Only a small cohort of the Class of 1983 were in Annapolis with the Plebes during Summer training, while most of their classmates and the entire Classes of 1984 and 1985 were deployed to various ships and bases around the world for training). When the seemingly traditional college portion of the Naval Academy experience began, it seemed conceptually impossible that all the things that were demanded of the Plebes during Plebe Summer could possibly continue within an academic year that typically had each midshipman required to register for twenty-plus credit hours of hard classroom work each semester.

And so, in due time, Jim, Eric, and most of their surviving classmates celebrated without fanfare, in their own small and tired ways, the end of Plebe Summer when it arrived, expecting that the most grueling part of their training was past, and that they had successfully navigated the worst that the Naval Academy had to offer.

They were very, very wrong.

(To be continued in the Epilogue . . .)

INTRODUCTION

Trials by Fire: The Roles of Crucibles in Defining Elite Groups and Cultures

"It is trial that proves one thing weak and another strong. A house built on sand is in fair weather just as good as if built upon a rock. And a cobweb is as good as the mightiest cable when there is no strain put upon it."
—Henry Ward Beecher

"How can we be in, if there is no outside?"
—Peter Gabriel

THROUGHOUT RECORDED HUMAN HISTORY, CIVILIZATIONS have stratified their citizens, by both implicit and explicit societal practices, beliefs, expectations, inheritances, and economics. Different civilizations have placed different members of their local social strata at the pinnacles of power and prestige through the establishment of selected, elected, or hereditary royal, priestly, and warrior classes, with some societies' leaders serving in all three roles. But in many times and many places throughout human history, there have been (and are) certain castes of citizens who have risen to positions of widespread authority, import, and power not by virtue of who they were born to, nor by virtue of their relative wealth, nor by popular acclamation, but instead by completing rigorous, codified rites of passage that demonstrate their commitment to their chosen vocations, their dedication to their organizations, and their exceptional physical, spiritual, or psychological capabilities in service to the causes they hold dear. The book you are reading is designed and intended to explore a

representative sampling of such elite organizations spanning multiple continents and centuries, with a special emphasis placed on
the onerous rituals and trials that were designed to separate the
wheat from the chaff, demonstrating for all and sundry that those
who completed such "crucibles" (as we dub them) were worthy of
esteem and acclaim, and capable of pursuing and achieving their
organizations' objectives.

Before digging into this collection of formidable (and hopefully interesting) formal rites of passage from a variety of historical periods and geographical locations, we wish to first consider the actual meanings of this book's title: *Crucibles*. Arthur
Miller's acclaimed and oft-performed 1953 play, *The Crucible*,
represents the most common modern usage of the word per
search engine results and popular cultural knowledge, though
there is a reason why "explain what *The Crucible*'s title means
in the context of the play" is also a common auto-populating
search string, likely due to its frequency as an essay or test question in high school English classes, and because the answer is
not necessarily instantly obvious.

As with so many things in our gloriously grabby English language, the word's roots are Latinate, *crucibulum*, perhaps first
meaning a lamp hung before a cross (*crux*) at night; *-bulum* is a
suffix denoting an instrument, place, or vessel. "Crucible" evolved
in the Middle English period (the word is documented before
1500) to refer to a vessel (typically ceramic) capable of withstand-
ing extreme temperatures, so that solid metals placed within it
may be rendered into liquid form, the better to mold and shape
them into useful or beautiful products. That element of temper-
ing-by-fire, perhaps compounded by contemplation of the horrors
of the crucifixion (derived from the same Latin root), led to the
emergence of the modern and metaphorical definition most ger-
mane to our purposes here: crucibles are trials by fire (and often
pressure) that result in transformational changes in form upon
all objects placed within them. Ideally, objects placed in crucibles

may then be worked in positive, productive fashions, but it is also the case that some objects placed in crucibles are permanently wrecked beyond use or repair, due to excessive or inadequate tempering, failure to act upon them effectively during their periods of maximum malleability, or imperfections and impurities in either the vessel or the subjects being tempered within it.

At bottom line, a key element of a crucible in any use of the word is an aspect of extremity, where confined and defined spaces and processes are created for the explicit purposes of softening solid objects so that they may be transformed into other, hopefully better or more useful, objects. The front end of the process involves raw materials in unrefined or chaotic states, the back end of the process involves worked and finished outputs, and between those points, all forms of violence and destruction are wreaked in the name of an expected worthy good emerging from the often-dangerous transitional phase of the crucible. Key to the process is an element of purposefulness: metalsmiths do not just melt materials because it is cool and fun to do so (even though it is!)—they melt materials in certain ways and in certain combinations, and they mold their malleable matter toward a desired outcome, which may be functional, creative, or both.

That purposefulness must have emerged slowly over the centuries since the Stone Age yielded to the Bronze Age some four thousand to five thousand years ago, anchored in humankind's inquisitive observational skills. The origins of metalworking and the crucibles used as part of that process are lost to time, though we can imagine some early innovators perhaps observing viscous silver or gold threads emerging from rocks serendipitously placed in a fire pit, which cooled and dried into beautiful, shiny, collectable, and trade-worthy shapes. Over perhaps generations or centuries of trial and error, in many different locations and circumstances, those original accidental creative steps were codified, so that they could be replicated, making objects that were not just pretty, but functional, around the hearth, in the public forum, in spiritual spaces, and on the battlefield. Those processes would have been passed from generation to generation, either via family connections or by some ancient forms of guilds, where arcane knowledge was shared only between those with a right and a need to know it, thereby protecting its economic value and the social stature associated with its possession.

In some cases, the terms, conditions, and structures of human crucibles, as rites of passage, are well-documented and available within ready public purview. In others, the crucibles are "black boxes" in part or in full, with their governing organizations testing their would-be members through secretive practices, mythologies about which often contribute to such organizations' mystery, mystique, and meaning within their societies. Some of our chosen subject organizations stand in history's telling as admirable, constructive members of their societies, while others have used their crucibles to build organizations that actively or passively contributed to the undermining or destruction of the civilizations that birthed them. The nature of these crucibles means that they are often developed and deployed by military or military-adjacent organizations, and so such organizations dominate our narrative, but we have worked where we are able to include civic, social, or fraternal entities as well, hopefully providing a meaningful civilian perspective on trials by fire and rites of passage. And, of course, because the world's militaries have for much of human history been male-only organizations, the subjects of this book also skew hard in that gender-specific direction, though once again, we have worked to identify and document cases where women have either organized or endured their own formal crucible-type rites of passage.

As described in the prologue to this book (the first part of a story to which we will return in the epilogue), your authors first met in the summer of 1982 as Plebes (i.e., freshmen) at the United States Naval Academy in Annapolis, Maryland, completing the grueling Plebe Summer program and then the (slightly less grueling) Plebe Year together, a ten-month crucible that irrevocably reshaped who we are, how we think, what we do, and why we do it. While our Plebe Year travails were certainly not of a piece with some of the more extreme, bloody, fervid, and dangerous crucibles described in other chapters within this book, our own small experiences with a process that welcomed approximately 1,400 young men and women, and weeded about four hundred of them out before our graduation, does give us a sense of experience in being able to tell these stories, with some idea of what it feels like to be at the whims and mercies of people whose sole purpose in life often seems to be punishing and tormenting their charges into failure. But having thwarted those tenacious taskmasters, and having survived and completed those experiences, we immediately became "links in the chain" within a relatively small and elite community, bound together by shared experiences with our classmates, with those who came before us, and with those who followed. The final stanza of the Naval Academy alma mater, "Navy Blue and Gold," evokes this sentiment as a core component of our shared experience:

> *Four years together by the Bay where Severn joins the tide,*
> *Then by the Service called away, we're scattered far and wide.*
> *But still when two or three shall meet and old tales be retold,*
> *From low to highest in the Fleet will pledge the Blue and Gold.*

One of this book's coauthors, Rear Admiral James R. McNeal, is also the coauthor (with Scott Tomasheski) of *The Herndon Climb: A History of the United States Naval Academy's Greatest Tradition* (U.S. Naval Institute Press, 2020), the first comprehensive history of the ceremony that has marked the end point of the Plebe Year crucible for the better part of a century. A couple of years later, Jim and this book's other coauthor, J. Eric Smith, wrote and published *Side by Side in Eternity: The Lives Behind Adjacent American Military Graves* (McFarland Books, 2022). Many of the subjects covered in that book experienced their own formally constituted crucibles or crucibles by circumstance, though many of those same subjects did not survive them.

During a 2021 Homecoming Weekend event at the Naval Academy promoting *The Herndon Climb* and other recently published Naval Institute Press books, Jim discussed the then-forthcoming *Side by Side in Eternity*, and was unexpectedly asked by the event's moderator to preview his next planned book project. We had not actually thought or talked about that yet, but being quick on his feet and reading his audience well, Jim posited a tome about the evolution of the Plebe Summer experience over the years. And as that which is said in public must be treated as truth, we soon began to churn that concept a bit, eventually deciding that instead of a single-topic deep dive of *The Herndon Climb* variety, a themed multi-topic tome in the *Side by Side in Eternity* style might serve the varied concept of crucibles better, for us as writers and researchers, and for the readers who may elect to acquire our work. (For those wishing to delve further into one or more of the topics covered in this book, we provide a full bibliography of sources and suggested additional reading to support such further exploration.)

After developing a long list of candidate crucibles for this project, we worked to develop a set of lenses through which we could research and assess each crucible, as well as a rubric through which we could process the totality of the topics tackled, hopefully gleaning some meaningful macro commonalities that bind crucibles across time and place, and ideally developing some carryforward takeaways on how, when, and why they work best, along with some cautionary tales into the ways that they fail as indoctrination pipelines or fail the governing organizations, civilizations, or societies in which they arise and function. We then developed a summary questionnaire to guide and hone our own research and to frame our discussions with subject-matter experts, including many who have completed the crucibles we will study. Our big-picture questions included:

1. What are the key purposes, both internally (i.e., for an elite organization itself) and externally (i.e., for the society served by the elite organization) of grueling, crucible-style training and indoctrination rites of passage?

2. In considering multiple types of crucibles, are there universal threads that can be potentially codified to define the tools and approaches used by elite organizations in choosing and training their members?

3. Similarly, are there any universally problematic threads that can be potentially codified to express ways in which such elite organizations may harm themselves or their societies?

4. Are there differences between elite organizations that make their crucibles widely and publicly known versus those who conduct their indoctrinations in a more secretive fashion? And is that a matter of marketing their "eliteness" to the greater society, or a matter of bolstering the elites within the organization, separate from the expectations or understanding of the greater society?

5. Are crucible approaches a dying phenomenon in modern times, or are they becoming more common and widespread in modern times?

6. How well do such crucibles really work? Are they simply a form of self-indulgent and ritualized sadomasochism, or are they valuable to creating meaningful elite organizations within any given society?

7. Are there selection biases to be considered in evaluating crucibles (i.e., are crucibles that funnel willing volunteers into the elite organizations fundamentally different from those that conscript members)?

8. Are there leadership principles to be found in crucible-centric elite organizations that can be applied, positively or negatively, to business, government, military, academic, or other less "extreme" contemporary organizations?

As a test of concept before embarking on specific research into our chosen crucibles, we reviewed our guiding questions and list of crucibles with Dr. Marcus Hedahl, professor of philosophy in the Department of Leadership, Ethics, and Law at the U.S. Naval Academy. Dr. Hedahl is an alumnus of Notre Dame (Navy's second-most-intense football rivalry, for what that's worth, ranking only after archrival Army) and Georgetown (located in a neighborhood where we used to party during our Naval Academy days because the drinking age in the District of Columbia was younger than in Maryland, and because the crazy early-'80s live music and club scene there offered a refreshing reprieve from our daily doses of crucible), and per his website, Dr. Hedahl's areas of research range from theoretical issues of meta-ethics to more practical ethical considerations, including environmental ethics, business ethics, and military ethics. The Naval Academy's Department of Leadership, Ethics, and Law, where Dr. Hedahl teaches and conducts his research, is designed to provide the Navy midshipmen with (per the Academy's website) the ability to:

- Understand human behavior as it pertains to leaders in military organizations.
- Demonstrate increasingly complex applications of leadership skills related to human behavior, character, ethics, and military law.
- Integrate, analyze, and evaluate acquired knowledge and experience and effectively use it in the decision-making process.

"I think the first thing you need to explore," began Dr. Hedahl after reviewing our proposal materials, "is why societies would want to have certain groups fill certain functions at all, and why societies would want to allow those groups themselves to regulate who gets to become a member. I come at this question from a military perspective, and from that perspective, there is a key book for me that came out in 1957 called *The Soldier and the State* by Samuel Huntington. Then in 1986, Brigadier General

Malham Wakin, a longtime professor of philosophy at the U.S. Air Force Academy, built off Huntington's foundation in a work entitled *War, Morality, and the Military Profession.* Both Wakin and Huntington focus on the distinction between those who are professionals, as they define the term, and those who are not. That does not mean that the second group is not necessary, or that they do not take their work seriously, or that they do not work hard in important roles, or that they do not get paid well, or that they do not make society better. But there is a difference between those groups. And in general, the work that professionals do is inherently rather than instrumentally required to make their societies better.

"Some paradigmatic examples of 'professionals,' as Huntington and Wakin use the term, are doctors or lawyers," Dr. Hedahl explained further. "It can be hard for people who are not doctors or lawyers to tell the difference between someone who is good and qualified, and someone who is not. If you think about the case of doctors, we can tell if they heal someone, of course, but obviously a lot of people who go to doctors are not going to get better. Because, let's face it, doctors aren't gods. They can't cure everybody. So, what differentiates a good doctor from a bad doctor? I don't know the answer to that, but other doctors do. Same thing with lawyers. For some cases, you might think they are up in the air and either side can win, and for some cases it's going to be much more obvious that one side's going to win than the other. But good lawyers can still increase the odds that their clients will win, or if their clients are found guilty, good lawyers may be able to mitigate the punishment received. And if you think about who passes the bar, and who gets disbarred, that's not up to us, that's up to other lawyers. So as a society, we let doctors and lawyers decide who gets to be a doctor or a lawyer because the rest of us are not qualified to do so.

"Now, contrast those roles with someone who is, say, a chef, or who styles hair," continued Dr. Hedahl. "Those are incredibly skilled activities that most of us could not ever begin to replicate. It certainly takes a long time to learn and perfect those skills, but the difference in this case is that I, as a layperson, can generally tell the difference between a good cook and a bad cook, or between a good haircut or a bad haircut and even more importantly, those who aren't chefs and who aren't hairdressers can tell what skills are required to keep the rest of us safe, to prevent cooks who will get us sick and to prevent those without the minimum skills required from using scissors and razors near our heads. So, if other people can tell what makes a good or minimally competent 'whatever,' then it follows that maybe we ought not allow that group to have sole responsibility over who gets to become a member of that group. And that's why you don't absolutely have to go to culinary school to start a restaurant or work in a kitchen, since if your cooking is very good, it will be recognized as very good. And if it's not, it won't. Same thing with styling hair. Other people can evaluate or license those professions. When it comes to military professionals, or for most of the groups you are considering in your book, it makes perfect sense that there is a benefit to society to having the people who best understand what it takes to fill those roles be the people who determine who will fill those roles. The rest of us just cannot tell."

Having affirmed that there is a logical reason for certain organizations to control the portals through which their inductees and recruits must pass, we then solicited Dr. Hedahl's perspective on why many of those portals take the form of crucible-style trials by fire. "The purposes of most crucibles, I think, are rooted in the fact that some things are just really tough to do," responded Dr. Hedahl. "Let's use the example of the military. It is very, very hard to be a member of the military in combat, and it requires you to make the best decisions you can at any given moment, in a stressful environment where people can get hurt. It makes sense that you might want to replicate that in some minor way to see who is good at it, so the point of the crucible is to answer that question, to see who is good at the thing. But again, we let the people who are good at the thing decide who can join them because those are skills that not everybody can judge.

"So, the first part of a well-designed crucible, and not just a crucible for crucible's sake, is to differentiate who's going to be good at the required skills from who's not," Dr. Hedahl continued. "But there is another part to a good crucible, too: they create common bonds within groups where everyone has been through the same crucible. And in many organizations where people must work closely together in stressful situations, having that common bond is very important to organizational success. Another important part of those types of indoctrinations is that they are often completed publicly in some way, even if the actual training itself is done behind a cloak of darkness. The public factors differentiate people who are in the profession from those who are not.

"In the academic world, even if I did not go to some doctor's White Coat Ceremony [n.b.: a topic covered in a later chapter of this book], I know that they had one. That's also why people put their credentials on their walls, so that people know that they really are one of those things. It is a way of differentiating a real doctor from someone who is giving me medical advice just because we have been through similar circumstances. 'Oh, you have this issue? What I would recommend is this.' So, crucibles are important for two reasons: to determine who is good at the required skills, and to bond people together in some way as part of the same organization. But it is important that the crucibles have something to do with the purpose of the organization, and what it does, and that those crucibles can evolve, rather than just being hazing for hazing's sake, or because 'we've always done it that way,' which is often the case in, say, college fraternity initiation rites. You have these crucibles to join a fraternity, and those initiation rites often require you to do things that are not related to the thing you're being asked to do as a member of the fraternity. The idea is merely to make it hard for the brute fact of making it hard, or because the ritual may be tied to a particular history. But we must be willing to change those rituals if it turns out the thing that a person is doing in the ritual is not what is related to the thing that people will do in the profession."

One interesting point that emerged in our conversation with Dr. Hedahl was his focus on distinguishing the acts of training or indoctrination themselves from the rites and rituals used to affirm successful completion of the crucibles. "Oftentimes we think of the training and the rites as being indelibly linked together, like in your case at the end of Plebe Year, where your class completes the Herndon Climb and you all know that you're done with Plebe Year," Dr. Hedahl explained. "So, while those things may be linked together, they serve different purposes. The indoctrination rite is not the crucible. It is what you do *after* the crucible, and it is equally important. Typically, the group will do the rite together, often in public, and it clearly defines the end of a stage. It tells the organization or the society that, yes, we have a role to play, we can do it well, we are bound together as a community, and we remind people who went through it before of the ongoing significance of the rite. We do the rite or ritual in a certain way because going through that reminds us, every time someone does it, of how we are to be excellent together. So, the crucible and the rite have different purposes. Sometimes we might do them together to reinforce the rite, and to reinforce that it is meant to be hard. But they have different purposes, and we can often see them broken apart, where we have the crucible, and then we have the rite."

In the chapters that follow, we will evaluate a variety of crucibles and their related rites through the lens of our guiding questions, supported by Dr. Hedahl's perspective and observations. As far apart in time and space as the various groups we will cover have been and are, and as seemingly at odds as their goals and philosophies may seem, we believe they may deploy common tactics and strategies in bringing their initiates into their "elite" societies. It is our hope that the act of documenting commonalities between (say) the Knights Templar and (say, again) the Mafia should make for an entertaining and educational journey, and we are delighted to have you join us in our exploration of history's most formidable rites of passage.

If you are inclined to drop and give us twenty to get in the proper headspace for what follows, please feel free. We have already done so, but we will be cheering you on.

CHAPTER 1

We Make Marines: Boot Camp at MCRD Parris Island

"The United States Marine Corps, with its fiercely proud tradition of excellence in combat, its hallowed rituals, and its unbending code of honor, is part of the fabric of American myth."
—Thomas E. Ricks

"A Marine is a Marine, there's no such thing as a former Marine. You're a Marine, just in a different uniform and you're in a different phase of your life. But you'll always be a Marine because you went to Parris Island, San Diego, or the hills of Quantico. There's no such thing as a former Marine."
—General James F. Amos, USMC

WE AND OUR CLASSMATES SPENT a surprisingly large percentage of our time during our Naval Academy Plebe Summer and through the four following years at Annapolis standing about and marching in formation. The Brigade of Midshipmen is organized into thirty-six companies, each composed of three platoons. Three times daily, midshipmen muster with their companies, typically in their respective home sections of Bancroft Hall for morning and evening meal formations, and often outside in the picturesque Tecumseh Court for noon meal formations, providing a favorite photo opportunity for tourists. The Academy also offered the tourists regular dress parades (always pronounced "PEA-raids" for no discernable reason), in which the formally attired Brigade would march, company by company, across the Yard to the Parade Ground, and once assembled, would perform a full manual of arms, then pass in

29

review before any visiting dignitaries in the grandstands. (The Academy's sailing team had a sweet duty assignment for such events, plying the waters of the Severn River behind the Parade Ground with spinnakers flying to make fan photos from the bleachers even more perfect and evocative).

Upping the public relations aspects of formation drill further, the entire Brigade of Midshipmen marched (and still marches) from the Academy across downtown Annapolis to Navy–Marine Corps Memorial Stadium for every Navy home football game, with the formal march-on to the playing field (often accompanied by combat plane flyovers and/or parachute jumps) standing as a beloved tradition for the Academy's football fans and supporters. The Brigade of Midshipmen and the U.S. Military Academy's Corps of Cadets also perform such march-on ceremonies at the annual Army–Navy football classic, held on neutral gridirons, most frequently over the years in Philadelphia. It is, admittedly, an impressive sight to watch four-thousand-plus young people in uniform moving in precision lockstep around a football field, or across a city, or completing the manual of arms, where the sounds of rifle stocks hitting the ground or being slapped from various presentation positions adds another otherworldly element to the ritual.

As precise as such parade events look from the grandstands, up close and from within, they are not always quite so accurate or consistent. Some people are indeed very good at marching, maintaining consistent pace and stride, seeming to glide forward, torsos motionless and heads fixed as legs and arms do all the work. Others are not quite so deft, bouncing up and down or bobbing heads as they progress, or with their rifles held at wonky angles, or their "covers" (uniform hats) tipped at inappropriately jaunty angles. It is not terribly uncommon, on hot and humid days, for midshipmen to pass out from standing at rigid attention with knees locked, nor are dropped rifles or bayonets or covers being knocked off by errant rifle moves out of the ordinary, nor are "illegal" tricks like hanging the heavy rifles off the buckles of the uniform watch belts while standing in the "present arms" drill position, relieving tired arms of undue strain. It is ultimately a matter of sheer numbers that make most Naval Academy parades look so impressive, as the ability to focus on any shoddy individual performance dissipates amid the overall spectacle of the thing.

While tourists might not notice substandard individual performance and behavior when presented with the Brigade passing by en masse, those entrusted with the training of the midshipmen certainly did, and there were frequent opportunities for practice, practice, practice to identify and rectify such discrepant behaviors in both company- and platoon-based drill scenarios. Plebes were given additional opportunities to hone their burgeoning marching skills via the imposition of "area tours," a form of punishment that involved marching in circles about prescribed portions of the Yard for as many hours as were deemed applicable for the myriad possible offenses that every Plebe could (and often did) commit, willfully or not.

Formation marching is ultimately a highly rhythmic activity, with some cadence required to keep units in step, and to pace the commands given for changes in direction, accelerations, decelerations, starts, and stops. For the more tourist-centric drill events at the Naval Academy, the Brigade was often accompanied by its Drum and Bugle Corps (D&B), providing the relentless marching rhythms and motivational melodies that propelled the midshipmen forward. But for other, often longer, drill events, the D&B could be either out of earshot or not participating in the procession, requiring members of each company to set the cadence, often with call-and-response-type marching songs.

To be clear: sailors do not often march about ships in formation, so the types of singalong songs that are endemic in nautical culture tend to be of the "sea shanty" variety, with lugubrious, liquid tempos and cadences that support such acts as pulling oars, trimming lines, or climbing rigging. Since most of those traditional shipboard songs do not lend themselves to marching, the Brigade of Midshipmen learned and marched to a variety of songs from more foot-centric cultures, most notably the United States Marine Corps and some elite Army units, with a variety of "Airborne Ranger" songs being particularly popular. Many of the songs that we sang in those days were, objectively speaking, a bit too bawdy and certainly too politically incorrect for modern sensibilities, and many of those cadences have left the current Naval Academy vernacular, rightly so.

But some of the very best marching songs, then and now, were Marine Corps classics that celebrate the spirit, energy, and culture of the Corps, with one of the most common and memorable beginning with these lines:

> *He was born on Parris Island, the land that God forgot;*
> *The sand is 86 inches deep, the sun is blazing hot.*
> *And when he gets to Heaven, St. Peter he will tell,*
> *"Another Marine reporting, Sir; I've served my time in Hell."*

Note that this is how our class would have sung it, injecting our graduation year (1986) into any numerical slot where it fit as a display of class pride; the default singing of the song absent that class spirit aspect tends to find the sand to be between twelve and eighteen inches deep, depending on who is doing the telling and the singing. But regardless of the sand's depth, the *"Born on Parris Island, the land that God forgot"* aspect of the chant captures the strange allure and mystique that Marine Corps Recruit Depot (MCRD) Parris Island, to use its complete name, holds on both military and civilian culture. The famed enlisted training center is featured strongly in such classic feature films as Stanley Kubrick's *Full Metal Jacket* (1987) and Jack Webb's *The D.I.* (1957), among others. Webb's film was made with enthusiastic support from the Marine Corps, who needed a positive public relations vehicle for the Corps in the aftermath of one of Parris Island's most ignominious historical moments, the Ribbon Creek incident, in which a drill instructor ("D.I.") marched his charges into a tidal creek, resulting in the deaths of six recruits.

While the images associated with grueling military rites of passage are often those from Parris Island, which is also likely to be the only military boot camp that most nonmilitary personnel could name if queried, all the military services have boot camp programs through which enlisted recruits must pass; officers go through different onboarding and training programs, generally in different locations. The Marines' program is the longest among the services at twelve weeks, followed by the U.S. Army's ten-week program, staged at Fort Sill, Oklahoma; Fort Leonard Wood, Missouri; Fort Moore (formerly Fort Benning), Georgia; and Fort Jackson, South Carolina. Air Force recruits go through an eight-week program at Lackland Air Force Base in Texas, while Navy recruits spend eight weeks at Naval Station Great Lakes in Illinois, and Coast Guard recruits are processed through the Coast Guard Training Center Cape May in New Jersey over an eight-week training cycle.

MCRD Parris Island's mission is stated simply and directly, consistent with the Corps' culture, in the command's official logo: "We Make Marines." Of course, it is not the only place that makes Marines, as enlisted recruits from west of the Mississippi River are assigned to MCRD San Diego by default, though they may (and many do) request assignment to Parris Island as a point of pride. Marine Corps officers ascend toward their commissions via various pipelines (e.g., the Naval Academy, Reserve Officers' Training Corps college programs, Officer Candidate School, or various Limited Duty Officer or Chief Warrant Officer programs for prior-enlisted personnel), before being funneled through The Basic School near Quantico, Virginia. While all

these programs are rigorous and share similar structures for the
physical, mental, and moral development of candidates, there is
no doubt that completion of the course at Parris Island carries
a certain cachet that other sources do not, such that the Parris
Island cohort often deride their West Coast counterparts, in a
friendly professional rivalry fashion, as "Hollywood Marines."

The close association between Parris Island and the Marine
Corps is long and deep. Located in the heart of the South Carolina
low country, near the historic city of Beaufort (also home to the
Marine Corps Air Station that featured strongly in Pat Conroy's
The Great Santini and its Robert Duvall–starring film adaptation), the island's earliest European settlements date to the latter
half of the sixteenth century; it was occupied intermittently by
various French and Spanish interests until the English secured
permanent long-term control in the early eighteenth century. In
the early days of the Civil War, Union Naval forces reclaimed Port
Royal Sound from the Confederates, with Parris Island serving
as an important coaling station for maritime operations in the
regional waters and beyond. The first permanent Marine presence was established in the 1890s, and the base's historical core
was largely developed prior to 1915, at which point Parris Island
was officially declared to be a Marine Corps Recruit Depot, a status it has maintained without stop to this day.

After four years of singing Marine Corps marching songs at
Annapolis, we both went into the Naval Supply Corps, largely
ending our drill and parade experiences for good, though we
both maintained strong personal connections to the Marines
through our fathers' careers in the Corps. One of our classmates
at Annapolis, Baltimore native Loretta "Lori" Reynolds, followed
a different, and remarkable, post–Naval Academy career in the
Marine Corps, retiring in 2021 as a lieutenant general (three
stars), after having become the first female Marine to command battle space during tours in Iraq and Afghanistan, and
then becoming the first female commanding general of Parris

Island, from 2011 to 2015, a role which also involved serving as the commander of the Marines' Eastern Recruiting Region.

"There's a whole culture in the Marine Corps of doing things the hard way," General Reynolds explained when we asked her about the cultural cachet of Parris Island. "So, some of that perception is probably just about the Marine Corps itself, about the ways that we build resilience, and build mental and moral toughness. Recruit training is where that all starts, and it's where we try to build that into every Marine, no matter what they're going to do in the Corps. Parris Island doesn't make infantrymen or riflemen, it just makes Marines. There's a lot of legends about Parris Island, a lot of lore, a lot of history. It is the second-oldest post in the Corps, and it's a hard place to train. But that's by design."

General Reynolds acknowledged the friendly rivalry between East Coast (Parris Island) and West Coast (San Diego) Marines, while also noting that structural differences between the depots do have actual impacts on the recruits' experiences. "Parris Island is just a tiny place, really, and when a lot of recruits become Marines and they're able to drive around it, they're shocked by just how small it is because it feels larger when you're deep in the training routine," she explained. "But MCRD San Diego is even smaller than Parris Island, so a lot of the field work that we're able to do on Parris Island, like the marksmanship training, the Crucible events at the end of the training program, and all of that, that actually happens up in Camp Pendleton. And that makes for a different kind of hard there because they have hills, and Parris Island doesn't. It's a fundamentally different kind of training environment. But at the end of the day, we have to be able to say that we achieved the same outcomes in both locations, and we do.

"Training and Education Command, TECOM, in Quantico is in charge of the training syllabus," General Reynolds continued. "We work diligently to make sure that Parris Island and San

Diego, week by week, are staying consistent, though that's a hard thing to do. For example, Parris Island is large enough that every battalion has its own physical training [PT] field, it has its own track, it has its own everything. And on Parris Island, because it's very, very hot, you get out there at five-thirty in the morning, you get your PT done, and then you move on with the rest of your training day. San Diego is a bit different because they don't have enough room for more than one or two PT fields, so sometimes they do PT in the afternoons. We can achieve the same outcomes, but we can't have identical training schedules, just because of the training environments being so very different."

The current Marine Corps recruit training process, via Parris Island or via San Diego, involves four discrete phases over a twelve-week period. For the first few weeks at the MCRD, recruits are trained in the basics of drill and the basics of PT, along with some academic testing and training for the swim qualification. "We're starting to get them into fighting shape, if you will," noted General Reynolds. In Phase Two, the recruits complete their swim qualifications, are sent to qualify on the rifle range, and begin their basic warrior skills training. Phase Three involves final drills and academic tests, as well as a built-in "catch up" week for any events that the recruits missed or failed to complete in a satisfactory fashion the first time around.

The capstone of Phase Three is known as the Crucible, a fifty-four-hour event involving forty-eight miles of hiking while carrying about fifty-five pounds of uniform items and gear. While the specific details and schedule of the Crucible are closely guarded, the event includes a variety of challenging test situations (often anchored around the stories of some significant moments in Marine Corps history to affirm those historical connections, and including simulated casualty evacuations), limited food, sleep deprivation, and utter physical exhaustion. The Crucible is intended to verify that every recruit has developed and can demonstrate the physical stamina expected of

Marines, while also proving the mental fortitude required to think and act critically while under myriad levels of stress. The final element of the Crucible is a night march of approximately ten miles; the San Diego contingent ends their route with "the Reaper," a steep seven-hundred-foot hill climb. Upon completing their final Crucible test, recruits receive their iconic "Eagle, Globe, and Anchor" insignia, and are finally able to proudly declare themselves Marines.

"What you get when you become one of us is you get to call yourself a Marine, that's what we give you. You get to wear this uniform and have the honor of calling yourself a U.S. Marine," explained General Reynolds. "At the end of the Crucible, the recruits march back in after these two and a half days and it is designed so that they arrive back on Saturday morning as the sun's coming up, right in time for morning colors. We line them up in formation in front of the Iwo Jima monument at Parris Island; they do it on top of the Reaper in San Diego. They are smelly and dirty and tired and hot, and all that stuff, but they are in formation and they are ready. And a first sergeant or a sergeant major from the regiment will come out and talk to them about what it means to be a Marine. About working through hardship and so forth. And then we do colors and sing "The Marines' Hymn," and then their drill instructors will show up again, and each of them is individually handed their Eagle, Globe, and Anchor for the first time. It is a *very* moving thing to see. There's not a dry eye; I'm even choking up thinking about it. These kids, this is all they really want. They want to be called a Marine. You'll see pictures of this grubby hand holding an Eagle, Globe, and Anchor and that's the culmination of the Crucible ceremony, and then we take them off to have their big warrior breakfast. They've made it, at that point, though now they have a Phase Four, which we call Marine Week, where they turn in their weapons, they get their final uniform fittings, and they're starting to transition to where they're not recruits anymore. Now they're not calling the people who trained them their 'senior drill instructors,' they're calling them by their ranks, 'staff sergeant,' and so on. We're really just trying to get them ready for service in the Marine Corps with that final twelfth week."

Given the challenges of the recruit training process at Parris Island and San Diego, some portion of those beginning the program obviously fail to complete it. "The experience is different for everybody, I would say, and to some extent it may hinge on how well the recruiters have prepared their candidates," said General Reynolds when asked about which elements of the training pipeline most often trip up recruits. "There are some folks who are PT studs. They may show up at recruit training and go, 'Man, that was way too easy.' But not everybody starts at the same level, so the key to the recruit training process is that we meet every kid, every recruit, wherever they are, and if we don't challenge them physically, then we're going to challenge them mentally or emotionally. They're going to be tested. Maybe they have never been in a swimming pool, so they're going to struggle in the swim tank. Maybe they're PT studs but have never been on a team before, or have never led before. They're going to struggle at Parris Island because it's all about the team. So it's hard to just say what the hardest part might be because it's different for everybody.

"The magic of recruit training is we're going to find your weakness. One way or the other, we are going to find it, we're going to figure it out. Because this place is purpose built to get you to where you need to be," continued General Reynolds. "But still, we lose some of them at the rifle range. They've never shot a rifle before. We lose some at the swim tank. We lose some who just don't have the character to be there, they can't keep themselves out of trouble, or they can't stay on a schedule, or they can't be part of a team. We try very hard to keep them because it is recruit training, by definition. We want them to succeed, and that's why the screening process with our recruiters is so important. We tell every brand-new arrival that the last time they show up at the recruiting station is their moment of truth. We have folks from the recruiting side of the house who will say to all of them, 'Okay, this is the last time where you're able to tell me if there's something we need to know, this is the very last chance that a recruiter will be able to help you.' And they have an opportunity to raise their hand and say, 'You know, I have an outstanding ticket, or I have a child that I didn't tell my recruiter about, or I never graduated from high school, or I have . . . whatever.' And then we try very hard to fix all of that before they enter training. But if any of that pops up after the moment of truth? After they have joined their company? They're gone. Because they didn't have the courage to do the right thing. They're gone."

Despite the rigors of its recruit training program, the efficacy and efficiency of the Marine Corps' recruiting processes are proven by the relatively small percentage of recruits who wash out at Parris Island, typically between 10 and 12 percent of each class. At the time of this writing, there are numerous current news stories about the difficulty that the Armed Forces are having with meeting minimum recruiting goals necessary to meet and sustain force needs and requirements. The one notable exception to this narrative is the U.S. Marine Corps, which continues to maintain extremely strong interest from quality recruit candidates.

General Reynolds attributes that ongoing success specifically to the ways in which the Marine Corps values its recruiters as one of the most important components of the Corps' sustained readiness to fulfill its mission, goals, and objectives. "First off, the Marine Corps has always acknowledged the importance of recruiting," she explained. "When you understand how young the Marine Corps is, by design, with about 60 percent of Marines in their first enlistment, then you understand why recruiting is doubly essential. We have always valued the quality of leadership that we put into recruiting because it is so essential. If you are selected to be a recruiting station commander in the Marine Corps, that means you are on an accelerated path to command. We put good Marines out there on recruiting duty because we know how important it is. Good Marines will recruit good-quality candidates, and I think that has always been part of our success.

"One of the things I kind of object to in some of these articles that you read about who won and who lost on recruiting duty, there's no mention of the premium that we place on selecting the right leaders to get after it," continued General Reynolds. "Because that is a big part of it, it is part of our culture out there. I don't know what the exact numbers are right now, but about 40 percent of our ground commanders at the General officer level typically have recruiting in their background. So, you have to put quality into the game. And, also, our commercials have always talked about the essence of being a Marine, and that continues to appeal to people. You know the ones: 'Are you willing to challenge yourself?' 'We don't promise you a rose garden.' 'The ethical warrior.' All of that. And then we hold to that through the process. If you go to any recruiting event, you might see the Army pull up with a trailer with high-tech wargames, and the Air Force will pull up with a jet simulator, and you know what we pull up with? A pull-up bar! Seriously, just a pull-up bar. And you know what? We'll have kids around the block. If you can do ten pull-ups, you get a Marine Corps T-shirt. And the Army just looks at us like, how the hell do you do that?"

Many crucibles designed and deployed by elite organizations seem to operate on the presumption that failure should be the default mode, placing barriers to entry that are so high that only the most extremely committed or absurdly skilled applicants have any chance of successfully completing the tasks set before them. The Marine Corps, for all its vaunted stature as one of the world's greatest fighting forces, has taken a different philosophical tack on that front, arguably to the betterment of the Corps and its alumni.

"There's so much about recruit training that is really about building confidence, and about proving to you that you can do what our nation needs you to do," concluded General Reynolds. "The process is to build you up, not to tear you down, and that is what the recruit training process, especially the Crucible, is all about. We have invested our leadership and our training in you. We are trusting you. Let us show you how it all comes together in a very difficult experience, but know that our goal is for you to get through it. Our goal is not to weed you out. That is not what a crucible is about. A crucible is about proving to you that you can do hard things. You can do this! We can take an average person who is committed to being better and we can make you better. That is what it's all about. We need more people to try this. Let us show you that you too can be a Marine. I just need good stock. I need good stock and a desire to be a decent human being who is willing to contribute in uniform. And then let us show you that you can do this. For me, do I think that the Marine Corps is an elite fighting force? Sure. But it's not like we're out there hunting for elite. We're hunting for the good. We're hunting for the good, and then we'll make you the elite."

With a better understanding of the ways in which MCRD Parris Island hews to its mission of "making Marines," we turned to one of its active-duty alumni to get a firsthand take on the ways in which the good become the elite, and how that process actually feels. Sergeant Thierno Mamadu Jalloh is a native of the West African nation of Guinea who emigrated with his family to the United States as a child, spending his school years in New York City's Bronx borough. Sergeant Jalloh completed the boot camp program at Parris Island, shipped off to Japan and served on a variety of Western Pacific deployments, then returned stateside to serve at MCRD San Diego, giving him a unique perspective on both the Marine Corps' pipeline training bases.

"Beyond the generic 'I want to be better, I want to better myself' aspects, I 100 percent joined the Marine Corps because it was the military branch that was seen as the hardest to get into," Sergeant Jalloh recalled. "Being born in Guinea, then coming here and having lived most of my life in the United States, I see the United States as having been the reason that my family has the life that we have here *and* back home, so this was my opportunity to give back. And as a kid from the Bronx, raised in the 'hood, it was one of those 'Hey, let me step out of this comfort zone and see what else is out there' things. I went into the Marines extremely motivated, ready to get into what I got into, and I changed entirely at Parris Island.

"One thing that changed for me, honestly, was that I became a little more religious," Sergeant Jalloh continued. "I did fine at Parris Island right up until the swim qualifications. That was when I was introduced to something that was hard for me to do. I really struggled there. I almost drowned and I had to be rescued from the pool, more than once. I'm Muslim, right, and a lot of my fellow recruits had never been in the presence of a Muslim before. Some of them came from small towns, and throughout training, a lot of them took an interest in what I did, how I prayed, so I made a lot of friends, and that was the first time I was exposed a lot to the Christian religion. They studied my religion, and I studied their religion. But anyway, when swim qualification came around and I was faced with something that I had never been faced with before, to the point where that was my brick wall, and I had to push through it. And my religion helped me: I remember I was up at night after struggling another day, and having only one more chance before I got recycled in training, so I prayed, tears in my eyes, all night, saying, 'Hey, if there's anything that you can do for me, this is the only thing I ever asked you, and if you give me this thing, then I will truly, truly believe in you and the fact that you have my back.' And the next day I passed with flying colors."

After successfully completing the MCRD Parris Island pipeline, one of Sergeant Jalloh's first efforts as an enlisted Marine was to facilitate the recruitment of those who followed him. "One thing we're offered after recruit training is ten days of leave, and during those ten days you can get extended leave. Your recruiter can grant you what's called 'recruiter's assistance,' where you extend your leave, but once your leave is done, you stay there to help your recruiter in finding others. For instance, you go back to your high school as a Marine and you talk to the individuals who are considering applying, and you can provide more insight from a different perspective. Even the last two times when I have been to New York, I went under recruiter's assistance. One of my buddies is also from the Bronx. We were applicants together, before becoming Marines, and he's working in the heart of the Bronx out there, 100 percent committed to recruiting quality Marines. He doesn't do it for him. He doesn't do it for promotion. He does it to help other individuals like ourselves. Kids from the Bronx, stepping out of their comfort zone. Stepping out of the 'hood and going out there and doing great things, being able to provide for their families, without doing it the usual ways that a lot of kids find themselves doing."

In addition to his recruiting activities, at the time of this writing, Sergeant Jalloh is "making Marines" himself in San Diego as a drill instructor, another activity that he sees as a key "giving back" aspect of his Marine Corps service. "You may leave boot camp hating your drill instructors for everything that happened, but eventually you come to realize that, at the same time, you respect them for what they did," said Sergeant Jalloh. "You go home, you see your family members, and they are telling you about the visible differences that they can see in you. You find yourself among regular folks and you're walking a little taller because you're used to marching. And you're walking a little faster because you're used to moving with intensity. You see life in a different way. The senior drill instructor I had toward the end of my time at Parris Island—I have nothing but extreme respect for him. He was a role model to me, the way he carried himself, the way he led us, the way he put pain in our bodies, he put fear in our hearts, but at the same time he was very motivated and passionate about the Marine Corps and what he does. So, everything you took for granted before you were in recruit training, you start to appreciate a little more after it. And I truly do feel like, in this world we live in, everyone needs to appreciate what they have a little more because so many others don't even have that."

CHAPTER 2

Kung Fu and Koans: The Shaolin Monks

"Strength is happiness. Strength is itself victory. In weakness and cowardice there is no happiness. When you wage a struggle, you might win or you might lose. But regardless of the short-term outcome, the very fact of your continuing to struggle is proof of your victory as a human being."
—Daisaku Ikeda

"Patience, Grasshopper."
—Master Po (as portrayed by Keye Luke in ABC's *Kung Fu*)

THROUGH HISTORIANS' LENSES POINTED BACKWARD a half century from the early 2020s, the view of the early 1970s in the United States may be summarized as a period of staggering social, cultural, and political change. The brutal tail end of the Vietnam War and totality of the Watergate scandal critically undermined the citizenry's faith in the honesty and competence of its elected leaders and their generals, widely disillusioning the eighteen- to twenty-one-year-old voters who had been freshly enfranchised in 1971 by the twenty-sixth amendment to the United States Constitution. Recessions in 1970 and 1974 were anchored in longer-term financial trends that saw the Dow Jones Industrial Average slowly and inexorably bleed more than two-thirds of its indexed value between 1965 and 1982. The Supreme Court declared abortion to be a constitutionally protected right in its landmark 1973 decision *Roe v. Wade*, seemingly settling that sticky social point in perpetuity, which turned out to mean "for five decades." The peace and love vibes of the hippie era yielded to the polyester and cocaine narratives that underpinned both the disco and soft-rock hit machines on the popular front, while nascent stirrings in Cleveland, Detroit, Los Angeles, and New York City foreshadowed the explosive emergence of punk and hip-hop and their offspring. Intel produced its first microprocessor in 1971 just as Disney World opened its gates in Orlando, and 1972 saw the debut of both HBO's cable subscription service and Atari's Pong video arcade game, collectively marking the emergence of key technologies and the brands that dominate American entertainment activities to this day.

In such extended periods of sociopolitical churn, the precious ties that bind shared public experience can often be woven from unlikely threads. One of the strangest of such fleeting focal moments in the nation's collective consciousness may have been the emergence of "the kung fu craze" from within the swirling turmoil of early 1970s America. Reaching with shocking rapidity across racial divides, age strata, and socioeconomic attainment levels, and fueled by an explosion of releases offered by a wide variety of global entertainment industry outlets, kung fu (or at least what most casual devotees understood kung fu to be) was truly a defining theme within American popular arts and culture at the peak of its same-named craze in and around 1973.

In May 1973, martial artist Bruce Lee's *Fist of Fury* (originally released in Hong Kong in 1972) sat atop the North American box office charts, eventually earning its producers nearly five hundred times its paltry production budget. Lee's tragic and mysterious death two months after *Fist of Fury*'s commercial American peak further fanned the flames of enthusiasm for Hong Kong–style kung fu films, including the joint Hong Kong–American coproduction *Enter the Dragon*, Lee's final completed film, released mere weeks after his passing. *Variety* magazine saw enough of a commercial trend line to feel like it needed a simple label, though their depiction of the genre as "chopsocky" was unfortunate in both its linguistic origins and its tenacity in film criticism in the years that followed.

The popularity of these films spilled over into other facets of American culture in both sublime and absurd ways. Hasbro's popular G.I. Joe action figures were redesigned with "Kung-Fu Grip" in their 1974 release to market, to cite but one example. Also in 1974, Jamaican musician Carl Douglas topped the *Billboard* Hot 100 singles charts with his disco-funk hit "Kung Fu Fighting," recorded in England, and culled from his hilariously titled debut album, *Kung Fu Fighting and Other Great Love Songs*. Hong Kong–style martial arts films earned particularly enthusiastic responses in America's Black and Hispanic communities, where themes of institutional oppression and principled players' fights against the many manifestations of "the man" resonated strongly, just as they did in many contemporaneous "Blaxploitation" films. Fast forwarding to the 1990s, the influential hip-hop collective Wu-Tang Clan (whose members were young boys at the peak of the kung fu craze) took their name from a 1983 Hong Kong action cinema film called *Shaolin and Wu Tang*, framed around the rivalry between two martial arts schools: Shaolin-style kung fu and Wu-Tang sword fighting.

One of the most-watched and best-remembered relics from America's kung fu craze was a television show that controversially (then and now) cast a white American actor in its lead role. ABC's *Kung Fu* ran from February 1972 through April 1975, with David Carradine starring as Kwai Chang Caine, a half-American, half-Chinese Shaolin monk, born in China in the mid-nineteenth century, and forced to flee to the American West after killing the murderer of his wise, old, blind teacher at the Shaolin monastery, Master Po. Caine spends his time fighting injustices through a variety of classic cowboy-era landscapes, and audiences are offered insights into the moral constructs under which he operates via flashbacks to his youthful days in the monastery, with Master Po (played by Keye Luke) and Master Kan (Philip Ahn) providing glib American distillations of the Buddhist philosophy underpinning the Shaolin way.

Various feature-length films and reboots have kept the franchise alive since its original run, and despite persistent concerns over the "yellow-face" aspects of his casting, Carradine continued to embrace the role of Caine proudly until his death in 2009. A 2005 box-set release of the series featured a mini documentary called *David Carradine's Shaolin Diary: Back to the Beginning*, where the actor visits meaningful Chinese destinations alluded to or referenced in the series itself. The staying power of the series beyond any hardcore cohort of martial arts devotees means that David Carradine's Kwai Chang Caine may well represent the most iconic image of a Shaolin monk in modern American culture.

But what, exactly, is a Shaolin monk? Or more to the point, what exactly is Shaolin? If you seek popular culture sources for an answer to that question, you would unquestionably be steered toward a definition that directly equates Shaolin with kung fu, as though "Shaolin kung fu" was just one of the many international flavors of popular martial arts forms, akin to American Kenpo (we will discuss that discipline further in a later chapter about the Hawaiian Koa), or Brazilian jiu-jitsu, or Muay Thai, or Bruce Lee's own "intelligent martial art" Jeet Kune Do, or countless other fighting forms from around the world that have been adapted for American consumption by various practitioners, both ethical and otherwise. For perspective, a current search of the term "Shaolin" on the Internet Movie Database returns 305 films, television shows, or video games featuring that word in their titles, and virtually every one of them features some form of martial art combat within its cinematic content.

Those popular perceptions aside, the most reductive and simple response to any "What is Shaolin?"–type inquiry is to anchor the word at its source: Shaolin is a place. Founded in 495 CE (in Gregorian calendar reckoning) by the Indian monk Batuo in what is now modern China's Henan Province, Shaolin Monastery is the ancient birthplace of Chan Buddhism, carried from India by Bodhidharma, whose roots in Central Asia and his legendarily fulsome beard earned him the sobriquet of "The Blue-Eyed Barbarian" in many Chan Buddhist texts. (Japan's Zen Buddhism, better known in the modern Western world, is a close philosophical descendant of Chan Buddhism, with "Zen" and "Chan" essentially representing different linguistic renderings of the same root sound.)

Bodhidharma is said to have arrived in the lands of the Northern Wei dynasty in 527 CE, some one thousand years after the Buddha, Siddhartha Gautama, first attained enlightenment and codified the Noble Eightfold Path that underpins the practices and beliefs of the modern world's 520 million Buddhists. Despite his foreign origins, Bodhidharma is considered the first Chinese Buddhist patriarch, the twenty-eighth representative of a lineage tracing back to Gautama Buddha himself, via his principal disciple Mahākāśyapa. (Prominent twentieth-century Buddhist scholar D. T. Suzuki argued that this lineage was created *ex post facto* during Chan Buddhism's first burst of widespread popularity and adherence in the seventh and eighth century CE, by way of giving the sect an air of rooted legitimacy that it might have otherwise lacked.) A seventeenth-century text called the Yijin Jing describes Bodhidharma implementing an extreme physical training for the monks of Shaolin Monastery, ostensibly forging the first connections between Shaolin and kung fu; more reliable contemporary sources also consider this linkage to be an apocryphal retrofitting of that connection.

While the strict historical details of the birth of kung fu within Shaolin Monastery remain shrouded in the thick mists of times long gone, there is no question of the historical importance of Shaolin in the Chinese telling and understanding of their martial arts history. The fundamentals of Shaolin-bred martial arts appear to have taken a codified, official form during China's Sui dynasty in the form of "The 18 Hands of Luohan," describing a set of simple movements inspired by those who had already achieved enlightenment; in India they were known as Arhats, in China, Luohan. Reliable historical sources recount the "soldier monks" of Shaolin defending their monastery from bandits in 610 CE and fighting in the Battle of Hulao in 621 CE, directly contributing to the emergence of the Tang dynasty. The 18 Hands of Luohan movements were later adapted to reflect eighteen martial postures, which were further expanded and codified over the centuries, eventually reaching a total of 324 (eighteen forms, each including eighteen postures) during the Ming dynasty.

Scores of documents from the late Ming period (sixteenth and seventeenth centuries CE) document the Shaolin monks' fighting prowess, which by that time had evolved to include the weapon most closely associated with the form: the long staff. (The oldest surviving Shaolin kung fu manual dates from approximately 1620 CE and is titled *Exposition of the Original Shaolin Staff Method.*) Shaolin reached its arguable apogee under the Ming dynasty, and its monks were recruited by Ming emperors at least six times to support its war efforts, largely against the Japanese. Unfortunately, this close association with Ming power meant that when peasant leader Li Zicheng sparked an uprising that led to the fall of the Ming dynasty in 1644, the destruction of Shaolin Monastery was part and parcel of his brief political ascendancy; Li died within a year of declaring himself emperor of the Shun dynasty. Shaolin remained a sparsely populated ruin until the early eighteenth century, when the Qing dynasty's rulers restored and rehabilitated it.

The Qing were the last of the imperial dynasties of China, collapsing during the Xinhai Revolution of 1911–1912, which led to the establishment of the Republic of China. During a lawless period following the establishment of the Republic, the Shaolin monks actively engaged in a variety of military sorties against various bandits and warlords, attempting to protect and preserve the villages surrounding their monastery. By 1928,

China's National People's Party (the Kuomintang) had consolidated ruling control of the nation; forces loyal to Kuomintang general Shi Yousan burned the monastery later that year, punishing the monks for their fealty to Shi's political enemy, General Fan Zhongxiu, who had once studied at Shaolin. But the reputation of the monks was once again restored in the early 1930s as Japan moved aggressively into China's Manchurian region, and the monks were publicly idealized and idolized for their long contributions to China's defense against foreign enemies. That period of relative acclaim lasted until the People's Republic of China was established in 1949. While the Communist Chinese government did not initially persecute the Shaolin monks as they did the Tibetan Buddhists and other religious sects, during the Cultural Revolution of the 1960s and 1970s, Shaolin's monks were required to return to their secular lives, the monastery was claimed by the state, and countless ancient religious artifacts and sacred spaces were destroyed in the name of maintaining an officially atheistic political culture.

As the tumult of the Cultural Revolution faded, Shaolin was rebuilt and restored yet again, largely replicating its historic configurations wherever possible. The monastery has largely been thriving in recent decades as China's leaders embraced (slightly) less centralized economic policies and allowed (slightly) more capitalist engagement within its many regional markets, fortified with booming numbers of foreign visitors and investors. The current abbot of Shaolin Monastery, Shi Yongxin, has embraced the spirit of the modern Chinese age in his own stewardship of the ancient compound and its resident monks, though not without pushback from unexpected directions. Shi has been widely derided as the "CEO Monk" in both global Buddhist and martial arts circles for his efforts since his ascension in 1999 to promote the monastery through commercial means, including the establishment of Shaolin branch temples outside of China, allowing advertising within the historic monastery, charging admission fees for tourists, and destroying villages near the monastery during its efforts to earn UNESCO World Heritage Site status and the funding that accompanies it; that goal was attained in 2011.

While the kung fu martial arts style certainly sits central to Shaolin's story in both popular and historical narratives (our own telling of the tale included in that reckoning), it is important to note that kung fu is by no means the only defining trait of Chan Buddhism as practiced by Shaolin's monks. Shaolin recognizes two distinct facets to its practices: Quan (which includes the martial arts) and Chan (the fundamentals of Buddhist faith upon which Shaolin's practices were built). The desired path to enlightenment involves unifying Chan and Quan, through immense, detailed, and highly prescriptive practices, passed down through written and oral means for the better part of 1,500 years.

Quan's contents include mastering the eighteen basic skills associated with improved stamina, balance, and flexibility, developing mastery of Qigong meditation (which includes both stationary "internal" forms and dynamic "external" forms) and the "72 arts," which are split between "hard" and "soft" categories and include such evocative titles as "Diamond Finger," "Pulling Out a Nail," "Iron Shirt," "Centipede Art," "Bullet-Like Fist," "Golden Cicada," and "Drawing in Testicles" (!). Chan's contents are anchored in Buddha's Noble Eightfold Path, which includes mastery of right view, right resolve, right speech, right conduct, right livelihood, right effort, right mindfulness, and right meditative awareness. Fundamental Buddhist monastic precepts related to the existential nature of suffering, the renunciation of physical pleasures (including meat and many other processed or cooked foods, material possessions, alcohol, tobacco, and, oh yeah, sexual relations), and the diligent, lifelong quest for enlightenment shape the lived experience of those resident at Shaolin and those practicing its tenets on a global basis.

It is also important to note that not every Shaolin monk becomes a warrior; only about 25 percent of those in residence at the monastery have been recognized as such. There are many other monks who serve primarily as scholars or in clerical roles, and the monastic traditions associated with Shaolin practice embrace all facets of life, including the most mundane and humble day-to-day tasks (housekeeping, gardening, farming, etc.), from which none are exempt. The creation and interpretation of traditional Buddhist art forms are also hard-baked into Shaolin tradition, as are a comprehensive knowledge and practice of traditional Chinese medicine. Taken together, the journey to knit Quan with Chan is a lifelong pursuit, with no guarantee of any fungible, transferable outcome, or passage beyond pursuing the elusive nirvana, an enlightened state within which a monk's desires and suffering are finally and completely vaporized, the individual rendered extinct before the immensity of the universal.

The controversial commercialization of the monastery and its practices over the past decade means that it is much easier today for the casual curious to participate in "Shaolin Lite" versions of the monks' experiences. Tourists can "train" at the monastery in watered-down versions of kung fu or become lay monks at the order's overseas properties, teaching the teachings without having to renounce their property, sexuality, families, and day-to-day secular lives. Countless political, sports, and entertainment celebrities have visited Shaolin to meet with Abbot Shi Yongxin, adding the exotic spice of adjacent fame to the possible tourism experiences for visitors to the monastery. Despite the growing Western awareness of, cachet associated with, and access to Shaolin Monastery, most of its many annual visitors remain Chinese, some small percentage of whom arrive hoping to enroll as disciples in training with the community of monks, some even smaller portion of whom are then accepted for training.

The rites of passage for admission into the Shaolin order are far more time-consuming and immersive than most of the others discussed in this book. Discipleship is a full-time job, without pay or prestige. Applicants are expected to spend years, sometimes decades, embracing a life of sacrifice in pursuit of atonement and purity. Before training in kung fu may even be considered, the would-be monks must develop humility, patience, and physical strength; the care and maintenance of the sprawling monastic complex falls on the shoulders of the trainees, among other time-consuming and strenuous manual labor. Meditation and study are also part of the daily routine, and students are expected to memorize, discuss, and interpret lengthy formative Buddhist texts, such as the ancient *The Blue Cliff Record* or *The Gateless Barrier.*

Young students of promise will (hopefully, and eventually) catch the eyes of senior monks, who will establish one-on-one master/disciple relationships to focus their training and will be the arbiters deciding when and if the disciples will be granted the opportunity to prove themselves before the abbot and a panel of his most senior monks. The final examinations involve a demonstration of both the Quan-side kung fu skills and the Chan-side ability to recite texts by memory, with the judges able to select any of the koans (lessons or stories) from within the prescribed sacred works, with the aspirants expected to deliver their contents on command, in flawless form.

If the students are not successful before their panel, they must wait at least three years before taking the tests again. If they are successful, they are acknowledged as monks, and they immediately return to their abstemious lives of prayer, work, and reflection, typically for the remainder of their days among the living. For those elite few who are recognized as warrior monks, the act of perfecting their skills at kung fu no longer represents a vital skill necessary to defend their homes and lives, but rather demonstrates the depths of their faith, the discipline of their bodies, and their quest to live harmoniously with all of nature, often by emulating the movements of the native animals of the lands around Shaolin Monastery. There are no Hollywood endings for most modern Shaolin monks, whose anonymity, despite their formidable fighting skills, is part and parcel with their commitment to humility and self-effacement.

Many of the crucibles investigated in this book involve relatively short, sharp moments, tests, or events, and the passage from "outside" to "inside" brings with it a fundamental change in the roles, responsibilities, and perceptions of those who complete the tests. The road traveled by the Shaolin monks, especially their warrior class, is far statelier and smoother, and its critical moment of transition brings no outwardly discernible change to the financial, social, or political status of the inductees, but is rather seen as simply one more step in a lifelong journey toward enlightenment. It is less a fiery melting pot crucible accordingly, and more of a sealed slow-cooker experience, as those contained within its chambers seek the transcendence required to release the overwhelming pressure of life's suffering, materiality, and desires. Membership in this elite society brings with it few tangible external rewards, though its focus on inner states of being, and on achieving a sense of psychic peace within the greater universe, may offer a more profound individual transformation than any other test we describe within this book.

Which, of course, is why Shaolin's true legacy, purpose, and meaning will always remain elusive to the multitudes of impatient and materialistic human beings living in these high-speed, high-connectivity, high-stimulation, and high-acquisition times. But at least we can all watch *Kung Fu* or *Enter the Dragon* on late-night cable TV some evening, or bust out our best moves when Carl Douglas's "Kung Fu Fighting" comes on the oldies-but-goodies radio station. We may not achieve enlightenment while we are nestled in our comfy chairs, but we might be entertained and perhaps even learn a lesson or two, if we are patient enough, and pay proper attention.

CHAPTER 3

Space Is the Place: The U.S. Astronaut Program

"The Earth is the cradle of humanity, but mankind cannot stay in the cradle forever."
—Konstantin Tsiolkovsky

"If I ever reach heaven, I expect to find three wonders there: first, to meet some I had not thought to see there; second, to miss some I had expected to see there; and third, the greatest wonder of all, to find myself there."
—John Newton

AMONG THE FAMOUS CRUCIBLES DEPLOYED as entry passageways by elite organizations, the one that has arguably permeated the most deeply into the collective public consciousness is the story of the travails endured by the original Mercury Seven astronauts, as described in lovely prose and delicious detail in Tom Wolfe's 1979 book *The Right Stuff*, later adapted into a popular Academy Award–winning film. Building upon an exploration into the insular and often extreme culture of military test pilots, *The Right Stuff* detailed the extensive screening and jockeying associated with the selection of the Mercury Seven from a pool of over five hundred highly qualified military test pilots, following the establishment of the National Aeronautics and Space Administration (NASA) in late 1958.

More memorably, and more entertainingly, *The Right Stuff* also provided glorious and graphic descriptions of the often-absurd physical rigors that the Mercury Seven endured through their pre-launch training programs. Among many other facets of the grueling regimen were repeated rides in the "Vomit

Comet" (a plane that flew a wave-like series of parabolic ascents and descents, creating short-lived microgravity), training in the "Gimbal Rig" (a gyroscopic contraption that could simulate roll, pitch, and yaw motions of approximately thirty revolutions per minute, requiring the astronauts to fire controls to stabilize the rotations), high-gravity endurance training in a centrifuge, survival training (in the event of an unplanned landing in hostile territory), academic and technical training associated with the Mercury capsule and its booster rocket, and a wide, gross, and often nearly sadistic variety of invasive medical tests and biological specimen collections.

Many of those endurance tests and physical indignities were imposed upon the original Mercury Seven astronauts largely because nobody knew truly what space travel would do to the human body, so that demonstrating the space pioneers' abilities to endure a variety of ludicrously invasive and baroque earthbound torments was seen by the program's physicians and administrators as the only way to ensure the Mercury Seven would not break and crack once they were placed in their tiny solo capsules and sent aloft. *The Right Stuff* followed the Mercury Seven through their six original launches (Mercury Seven astronaut Donald K. "Deke" Slayton was grounded for an irregular heartbeat before he could fly his scheduled mission; he eventually made it into space in 1975 as a member of the Apollo-Soyuz Test Project), and the book also documented the ways in which the Mercury Seven eventually rebelled against their training tormentors, demonstrating their own senses of what "the right stuff" entailed by demanding to be treated as more than "spam in a can" for their programmatic higher-ups to market and manipulate.

While the Mercury Seven came to demand and assert more active control and engagement with their space craft, their qualification regimes, and their ultimate flight assignments, they also played key roles in the evolution of training protocols

through the ensuing Mercury, Gemini, and Apollo flight programs, in part to reflect and incorporate knowledge gleaned
from actual space flights, and in part to preclude comparisons
being made between the successes (or lack thereof) of the original Seven versus those who followed them. Six additional astronaut classes with a total of seventy-two members (all white men)
were recruited and trained by NASA between Alan Shepard's
first suborbital flight on May 5, 1961, and the final Apollo-based
Skylab missions (1973) and the Apollo-Soyuz Test Project (1975).
Group 3 (known as "The Fourteen") abolished the strict requirement that astronauts be qualified test pilots, allowing military
fighter jet experience to suffice. Group 4 ("The Scientists") were
selected based on their academic and research histories, with
previous flight experience optional. By the time Group 6 ("The
Excess Eleven" of 1967) and Group 7 (a 1969 transfer cohort
from the U.S. Air Force's secretive Manned Orbiting Laboratory
[MOL] program) were recruited, the handwriting was on the
proverbial wall regarding the limited flight opportunities for the
pool of available astronauts, many of whom did not fly until after
the dawn of the Space Shuttle era in 1981.

While the original Mercury Seven astronauts (and their
families) were accorded celebrity superstar status in the popular
media of their day, and the crews of certain later missions (e.g.,
those who died in the fatal Apollo 1 fire and crews on the first
journey to the Moon on Apollo 8, the first Moon landing on
Apollo 11, and the ill-fated Apollo 13 mission with its attendant
amazing rescue efforts, where "failure [was] not an option," in
the inspirational and immortal words of Flight Director Gene
Kranz) have permeated popular consciousness in somewhat
permanent fashion, many of the working astronauts of the early
Mercury, Gemini, and Apollo programs were and remain less
well recognized today, their formidable efforts and achievements notwithstanding. Equally obscure to most modern
American readers were the numerous Soviet cosmonauts who

flew after Yuri Gagarin became the first man in space on April 12, 1961, and the twelve pilots in the North American X-15 program, which pioneered high-speed and high-altitude suborbital flights. Eight X-15 pilots were awarded their astronaut wings for flights above the U.S. standard of fifty miles, while one of them (Joseph A. Walker) twice flew above the Kármán line (one hundred kilometers), the point defined by the Fédération Aéronautique Internationale (FAI) in its recognition of who has, and who has not, traveled into space.

Since 2002, a new class of space travelers, "commercial astronauts," have emerged, their flights controlled by business interests (e.g., Axiom Space, Blue Origin, and SpaceX) rather than governmental entities, with launches supporting both traditional scientific activities as well as simple "space tourism." China became the third nation to launch and maintain an independent human space flight program with the journey of Shenzhou 5 in 2003; while Western media have adopted the term "taikonauts" to describe the Chinese space travelers, they are known as *hángtiān yuán* ("navigating celestial heaven personnel") in their native language.

Given the slowly growing number of pipelines for astronauts (in the broadest sense of that word) to travel into space, with each agency and organization possibly hewing to different standards for recruitment, training, and flight assignments, in evaluating the crucibles associated with spacefaring programs, we have elected to focus on the best-known and longest-running current pipeline, that administered by NASA through the Space Shuttle and International Space Station (ISS) eras and the planned Artemis missions (2025–29) designed to carry humans back to the Moon for the first time since 1973. (For side perspective, fifty-eight years passed between the time when the Magellan-Elcano expedition first circumnavigated the globe under sail in 1522, and the time when Sir Francis Drake completed the second global circumnavigation in 1580. If we consider the Apollo lunar missions to have been sequential steps on a single exploratory adventure, a return to the Moon by 2031 will match Drake's achievement. We consider the lesson here to be a demonstration of the utter audacity of the Magellan-Elcano expedition and Project Apollo, both of which achieved extraordinary goals, so formidable that a half-century's worth of technological progress was required to replicate their achievements.)

The modern era of the American manned space program began with NASA Astronaut Group 8, announced in January 1978. Group 8 featured thirty-five members, including the first female, African American, and Asian American astronauts. (The group's nickname was "TFNG," which for public and media purposes was explained as "Thirty-Five New Guys," but in standard military parlance was understood in a deprecatory fashion to mean "The Fucking New Guys.") Group 8 was the first astronaut class to distinguish between pilots and mission specialists, waiving the requirement for the latter group to complete flight training; the pilot-versus-mission-specialist distinction remained through Group 20's selection in 2009. Group 8 was also the first cohort whose members were not categorized as astronauts upon selection, but rather remained astronaut candidates until completion of their training programs. The relatively large size and flexible configurations of the Space Shuttles, compared to the smaller capsules of the Mercury, Gemini, and Apollo eras, also allowed a widening pool of candidates to apply for the program, including larger men and smaller women than had been possible in earlier programs, which limited applicants to a fairly narrow range of body shapes and sizes.

NASA Astronaut Group 9, announced in May 1980, was the first to include non-American personnel, with the European Space Agency's Wubbo Ockels (Netherlands) and Claude Nicollier (Switzerland) joining the force as mission specialists. Group 9 also included Charles F. Bolden Jr., a Naval Academy graduate and a highly decorated and combat-tested U.S. Marine aviator who went on to fly four Space Shuttle missions between 1986 and 1994; he was the fourth African American astronaut to fly a space mission. Following his time as an astronaut, Bolden returned to active service with the Marines, eventually retiring as a major general in 2004, following combat command tours in Kuwait during Operation Desert Thunder, among other high-level duties and assignments. In July 2009, General Bolden was appointed as administrator of NASA by President Barack Obama, a role he filled admirably until January 2017. General Bolden was the first African American NASA administrator and second astronaut to fill that role, following Richard H. Truly (1989–1992); Truly had joined the NASA Astronaut Corps as part of the Air Force MOL program transfer in 1969.

As our research for this book was in progress, National Geographic Documentary Films released an exceptional documentary called *The Space Race*, exploring the unique challenges and obstacles faced by Black astronauts at a time when the community seemed inexorably closed to all but white male test pilots of certain ages and body types. General Bolden was both a key character and a cornerstone interview subject in the documentary, with the filmmakers granting him their work's final, summarizing words, reflecting both on NASA's African American history and its future as a multicultural, multinational, and multi-gendered organization, both within its ground control centers and on its manned spacecraft. We ourselves elected to interview General Bolden to further explore the structure, role, and importance of crucibles in NASA's astronaut program, recognizing his unique perspective as both a Space Shuttle pilot and crew member, and the federal executive ultimately responsible for the American space program at large during a particularly challenging era in its history, as the cessation of the Shuttle program and limited commercial launch platforms available made the United States dependent on Russia's Soyuz spacecraft for access to the ISS.

"The three types of astronaut experiences, first the Mercury-Gemini-Apollo era, then the Shuttle era, and now what I call the Space Station–Moon-Mars era, are dramatically different in a number of ways," explained General Bolden. "And in some ways, I would not call the astronaut experience today a crucible-like experience at all. It is a very gentlemanly process, and I use that term loosely, where you apply through your parent service, and then your parent service considers the applications and submits a list of names to NASA that they want considered, and then NASA's selection committee goes through the list and picks people that they think they want to talk to. Having served on a couple of astronaut selection boards while I was there, we started out by looking for the whole person, just like you would imagine the Naval Academy or any other place, looking for somebody who has the right academic background, the right technical background, and the necessary operational experience. That operational component is a key discriminator for the current astronaut program. Operational experience includes flying as a test pilot, or serving as a military person, or as a test flight engineer, or as a test NFO [naval flight officer], or as a researcher. So, anybody with a PhD, they automatically get credit for three years of operational experience because the assumption is that they have done three years of research to earn that PhD. A master's degree credits applicants with two years of operational experience, and so on.

"So that's why I would not call the present-day astronaut process much of a crucible experience at all because there's not the physical component that you would see in, say, a Navy SEAL qualification, or even just getting into the Naval Academy," General Bolden continued. "It was very physical when we got to the Academy through Plebe Summer, but also psychological, to a great extent. Today, I would say there is neither the physical stress nor the psychological pressure with the astronaut program that we were accustomed to going through Plebe Summer and Plebe Year in Annapolis. I think that is part of the times we live in, and I do not see it being to the detriment of the program at all. I mean, we are looking for ways to screen out people who obviously would not be able to handle the strenuous program for training for flights; it can be up to two years of training before you fly your first mission, and not everybody can handle going through that kind of stuff. Not everybody's patient enough to do that. And today everybody also learns Russian because we are flying frequently on Russian vehicles as crew members, so everybody needs to be able to read, speak, write, and understand Russian."

One of the more amusingly common traits within elite organizations is the pervasive belief that entry crucibles get easier over time, allowing the "elders" to scoff at the purportedly easier travails endured by those who followed them. General Bolden's Naval Academy peers from the late 1960s would scoff at the experiences we endured in the early 1980s, and all of us tend to look at today's midshipmen's experiences and see many familiar hard elements dropped, without fairly considering the new hard elements added after our respective times in Annapolis. When General Bolden joined NASA as an astronaut, that dynamic was in play, as there were still numerous holdovers from the earlier Mercury, Gemini, and Apollo eras, and they were not at all shy about sharing their comparative senses of the different regimens experienced by the astronaut classes and cohorts over time.

"If you go back to the Mercury-Gemini-Apollo era, that was really all about physical and medical testing, all the stuff they had to do that made *The Right Stuff*," General Bolden said with a chuckle. "And those guys would explain to us when we came in that all that stuff was doggone challenging and taxing. But we did not have anything at all like that. Our experience was more heavily weighted toward psychological and mental testing, looking at how you could handle isolation and how you worked as a team. And it is even more so that way today, since everybody flies now on anything from a four- to seven-person crew. If you are not a team player, you just are not going to be able to contribute to the success of the mission, and you are probably not going to do very well if you are spending six months on the International Space Station the way that crew members do today. We saw two psychiatrists for an hour each, a good cop and a bad cop, as was generally the way that NASA did it back then, and that was it for our psychological screening. Today, if somebody passes the first week of initial screening, then they go through a second week that is almost all psychological tests and written evaluations. We did not really do any of that, but today, that is the heaviest part of the second week of candidacy."

While NASA's Human Health and Performance (HH&P) Directorate can be cagey about the detailed specifics of the current psychological evaluation programs used to screen astronauts for what they euphemistically term "behavioral health," their public-facing materials note that they are seeking to identify who may, and may not, adapt to and perform within extremely demanding, close-quarters situations. Lack of privacy, variable workloads, long moments of boredom potentially interrupted by instants of extreme terror, and long separations from family members and friends are givens among those seeking to travel into space, especially as NASA considers new long-term missions to the Moon and, eventually, to Mars; the latter journey is expected to involve crews living and working in the space of a small studio apartment for up to thirty straight months.

Specifically, HH&P's website on behavioral health explains that "astronauts solve problems and encourage one another during long missions. The conditions of spaceflight can make teamwork difficult. Astronauts must maintain situational awareness in an ever-changing environment, so they know what information needs to be shared with one another and ground control. They also need to be able to effectively communicate complex information to people with different professional backgrounds.

Astronauts aboard the ISS are roommates. They must be considerate of others and be able to effectively resolve disagreements. . . . The small crew will need to solve problems and seamlessly coordinate on complex tasks such as landing on Mars with no real-time support from Earth. The BHP [behavioral health and performance] team conducts research to identify which combinations of astronauts will most likely work well together, where teamwork problems are likely to occur over the course of a mission, and the training and in-mission interventions that help the team accomplish amazing feats such as safely landing humans on Mars."

The rigorous evaluation processes, with their extremely high attrition rates, are intended to weed out candidates with latent mental health disorders via written and interview-based evaluations supplemented by field exercises designed to simulate the rigors of space travel and the unpredictability of events that astronauts may face between launch and landing. Good social skills, an easygoing nature, and emotional resilience are cited as key positive attributes closely correlating to programmatic success, while subordinance, gullibility, impatience, irritability, low openness to new ideas and experiences, and egotism are deemed detrimental to candidates' applications. And even after acceptance into the astronaut program, testing and evaluation continues, most notably through various ongoing studies of the physical and psychological health challenges faced by astronauts serving long-duration missions on the ISS. (Astronaut Frank Rubio holds the current American record for uninterrupted time in space, having clocked 371 days aloft in the ISS between September 2022 and September 2023. Rubio's impressive feat still pales against the all-time aloft record of 437 continuous days aloft, set by Russian cosmonaut Valeri Polyakov between January 1994 and March 1995. Missions to Mars will be longer yet.) These data-driven feedback loops that balance real space experiences against predicted results are key to honing the tests and trials faced by would-be astronauts, now and in the future. It is safe to presume that they won't be getting any less rigorous.

While the modern psychological testing aspects of the astronauts' crucibles are an ever-evolving work in progress, General Bolden did affirm our sense that many of *The Right Stuff*–era training requirements were less anchored in any practical need than in the mysteries and uncertainties associated with manned space flight at the time, plus the fact that only the astronauts were (eventually) willing to tell the doctors when enough was enough. "You know, back then with the Mercury-Gemini-Apollo guys, it was all about them going into the great unknown," he said with a laugh. "But once they had done that, and the Shuttle rolled around, there were not that many questions about what kind of person do we need to be able to withstand the physical stresses of launch. We had already learned that: launch is eight and a half minutes, and almost anybody can do that, so long as they know what to expect and they are taught how to do the Valsalva maneuver [exhaling forcefully against resistance, either with the nose pinched shut or the glottis closed] to equalize pressure and withstand high G's and everything.

"The Space Shuttles were really nothing like the Mercury-Gemini-Apollo or the Soyuz spacecraft that we fly with the Russians," General Bolden continued. "I would not say they were exactly a G-less spacecraft, but I always referred to the Shuttle as a 'gentleman's airplane' or a 'gentleman's spaceship.' It launches, and the maximum number of G's [one G = the downward pull of gravity against our bodies at rest at sea level] you experience through launch is about three. Lift-off is about a G and a half, nowhere close to an aircraft catapult shot even. That is like being with your teenage son or daughter in the car when they take off from a stop sign. You experience three G's for about forty-five seconds or so, just prior to the main engines cutting off, when a four-million-pound vehicle with seven million pounds of thrust is reduced to a two-hundred-thousand-pound vehicle with about a million and a half pounds of thrust. They reduce the power on the engines as much as they can, but they really cannot get it below an acceleration of about three G's, for maybe forty-five seconds. Coming back home, the maximum you feel is about two G's. And that's it. Unlike, you know, Soyuz being a ballistic vehicle for all intents and purposes. Sometimes we have had crews that have experienced a nine G reentry on Soyuz. That would have been devastating in the Shuttles."

To provide training in how to handle Soyuz-level gravitational forces, the centrifuge remains one of the training relics familiar to both the original Mercury Seven astronauts and their contemporary descendants. "Because we select far more civilians than we do military personnel today, and because we select a lot of people who have not been in high-performance aircraft, everybody today goes through the centrifuge, no matter what," explained General Bolden. "When I applied, unless you were a nonmilitary person, there was no centrifuge training. Everybody does that today, and I think it is mainly because we are going back to capsules, and so they try their best to get everybody accustomed to what a high-G environment is going to be like by putting them through the centrifuge. The Russians still use the centrifuge for high-G training too, and I would say probably going through the Russian system is much more physically demanding than our system at this point because the Russians are still old-fashioned in a lot of ways. They do a lot of the same old stuff they always did because their spacecraft have not changed significantly from the beginning; Soyuz is basically the same vehicle they have always flown."

For most of the history of American space travel and exploration, NASA was the only game in town, and what NASA directed, and what NASA wanted, were what the various would-be space travelers did. While the dawn of the commercial astronaut era has begun to nibble away at that singular hegemony, NASA's collective experience and knowledge still allow it to shape the ways in which American astronauts and their international colleagues train for spaceflight, though the commercial Axiom Space (for which General Bolden serves as senior strategic advisor) is beginning to peel away some of that NASA-centric training focus. "Up until the birth of Axiom Space, everybody who went to space, from whatever country, everybody flew either with us or they flew with the Russians because the Chinese still have not gone out and brought in foreign flight participants," observed General Bolden. "But beyond Axiom, everybody else comes to Houston, is integrated into the NASA training program, and so they do whatever NASA astronauts do. It does not make any difference where they came from, whether they are military or hard science or what, they are integrated into the class. I had two Europeans in my own astronaut class, one from the Netherlands and one from Belgium, and from day one they did everything that we did. All the physical training, everything that we did, they did right alongside us. And that is still the way it is. So even the commercial guys who fly now with Axiom and SpaceX, SpaceX gives them the training on the Dragon—you know, on the capsule that they are going to ride to space—but NASA provides them a lot of the prelaunch training and stuff that they are going to do on the International Space Station, what equipment is on the station, how do you activate it, all that kind of stuff. So, it's kind of a hybrid today, where whoever you're flying with gives you the training on the launch vehicle and entry, but NASA gives you the mission training."

Beyond his own involvement with Axiom Space, General Bolden sees the emergence of the broader commercial space sector most favorably. "The commercial programs have had a very positive impact," he noted. "The most important impact is getting the cost of launch down, especially with SpaceX entering the mix, so that has allowed more people to think about sending humans or payloads into space. I am going to guess here, but I think the price of a launch now is about a fifth of what it used to be with the big guys running everything for the government. Axiom Space has a crew on the International Space Station right now [Axiom Mission 3] that is completely commercial, and is the first all-international crew, with five nations represented by the four astronauts." (Mission commander Michael [Mike] López-Alegría is a dual U.S.–Spanish citizen; he was a member of NASA Astronaut Group 14, announced in 1992, and Axiom Mission 3 is his sixth trip to space—four with NASA, and two commercial flights.)

"Axiom Mission 3 also has an Italian air force jet fighter pilot who's Mike's copilot. They have a Turkish pilot who is one of the mission specialists, and they have a Swedish pilot who represents both Sweden and the European Space Agency. ESA has realized that by going to the commercial sector, they can get more of their astronauts flown than they were able to do before under the agreement with NASA, which really delegates a small number of astronauts from any country outside of the United States to go to space. The advent of commercial space flight has benefited everybody, all around. And the astronauts, as they always do, they have adjusted well," General Bolden concluded, with a wry and knowing laugh.

While General Bolden's sense of the current training experiences for NASA, Axiom Space, and allied astronautical programs may not paint them as the grueling crucibles that the early Mercury, Gemini, and Apollo astronauts faced, he feels that it is important to note that the lightening of the physical, mental, and psychological loads required to get from astronaut candidate to astronaut are possible because, in some ways, the key crucible pipeline process associated with becoming a space traveler has moved from the post-acceptance training period to the pre-acceptance screening and vetting period.

"I don't know the exact numbers off the top of my head, but the percentage of non-selection is massive compared to the applicants," General Bolden noted. "In my class, I think there were 1,800 applicants and there were nineteen of us selected. Then for my first class as NASA administrator, I want to say twenty-eight thousand applied and we picked eight. And that is not unusual to have tens of thousands of applicants and single-digit selections. The Class of 1978, just before my class, was an exception to that rule because we were really getting down to very few astronauts left in the office from the early days, coupled with unrealistically massive plans for the Shuttles; people foolishly thought we were going to hit fifty flights a year. That never happened, obviously, but nonetheless, if you hung around, even if you were part of those big groups, you flew. Everybody flies, with very, very few exceptions, and that is by design. NASA prides itself on its ability to select winners, which means the ability to select people who are going to have the fortitude to stick through the training program, and the patience to wait years to fly. They very seldom have someone who does not fly, voluntarily or otherwise, other than people who were killed or died in training or something." (Note that astronauts routinely use the word "fly" to describe their space travels, a relic of the days when astronauts were pilots first, and did not wish to be perceived as passive "spam in a can" payloads fully guided by ground control, but rather worked to be active drivers of all actions associated with their spacecraft, just as conventional pilots have full control and command oversight over their own atmospheric craft.)

"Even the guys from the Apollo era who did not fly after Apollo 18 and the subsequent flights were cancelled, if they stuck around, they flew," continued General Bolden. "Some of them were flown on Skylab, but everybody else that stayed around came back and flew on Shuttles in the earlier days of the program. When we moved to flying anywhere from five to eight people per flight, that gave NASA the opportunity to fly everybody that was there and waiting for twenty years. There was a guy named Don Lind who became the oldest person to fly at that time when he flew at the age of sixty-six, and that was his first time!"

Those extremely tight recruiting numbers, and NASA's organizational commitment to making sure that those who are selected are given the opportunities to do the jobs they were hired to do, serve to keep the astronaut community a most exclusive one, even if every applicant is not poked, prodded, tortured, and tormented in the ways that the Mercury Seven were. The total number of people who have flown in space (using either the U.S. Armed Forces rubric of fifty miles aloft or the FAI rubric of one hundred kilometers aloft) is about 675 at the time of this writing, keeping astronaut, cosmonaut, and "navigating celestial heaven personnel" among the most truly exclusive professional vocations in human history. The NASA Astronaut Corps currently counts only about forty members in its ranks, about 40 percent of them women; the highwater mark for the Astronaut Corps occurred in 2000, when there were 149 members in the cohort.

While General Bolden enthusiastically embraces the tight access paths that have shaped the American space program since the dawn of the Space Shuttle era and beyond, he also recognizes both the vast backlog of interest and desires swirling around space travel as well as the benefits that might accrue should more people be admitted to his most-esteemed and elite professional community. "I really do want to stress how important I think the value of having people go to space has been and continues to be," he concluded. "In your writing about crucibles, I suspect a lot of them are going to sort of be about these types of clubs where everybody is fighting to get in, just so that they can demonstrate that they can do all this amazing stuff. But I think there is a slight difference in what drives people to become astronauts. Most astronauts and astronaut candidates that I have met want to make a difference in the world, and they have heard how going to space dramatically changes your perspective on the planet. If you go to the NASA website, they have a feature on there right now called 'Astronaut Perspectives.' And they go through probably twenty or so astronauts, from the beginning of the Shuttle era to today, people who have spent six months on the International Space Station, or whatever else. And they all, to a person, talk about how their perspective on the planet dramatically changed by going into space, and they all want other people to fly so that they will have that same experience. In fact, Reid Wiseman, who at one time was the chief of the Astronaut Office once said to me that 'I just cannot believe that anybody who has an opportunity to go to space, whether it is for twenty seconds or for twenty months, cannot help but be moved by the planet and the impact that we have on it. Good and bad.' Everybody who has been to space believes that if we could just get more people off the planet, we might be able to get along better while living here."

CHAPTER 4

Poor Fellow Soldiers of Christ: The Knights Templar

"Power is not an institution, and not a structure; neither is it a certain strength we are endowed with; it is the name that one attributes to a complex strategical situation in a particular society."
—Michel Foucault

"History is an account, mostly false, of events, mostly unimportant, which are brought about by rulers, mostly knaves, and soldiers, mostly fools."
—Ambrose Bierce

GERALDINE BROOKS IS A COMMERCIALLY successful, critically acclaimed, Pulitzer Prize–winning author whose six novels sit comfortably as contemporary exemplars of the "historical fiction" literary genre. In an archival interview on her website, Brooks explains her passion for her chosen creative idiom thusly: "The thing that most attracts me to historical fiction is taking the factual record as far as it is known, using that as scaffolding, and then letting imagination build the structure that fills in those things we can never find out for sure." The flexibility and creative potential of the idiom has fueled a significant rise in the genre's profile and popularity throughout the English-reading world in the first two decades of the twenty-first century, perhaps creating the impression that it is a modern literary form, the product of Google-era access to historical facts and records, atop which audience-pleasing fictional elements can be built. But such an interpretation would be wrong, as Scottish polymath Sir Walter Scott essentially created the form, as we now understand it, in the early nineteenth century via a long series of works collectively known as the Waverley Novels.

Between 1814's *Waverley; or, 'Tis Sixty Years Since* and 1831's *Castle Dangerous*, Scott published twenty-six novels, temporally set between the eleventh and nineteenth centuries (one book in the series, *St. Ronan's Well*, was essentially a "current-time" work), with various plots set in Scotland, England, France, Belgium, Wales, the Holy Land, the Netherlands, Switzerland, and Turkey. For reasons still argued by literary scholars, with no definitive answer forthcoming, Scott did not acknowledge his creations by name until 1827, with the works he crafted before that time being mysteriously credited to "the author of *Waverley*." Despite their strange original attributions, Scott's novels were among the most widely read and frequently reprinted books in Europe and beyond until well into the twentieth century, at which point they also often became fodder for film and television adaptations.

Arguably the most influential and beloved of the Waverley Novels was the tenth in the series, 1819's *Ivanhoe*. Originally published in three standalone installments, *Ivanhoe* is set in the closing years of the twelfth century in northeastern England, and features such leading characters as King Richard the Lionheart, his brother John (a prince during the novel's narrative scope, though later King of England in his own right), and Robin Hood, Friar Tuck, Alan-a-Dale, and their Band of Merry Men. While the quasi-historical Robin Hood mythos had existed for centuries in England, our modern understanding of its principles and principals alike is almost completely anchored in Sir Walter Scott's *Ivanhoe* treatment, as are the commonly understood narratives associated with "Good King Richard" and the villainous-to-weaselly Prince John.

Ivanhoe's chief antagonist, while perhaps not as well remembered by name as his previously mentioned character counterparts, also set a modern template for a particular class of stock medieval characters: the Knights Templar. Scott's representative Templar is Sir Brian de Bois-Guilbert, introduced in *Ivanhoe*'s text thusly: "That name has been spread wide both for good and evil. They say he is valiant as the bravest of his order; but stained with their usual vices, pride, arrogance, cruelty, and voluptuousness; a hard-hearted man, who knows neither fear of earth, nor awe of heaven." Later, Scott elaborated further on de Bois-Guilbert's appearance and character: "His dress was as rich, and his appearance far more commanding, than that of his companion. He had exchanged his shirt of mail for an under tunic of dark purple silk, garnished with furs, over which flowed his long robe of spotless white, in ample folds. The eight-pointed cross of his order was cut on the shoulder of his mantle in black velvet. The high cap no longer invested his brows, which were only shaded by short and thick curled hair of a raven blackness, corresponding to his unusually swart complexion. Nothing could be more gracefully majestic than his step and manner, had they not been marked by a predominant air of haughtiness, easily acquired by the exercise of unresisted authority."

Sir Brian the Knight Templar is an epically serious villain in Scott's *Ivanhoe*, evincing and engaging in a wide variety of sociopathic beliefs and behaviors, shrouded beneath, and justified by, multilayered cloaks of wealth, privilege, political connection, and self-righteous spirituality. As typically happens with most literary Big Bads, de Bois-Guilbert eventually gets his comeuppance, done in by the great beast hubris in his dramatic final reckoning, his complicated skein of skewed principles eventually creating a circle of peril from which he cannot escape. But Scott's skilled depictions of Sir Brian's high-handed blend of power, brains, spiritual strength, and malefic menace made for great and memorable reading, another codified character study that has echoed throughout English-language literature for two centuries and counting.

Mysterious and often malignant Knights Templar characters have appeared in such popular modern novels as Dan Brown's

The Da Vinci Code and Umberto Eco's *Foucault's Pendulum*. The pseudo-historical *The Holy Blood and the Holy Grail* by Michael Baigent, Richard Leigh, and Henry Lincoln has been a steady international bestseller since its original release in 1982, knitting Templar-based myths into a vast conspiratorial web that includes, among other things, the French Merovingian dynasty, allegedly the extant sacred royal bloodline of Jesus of Nazareth and Mary Magdalene. Knights Templar motifs and references also appear regularly in the literature and practices of a variety of modern fraternal orders (many of them secretive) including Freemasonry, temperance organizations like the International Order of Good Templars and the Tempel Riddare Orden, and "neo-Templar" groups of various styles, types, and reaches, including Knights Templar International, the Sovereign Military Order of the Temple of Jerusalem, the Order of the Solar Temple, and the Priory of Sion.

On some plane, "Knights Templar" is now as evocative a sobriquet as "Illuminati" or "Deep State" when it comes to creative shorthand for secretive cabals allegedly pulling the strings that make the world go 'round, primarily for their own nefarious purposes, and typically powered by secret or arcane rites, objects, treasures, or talismans beyond the reach or ken of the uninitiated. (While the modern use of "Illuminati" is largely fanciful, like the modern use of "Knights Templar," the name is drawn from the history of a real organization, the Bavarian Illuminati, founded in 1776 to resist religious influence in the public sphere and to shine the proverbial spotlight on abuses of state power.) Holy Grail? Shroud of Turin? Ark of the Covenant? All of them have been claimed to rest in the hands of the Knights Templar.

The passage of time, the prominence of the Waverley Novels and the panoply of later works they inspired, and Hollywood mythmaking have created a situation where much popularly accepted conventional wisdom about the medieval period in which the Knights Templar thrived is, in fact, far more anchored in historical fiction than in history. Dr. Eleanor Janega, professor of medieval and early modern history at the London School of Economics, has diligently worked to rectify such misperceptions about the Middle Ages, deploying a variety of academic and popular outlets. Her Going Medieval website, which promises (and delivers) "Medieval History, Pop Culture, Swearing" is a stellar resource for separating historical wheat from quasi-historical chaff on a variety of fascinating topics, both highbrow and low.

"When it comes to the Middle Ages, we tend to know more today about the fanciest guys," Dr. Janega explained in an interview with us. "And that is super, super normal if you think about it because, you know, eight hundred years is a long time ago, people did not always bother writing things down because parchment was expensive, and it was expensive to just have enough room to keep books around for eight hundreds of years. So, the stuff that ends up surviving is the stuff about the fanciest guys, which means we know a lot about the Knights Templar, because those guys were almost like a form of superstar for regular old medieval people. They represented a romantic thing that medieval people wanted, an idea that there were people on their side who were going to look after them, and who could facilitate their wildest dreams, which often involved going to Jerusalem as pilgrims. There was a real reverence on the part of ordinary people for the Knights Templar, which is ultimately what brought them down, because the kings came to hate their power and popularity."

So, who, really, were the Knights Templar, factually and historically speaking? The Poor Fellow-Soldiers of Christ and of the Temple of Solomon (to provide their full name) were established in approximately 1120 CE by a group of seven French knights who took monastic vows, created a fraternal brotherhood, and pledged to defend Christian pilgrims and their chosen destinations in the Holy Land. Four Crusader states (often collectively referred to in contemporary literature as Outremer, French for "overseas") had been established in the Levant in the early twelfth century to formalize and solidify territorial gains made in the region by Christian armies during the First Crusade against the Seljuk Empire (1095–1102). The most powerful and influential of the Crusader states was the Kingdom of Jerusalem, and in 1120 its king, Baldwin II, granted a former mosque on the Temple Mount of Jerusalem to the nascent order of fighting Christian brothers. The ancient mosque site was grandiloquently rebranded as the "Temple of Solomon," bestowing the monastic knights who established their headquarters there with the name "Templars," which has stuck to and with them, for better and for worse, for the better part of a millennium.

"Pilgrimage was such a much bigger deal for medieval Christians than it is now," Dr. Janega explained. "For people in the Middle Ages, being in the places where those awesome holy things happened, communicating with these things in person, that really mattered on a very deep, spiritual level for them. The Knights Templar essentially represented the possibility of that happening. Because travel was very dangerous in the Middle Ages. There were no such things as police, right? If you were walking down a road in the well-run kingdoms and places, there might have been people watching to make sure that nothing happened to you, but beyond that, it was pretty dangerous out there. And it was doubly dangerous if you were going over to the Middle East and you didn't know where you were going and you were surrounded by people that you couldn't communicate with. So, the Knights Templar kind of set up a network of places where you knew that if you made it to one of their *krak des chevaliers*, kind of like castle hotels, then there would be a place to stay where you were going to be protected. And the Knights Templar really were fearsome guys who actually did get into fights for people. They would bust some heads, if that's what they felt like they needed to do, on the part of their Christian pilgrims."

In 1128, the influential Cistercian abbot Bernard of Clairvaux attended the Council of Troyes, where the outlines of the emergent Templar order were brought into focus, in large part through Bernard's *Liber ad milites Templi: De laude novae militae*, a treatise crafted "in praise of the new knighthood." Bernard's text opened with grand words of exhortation for the Knights of the Temple, seeing them as the sacred and necessary replacement for the members of the "worldly knighthood," which Bernard concisely equated with "knavery." The abbot then further discredited worldly knights by asking of their finery and pomp, "Are these the trappings of a warrior or are they not rather the trinkets of a woman? Do you think the swords of your foes will be turned back by your gold, spare your jewels, or be unable to pierce your silks?"

Compare and contrast those dismissive remarks with Bernard's florid praise for "the new knighthood," as he dubbed it: "The knight of Christ, I say, may strike with confidence and die yet more confidently, for he serves Christ when he strikes, and serves himself when he falls. Neither does he bear the sword in vain, for he is God's minister, for the punishment of evildoers and for the praise of the good. If he kills an evildoer, he is not a mankiller, but, if I may so put it, a killer of evil. He is evidently the avenger of Christ towards evildoers and he is rightly considered a defender of Christians. Should he be killed himself, we know that he has not perished, but has come safely into port. When he inflicts death, it is to Christ's profit, and when he suffers death, it is for his own gain."

And lest people, common and exalted alike, question the theological soundness of a priestly soldier class, Bernard answered rhetorically that "if it is never permissible for a Christian to strike with the sword, why did the Savior's precursor bid the soldiers to be content with their pay, and not rather forbid them to follow this calling?" He then summarized his case, explaining, "Thus in a wonderous and unique manner [the Templar Knights] appear gentler than lambs, yet fiercer than lions. I do not know if it would be more appropriate to refer to them as monks or as soldiers, unless perhaps it would be better to recognize them as being both. Indeed, they lack neither monastic meekness nor military might. What can we say of this, except that this has been done by the Lord, and it is marvelous in our eyes. These are the picked troops of God, whom he has recruited from the ends of the earth; the valiant men of Israel chosen to guard well and faithfully that tomb which is the bed of the true Solomon, each man sword in hand, and superbly trained to war."

His arguments were enthusiastically received, and Pope Honorius II formally recognized the order in 1129, the first such Catholic monastic military organization to be created. Within two decades, the Templars were engaging in their first significant military campaigns during the Second Crusade, and they were also well upon their way to becoming one of the most important religious, military, and financial organizations in late-medieval Europe, with gifts of money, livestock, land, comestibles, and armaments pouring in from donors across the continent's socioeconomic strata. While some benefactors clearly supported the Knights Templar because they recognized and believed in the importance of keeping the Holy Land open to pilgrims, others saw support of such an apparently blessed organization as a means of buying themselves a better afterlife, or at least a way to benefit in this earthly sphere from the prayers offered by the Knights on behalf of their generous donors. So fortified with various forms of capital, the Templars were also able to expand their geographic and political sphere of influence by exacting tribute from conquered cities (in addition to their activities in the Levant, they were also active in Iberia during the *Reconquista* against Moorish states and armies, and in the Baltic Crusades) and through the acquisition of convents and priories across the continent.

"The Templar marketing motto could have been: 'We'll fight for you, and we'll pray for you,'" Dr. Janega summarized evocatively. "That's what the Templars were all about, really. And that was compelling for people. When you saw them walking down the road, they were impressive, especially in the Middle East, where they're tromping around in fifty pounds of plate armor, head to toe, consciously choosing to never stop being Europeans, so that when people came over and saw them, they would say, 'Ah, yes! A Knight! I know what that is, I can go to them for help.' I mean, if they dressed like the locals, they probably would have been less prone to pass out in the heat so easily, but they would have lost that connection, that ready ability to say, 'Hi, I'm here to bodyguard any Europeans who show up.'

"To their credit, the Knights Templar really did live a grueling lifestyle, in their 'fight for you and pray for you' mode," Dr. Janega continued. "Because since they were part monk and part knight, beyond the fighting stuff, they followed an intentionally difficult daily plan where they had to be praying at certain times of day, singing at certain times of day, and that meant getting up all night long, every couple of hours, for matins, for lauds, whatever. And they did that on purpose, because they're like, 'This sucks, you know? And everyone hates it, right? This is such an awful thing to do, so we must really be devoted to God, to do this thing.' And it never stopped. The idea was that they were breaking you from the ordinary world where people went to sleep when the sun went down and then they got up before the sun came up, but the Knights Templar were not normal people. And a lot of them eventually came to love that aspect of their lives. It felt like an initiation at the beginning and then at the end they were like, 'Oh, this is just how we organize our days. We just have a really messed up sleep schedule.' They were very devoted to the idea of *ora et labora*, prayer and work, where everything they did was for the glory of God."

Extreme piety notwithstanding, the combination of the Templars' financial wealth, military strength, and eventual ubiquity across the continent's metropolitan centers led to their castles becoming repositories for a variety of assets, held both in and for their own interests, as well as for those of their secular and religious neighbors. By the thirteenth century, the Templar organization essentially functioned as a massive cross-continental banking institution, one of the most important and sophisticated financial pedestals of late-medieval Europe's economy. While the number of actual Templar Knights was modest (at most, there were probably about five hundred knights active at the organization's apex), the number of "sergeants" (e.g., lay support staff, administrators, noncombatant religious members, tradesmen, and craftsmen, etc.) was much larger, allowing the wishes and reach of the order's grand masters to be fostered and executed far more readily and effectively than would have been the case within an all-military, all-monastic organization. The model pioneered by the Knights Templar was mirrored by later, often competing, military orders, including most prominently the Order of Knights of the Hospital of Saint John of Jerusalem ("Knights Hospitaller") and the Order of Brothers of the German House of Saint Mary in Jerusalem ("Teutonic Knights"), among others.

While the Knights Templar's economic strength was unparalleled in Europe throughout the thirteenth century, their military fortunes and successes in the Middle East were often less noteworthy, with occasional tactical successes failing to stanch the slow and steady erosion of Crusader holdings in the Levant. Following the Siege of Acre (1291) and the Siege of Ruad (1302), the Kingdom of Jerusalem fell, and Christian forces no longer controlled any significant holdings in the Holy Land. As their ostensibly foundational purpose collapsed, various European heads of state and leaders in the Catholic Church began to question the wisdom of the Templars' independent control of such formidable assets, and pressure built across Europe's courts and palaces for the Church to dilute Templar influence and power by merging the order with the Teutonic Knights and Knights Hospitaller.

As these political machinations unfolded, accusations began to circulate across various European courts about the Templars' secret rites and rituals, specifically that their initiation crucible for would-be Knights involved spitting and urinating on a crucifix, the denial of Jesus as the human aspect of a triune God, "indecent kissing," "unnatural lust," and various forms of sanctioned idolatry, including the worship of a graven head of a dark deity called Baphomet. In 1307, France's King Philip IV actively moved on these charges and sentiments by ordering the arrest of all Templar Knights in France, with their property confiscated by agents of the state. (Philip and France were both in significant and unsustainable debt to the Templars, which no doubt played a role in the King's decision-making regarding the order.)

While Pope Clement V initially defended the Knights, after King Philip presented the pope with confessions from leading French Templars, including Grand Master Jacques de Molay, Clement had a change of heart and ordered the arrest of all Knights Templar in Western Europe. Following a mass trial in 1310, over fifty Templars were burned at the stake, and Pope Clement formally and finally terminated the order in 1312; its final grand master, de Molay, was burned at the stake in 1314, protesting both his own and his order's innocence until the flames silenced him. While some Templar assets were transferred to the Knights Hospitaller, many others ended up in the hands of the various governments that had long benefited from the Templars' financial services, the nobles' debts conveniently erased, their coffers conveniently restored by the assets that had once secured those debts.

Legends of surviving secretive cells of Templar Knights began flourishing soon after their demise, tied in part to presumptions that their long stewardship of the "Temple of Solomon" must certainly have allowed them to access various powerful and sacred relics from its depths, none of which were publicly disclosed or displayed by the organizations that were otherwise happy to flog their forebears' remnants. The titillating nature of the public charges against Templar initiation rites and

practices further entrenched and enhanced the sense of secretive sacred depravity associated with the order, and those narratives have been baked deeply into popular consciousness over
the centuries, occasionally bumped into front-of-mind cultural
space by the success of works like *Ivanhoe*, *The Da Vinci Code*,
and *Holy Blood, Holy Grail*.

"Do I think that some Knights Templar influence survived at
the time? Yes, 100 percent," Dr. Janega averred. "The kings and
the church did not manage to get them all. It was a huge organization and a lot of them just kind of snuck away. There were
also places where the tradition of being a Templar held out longer, like the Temple in London, which hung on for a while after
the Templars in France went over like a house of cards. And it
really was the kings more than the church that did them in. The
medieval church was a lot more higgledy-piggledy than people
realize. It took a long time in the Middle Ages for the church
to get its ducks in a row. They spent centuries just being like,
'Guys! We are important, we're really important!' before anyone
really kind of cared what the pope thought, right? So, the kings
had a lot more power than people may realize, compared to the
church. And kings just do things because they can."

The only (known) organization with any legitimate claim to
being a true (if wan) successor to the Templar order would be
Portugal's Military Order of Christ, founded in 1319 under the
protection of King Denis, and joined by many of Iberia's surviving Templars; Denis refused to follow Paris and Rome's lead on
persecuting the former Templars as an expression of gratitude for
their efforts in Iberia during the *Reconquista*. The Military Order of
Christ was secularized in 1789, briefly abolished in the early twentieth century, and now serves primarily as an honorific and advisory body under the ultimate supervision and control of Portugal's
president, who serves as the order's honorary grand master.

In a book focused, as this one is, on initiation crucibles
as rites of passage, the fact that the Templars' downfall was

directly attributed to their own practices on such fronts could certainly be posited as a cautionary tale. But a more important lesson to be taken from the Templars' demise is that it remains vitally important to separate historical fiction from history itself because the charges against the Templars were almost certainly falsified, and the confessions that confirmed them were the results of torture, as many leading Templars' confessions were recanted after they had been sentenced to death.

While the ancient nature of Templar history makes it more difficult to ascertain exactly how they initiated their novices into the order, there was indeed a formal initiation ceremony known as *Receptio*. Non-Templar involvement in the ceremony was discouraged, a fact that allowed the fabrications against the order to stand because they had few if any non-Templar allies who could rebut the claims of their persecutors. Initiates turned their own personal assets over to the order and took formal vows of obedience, chastity, piety, and poverty. Bernard of Clairvaux provided what is likely an idealized, but at least conceptually more historically accurate, record of what the Knights Templar experience may have looked like to its incoming initiates.

"Discipline is in no way lacking and obedience is never despised," wrote Bernard in *Liber ad milites Templi: De laude novae militae*. "As Scripture testifies, the undisciplined son shall perish and rebellion is as the sin of witchcraft, to refuse obedience is like the crime of idolatry. Therefore, they come and go at the bidding of their superior. They wear what he gives them, and do not presume to wear or to eat anything from another source. Thus, they shun every excess in clothing and food and content themselves with what is necessary. They live as brothers in joyful and sober company, without wives or children. So that their evangelical perfection will lack nothing, they dwell united in one family with no personal property whatever, careful to keep the unity of the Spirit in the bond of peace. You may say that the whole multitude has but one heart and one soul to the point that nobody follows his own will, but rather seeks to follow the commander.

"They never sit in idleness or wander about aimlessly, but on the rare occasions when they are not on duty, they are always careful to earn their bread by repairing their worn armor and torn clothing, or simply by setting things to order. For the rest, they are guided by the common needs and by the orders of their master," Bernard continued. "There is no distinction of persons among them, and deference is shown to merit rather than to noble blood. They rival one another in mutual consideration, and they carry one another's burdens, thus fulfilling the law of Christ. No inappropriate word, idle deed, unrestrained laugh, not even the slightest whisper or murmur is left uncorrected once it has been detected. They foreswear dice and chess, and abhor the chase; they take no delight in the ridiculous cruelty of falconry, as is the custom. As for jesters, magicians, bards, troubadours, and jousters, they despise and reject them as so many vanities and unsound deceptions. Their hair is worn short, in conformity with the Apostle's saying, that it is shameful for a man to cultivate flowing locks. Indeed, they seldom wash and never set their hair, content to appear tousled and dusty, bearing the marks of the sun and of their armor."

While Bernard, a strong advocate for the Poor Fellow-Soldiers of Christ and of the Temple of Solomon in their formational years, certainly had his own propagandistic motivations in so stylizing and idealizing the Templars, his depictions of life within the order are likely far less fanciful than the trumped-up charges upon which so many of the order's leaders were executed. Of course, such bland and simple virtue tends not to be remembered over history's long arc, and it certainly would have made Brian de Bois-Guilbert a far less compelling dramatic character five hundred years later in *Ivanhoe*, while a whole cottage industry of conspiracy theorists would have been forced to turn to or create other unsavory organizations in their quests to codify linear causes, correlations, and connections where none may truthfully exist. At bottom line, the ability to segregate historical fiction from history is the key to recognizing that the literary Knights Templar and the historic Knights Templar are not one and the same at all, but that as long as the former sells and thrills more than the latter, their narrative is likely to be the one that sticks in public perception.

CHAPTER 5

Knives in the Mountains: The Gurkhas

"One fears death because of ignorance, but when the 'flame of knowledge' is enkindled in the mind then the 'fear of death' ceases to exist."
—Atharva Veda

"If a man says he is not afraid of dying, he is either lying or is a Gurkha."
—Field Marshal Sam Manekshaw

THE FEDERAL DEMOCRATIC REPUBLIC OF Nepal is a geographically elongated, landlocked nation hugging the vertiginous terrain between the mighty and austere Himalayas and the fertile Indo-Gangetic Plain. Bordered on the north by the Chinese-ruled Tibet Autonomous Region, and otherwise surrounded by India, Nepal's relative isolation kept it free of direct European political and economic control through the long English colonial era in South and Southeast Asia (roughly 1612 to 1947), beyond its perceived utility to both the Imperial Chinese government and to British India as a buffer state between those competing regional mega-powers. The nation is ethnically and linguistically diverse and holds a place of prominence in the histories of two of the world's great religions: Siddhartha Gautama, the Buddha, was born in Lumbini, near Nepal's border with India, while the Kingdom of Nepal stood as the last surviving Hindu kingdom until 2008, when the monarchy (established in 1768) was abolished in the aftermath of the brutal Nepalese Civil War, which raged from 1996 to 2006.

Despite its success in resisting formal political control by distant European interests, Nepal has long exerted a pull and a fascination for Western travelers, in large part because of its extraordinary geological features. Eight of the world's ten tallest mountains are partially or entirely within its national borders, including Everest, the world's highest point, which was opened to foreign mountaineers in 1950. Since being summited in 1953 by Sir Edmund Hillary of New Zealand and Nepal's own Tenzing Norgay, of the Sherpa people, over twelve thousand subsequent summit ascents have been recorded by over six thousand different climbers, each one of the expeditions involving significant financial resources being poured into the Nepali economy. As of the time of this writing, thirty-six individuals have summited Everest ten or more times, twenty-eight of whom were or are Nepali guides, led by Kami Rita Sherpa, who completed his thirtieth ascent in May 2024. While "Sherpa" and "Nepali" are not synonymous (some Sherpa are from Tibet, and some Nepali guides are not Sherpa), the omnipresence and crucial importance of local guides in Himalayan mountaineering has transmuted the name of a proud and distinct ethnic and linguistic group into a catchall caste descriptor for "helpful locals" who assist outsiders with achieving glories that are rarely equitably shared with those who made them possible.

Beyond the draw of Everest and its neighboring Himalayan massifs, Nepal's capital city, Kathmandu (the preferred modern spelling, supplanting the obsolete Katmandu), has also served as a focal point for a particular form of Western interest, as the onetime terminal point of the so-called "Hippie Trail," an alternative tourism route from points in Europe and West Asia, involving an overland journey to Istanbul, then a trek across Turkey, Iran, Afghanistan, Pakistan, India, and ultimately into Nepal. Kathmandu's Freak Street (now known as Jhochhen Tole) served as a key point of arrival for the weary, hairy travelers, in large part because of its legal, government-licensed, and plentiful hashish shops. Kathmandu's standing as a hippie mecca unraveled in the early 1970s, when the Nepali government, losing patience with Freak Street's excesses, implemented strict dress codes for tourists and began deporting noncompliant visitors to India, allegedly with the strong encouragement of President Richard Nixon's State Department.

The demise of Freak Street, coupled with the Iranian Revolution, the Soviet Union's invasion of Afghanistan, and simmering territorial disputes between China, Pakistan, and India in the Kashmir region resulted in the collapse of the Hippie Trail, but not before a variety of Western artists and musicians had idealized it in perpetuity as a sort of countercultural nirvana, the place to go when no other places would do. That lingering resonance permeates into modern times through the music and lyrics of such diverse classic rock talents as Bob Seger, Cat Stevens, and Rush, among others. Tourism remains an important component of Nepal's economy accordingly, though modern visits to Kathmandu are less defined by cheap eats, plentiful drugs, and grotty lodging than they are by haute cuisine, modern hotel chains, and shopping sprees.

While the twin pulls of mountaineering and cultural tourism would seem to provide modern Nepal with a potentially robust economic base, the reality at ground level is that the benefits achieved by those draws from abroad are highly localized, often to the severe detriment of the local environment and culture. Far from the slopes of mountains with Western appeal or the urban center of Kathmandu, much of the nation exists and functions at near-subsistence levels, resulting in Nepal's consistent standing as one of the world's most impoverished countries, ranking unfavorably in various global hunger, literacy, and quality of life indices. Roughly two-thirds of the nation's population is engaged in agricultural work, though their efforts generate less than one-third of Nepal's gross domestic product. Nepal's tangible export activities are dominated by fabrics (especially

carpets), food stuffs (legumes, spices, juices, and teas most dom-
inantly), and products derived from its tough-to-extract natural
mineral resources. But in terms of direct impact on the lives and
well-being of many Nepali people, the most important export is
the sweat equity of their fellow countryfolk.

A comprehensive 2016 report by the International Labour
Organization (ILO) estimated that one in every four Nepali families has at least one member living outside of the country and
sending home "remittances" (defined as noncommercial trans-
fers of money by foreign workers) to support their own families and communities. Nepal is estimated by the ILO to be the
third-largest receiver of remittance income among the world's
nations, with over a quarter of the country's gross domestic
product coming from such extra-governmental and noncorpo-
rate monetary flows, offering far more expansive relief and benefit to the country's people than formal international investment
or local governmental involvement combined. Unfortunately,
the costs associated with securing foreign work permits and
travel expenses abroad are well beyond the means of most families, requiring their migrant workers to secure loans with interest rates as high as 35 percent, meaning they will need to work
far from home for years before their remittances benefit their
families, instead of their loan sharks.

Most Nepalis abroad work in the Middle East and Malaysia,
typically in low-paying, low-skilled jobs in the manufacturing,
construction, services, security, and domestic sectors. Nearly
three-quarters of the Nepali foreign workers have no training
prior to their employment abroad, and like most of the world's
169 million migrant workers, they labor in obscurity, enduring
living and working conditions that would appall most European
and American laborers and white-collar professionals alike. But
one group of Nepalis working abroad largely buck those trends
and perceptions, holding a highly respected stature both at home
and abroad, demonstrating the ways in which the completion of

strenuous crucibles defined by established elites can truly and fundamentally change the course of otherwise seemingly unremarkable lives. That select group are known as the Gurkhas, a highly regarded military order composed exclusively of Nepalis and Nepali-speaking residents of Northeast India.

Both the history and the name of the Gurkhas are closely knit within the history of Nepal itself. Prior to the mid-eighteenth century, Nepal's territory was fragmented into dozens of isolated fiefdoms and kingdoms, aligned at various times into a shifting tapestry of confederations. The Kingdom of Gorkha was founded within this vast regional checkerboard by Prince Dravya Shah in 1559, the kingdom's name derived from Gorakhnath, an eleventh-century Hindu warrior-saint. In the mid-eighteenth century, the Kingdom of Gorkha began a large-scale military campaign to subdue or annex its neighbors under the leadership of Prithvi Narayan Shah, who declared himself the first king of Nepal in 1768, having effectively unified the mountain hinterlands between Tibet and the holdings of the East India Company, England's quasi-governmental corporation that effectively ran its South and Southeast Asian land holdings. The Kingdom of Nepal's capital city was moved from rural Gorkha to cosmopolitan Kathmandu soon thereafter.

Prithvi Narayan Shah died in 1775 and was succeeded by his son, Pratap Singh Shah, who died of smallpox a mere three years into his reign, to be succeeded in turn by his two-year-old son, Rana Bahadur Shah, under the regencies of Queen Rajendra (Pratap Singh Shah's widow) and his uncle, also named Bahadur Shah. The regents and King Rana Bahadur Shah (once he came of age) continued the press to expand Nepal's borders, eventually invading Tibet, which sparked a counterinvasion by the Chinese Army on Tibet's behalf. With their territorial aspirations foiled northward, the Nepalis (now under the rule of Rana Bahadur Shah's son Girvan Yuddha Bikram Shah, who also became king at the age of two when his father abdicated to ensure his son's ascension) turned their gaze southward, an expansion that put them at direct odds with the

East India Company, eventually sparking the Anglo-Nepalese War in 1814. While the Nepalis fought gallantly, they were eventually overwhelmed by England's superior numbers and battlefield technology, and the Treaty of Sugauli in 1816 terminated Nepal's expansionist tendencies, forcing the Shah dynasty to yield vast swaths of their territory to the English, leading to an uneasy border situation that was not firmly resolved until 1830.

While the English were victorious in the Anglo-Nepalese War, their struggle against the Nepali forces was more difficult than initially expected, given their ostensible military superiority and greater troop numbers. Major-General Sir David Ochterlony, one of the more successful English commanders in the campaign, wisely recognized and celebrated the extreme military skill and stamina of the soldiers facing his own units. The Nepalese warriors fought in traditional garb and were most deft in melee situations, where the *khukuri*, a curved short sword, could inflict fearsome carnage; the blade was then and remains today a key symbol of the Nepalese military, both at home and throughout its global diaspora.

During the Anglo-Nepalese War, Ochterlony was quick to court and deploy defectors from the Nepalese Army to serve in irregular forces supplementing his own regular troops, eventually recruiting nearly five thousand men from a variety of Himalayan communities, all of whom were eventually lumped together in English parlance as "Gurkhas," even though many were not actually Gorkhalis (as natives of Gorkha were then known), just as "Sherpas" has become a catchall title not directly linked to its ethnic roots. In 1815, Ochterlony formally organized a unit dubbed the 1st Gorkha Rifles, leveraging the Nepalis' knowledge of their home region, military skill, and endurance in high-altitude battle to the benefit of English interests in India.

Under the terms of the Treaty of Sugauli, Gurkhas continued to be recruited for service with the East India Company, fighting successfully in a variety of campaigns through the first half of the nineteenth century. The Indian Rebellion of 1857, largely sparked by discontent with the East India Company's meddling in traditional religious and economic models across the Indian subcontinent, ended with the dissolution of the Company via the Government of India Act of 1858, with the Company's powers being transferred in whole to the British Crown; in 1877, Queen Victoria formalized this transition by declaring herself the Empress of India. The Gurkha regiments fought for the English during the Indian Rebellion, and, as a reward for their service, they were formally incorporated into the British Indian Army, rather than continuing to serve as irregulars or adjunct units.

In the early twentieth century, the Gurkha regiments were reorganized and redesignated as the Gurkha Rifles, with twenty battalions in ten regiments collectively branded as the Brigade of Gurkhas. Their performance in World Wars I and II directly contributed to their reputation as one the world's most effective and ferocious fighting units, with their members receiving a statistically improbable number of Victoria Crosses, the British equivalent to the U.S. Medal of Honor, the highest recognition offered for battlefield valor. As one of many possible representative examples, consider the case of Lachhiman Gurung, the famed "Gurkha who took on 200 soldiers with only one hand." In May 1945 in Burma, Rifleman Gurung's platoon was attacked by at least two hundred Japanese combatants. He successfully threw two Japanese grenades back at the enemy before the third exploded in his hand, grievously injuring him and his comrades. Seemingly undeterred, Gurung held off the Japanese assault for four hours, firing his rifle with his left hand, while taunting the Japanese with the Gurkha battle cry: "Ayo Gorkhali!" ("The Gurkhas are upon you!"). The Japanese eventually retreated, and it was estimated that thirty-one of the eighty-seven Japanese dead counted on the battlefield were killed by Gurung after his injury.

Lest that story feel a bit of an old-fashioned "that could never happen today" anecdote of simpler battlefield days, consider too the case of Corporal Dipprasad Pun, a third-generation Gurkha awarded the Conspicuous Gallantry Cross in 2011 for his actions against the Taliban in Afghanistan's Helmand province. As a sole sentry at a remote checkpoint, he witnessed Taliban forces surrounding his position, apparently planting bombs, after which he proceeded to unleash four hundred rifle rounds, seventeen grenades, and one landmine to drive his foes back, eventually resorting to beating one of them with his rifle tripod when he ran out of ammunition. The Taliban counterattacked him with AK-47s and rocket-propelled grenades, but Corporal Pun was able to evade their assaults, all the while moving into positions that maximized his ability to inflict carnage on his foes. It is stories like these that have framed the perception of the Gurkhas as nearly mystically gifted warriors, a sentiment accurately, if unexpectedly, voiced by England's now-controversial Prince Harry, who served with the Royal Gurkha Rifles' 1st Battalion in Afghanistan in 2007–2008: "When you know you are with the Gurkhas," Harry noted, "I think there's no safer place to be."

Following India's independence from its English overlords in 1947, the enlisted Gurkhas were given the opportunity of serving in the British Army or the newly organized Indian Army; six regiments worth of soldiers chose the latter option, while the remaining four regiments chose to serve with the British. In current times, Gurkhas serve in the Nepali Army, in the Indian Army, in the British Army, as security/police forces in Singapore and Brunei, and on a variety of UN Peacekeeping missions. While the unusual nature of their service model brings them perilously close to the definition of mercenaries under the provisions of the Geneva Conventions, they have been specifically exempted from bearing such a designation, and the negative connotations associated with it, along with the French Foreign Legion, which is discussed at length in another chapter of this book.

So how does Nepal "make" a Gurkha? Even before any formal crucibles are enacted, a key component to the process is one of high selectivity, given the vast numbers of young men (while England authorized female members for its Gurkha units in 2018, the Nepalese government put that change on hold in 2020, so the units remain entirely male at the point of this writing) who seek to join the forces, for both the prestige and for the life-changing opportunities for themselves and their families, their remittances unencumbered by the need to pay loan-sharking labor travel providers. A comprehensive 2019 report by the British Forces Broadcasting Service estimated that ten thousand men aged eighteen to twenty-one applied for that year's Gurkha recruitment campaign for the British Army, from which only 320 would be selected for service. While the COVID pandemic resulted in lightly amended recruiting procedures in subsequent years, the number of applicants has been increasing on a long-term trend for many years as Nepal's more remote corners gain mobile phone and internet access, allowing the government's recruiters to reach further than they have in the past in pursuit of the perfect candidates.

The "PRs" (potential recruits) identify which of the units (i.e., England, Nepal, India, Brunei, or Singapore) they wish to serve at the front end of the registration process, and those invited to move forward are first screened through regional centers in Dharan and Pokhara, with finalists invited to the headquarters of British Gurkhas Nepal, in the Kathmandu suburb of Jawalakhel. PRs may not register for consideration without a School Leaving Certificate and proof of Nepalese citizenship, which are strenuously screened and checked through multiple review steps to avoid fraudulent applications and any appearances of favoritism or bribery. The candidates must be at least five feet two inches tall, weigh at least 110 pounds, have a chest circumference of at least thirty-one inches, have passable vision and hearing, possess healthy teeth (no more than four fillings), and meet a variety of other quickly and readily evaluated physical evaluations, e.g., tuberculosis screening, hyper-extending joints, heart murmurs, bloody stool or urine, etc.

Once the PRs have satisfied the documentation and basic health requirements, they are put through a series of physical tests, involving a half-mile sprint, sit-ups, "underarm heaves" (pull-ups in American parlance), a seventy-five-pound standing weight lift, and a carry of two water jerry cans weighing over eight pounds together across a pitch that is about 30 percent longer than an American football field. Some of the physical components are simple pass/fail, others reward superior performance beyond the required minimums. At each step of the process, PRs who fail to satisfy the requirements are culled from the ranks and quietly escorted from the premises, their departures being screened away from their successful colleagues to reduce the public hurt and humiliation they may be feeling.

Next up, the surviving PRs are offered a series of educational written tests, in English, assessing both their language and math skills. Survivors of that round are then interviewed by a Nepali Gurkha officer and an English Gurkha officer, who seek to explore the candidates' characters and commitments to the core tenets of teamwork, discipline, integrity, maturity, resilience, and knowledge of military duties and history. The regional applicants are then ranked, with the highest performers being invited to the final round at Jawalakhel, where they endure further rounds of physical and language tests, a second interview, and an enhanced medical screening. At that point, the remaining PRs queue up for the notorious final crucible: the *doko* race, in which the aspiring Gurkhas must run five kilometers up the foothills of the Himalayas, carrying fifty-five pounds of rocks in rattan baskets on their backs, secured by straps wrapped around their heads. The *doko* race must be completed in no more than fifty-five minutes, though faster times increase the probability of success and selection. Upon completing the course, the PRs' baskets of rocks are reweighed; losing one along the route and reducing the load below the fifty-five-pound (twenty-five kilogram) minimum is instantly disqualifying.

Following the *doko* race, the candidates are then re-ranked, and those at the top of the screening process are offered positions within their selected units, an utterly transformational experience for them and their families alike, as they are looking at up to fifteen years (for the British Army recruits) or up to twenty-seven years (for the Singaporean security recruits) of guaranteed income at a compensation level approximately thirty-five times that earned by the average Nepali worker. Since 2009, an additional benefit has been provided to Gurkhas serving in the British Army: after four years of service, the Gurkhas are eligible to remain in Britain with full benefits of citizenship, a step which followed the English government's 2007 decision to finally provide the Gurkhas with pensions comparable to their British colleagues, after nearly two centuries of inequity on that front. For those successful PRs joining the British Army, they will likely leave for England within a month of their selection for service. The freshly minted Gurkha recruits then endure an eleven-week training course unique to their unit, followed by the standard twenty-eight weeks of training with other non-Gurkha enlistees in the combat infantry course and training for their selected areas of military specialization. Three years after their arrival in England, the Gurkhas are typically granted five months' leave and provided with transport, at no personal expense, back home to Nepal for the first time since their selection.

Given that the Gurkhas are one of the extant organizations that we have studied and documented in this book, it had seemed to be an easy research task to find members of the elite organization willing and able to discuss the transformational nature of their experiences. Interestingly enough, though, while there are no strict tenets regarding silence or secrecy, the number of documented interviews with members of the group is surprisingly small, and few, if any, of them dig into the sorts of inward-looking Western self-improvement, self-help, or self-actualization narratives that often anchor texts like this one. This counterintuitive fact is likely a byproduct of the primary religious traditions of the majority of contemporary Nepali people, who embrace a unique blend of animism with (mostly) Hinduism and (to a lesser extent) Buddhism. Central to those faiths is belief in the concept of reincarnation, with repeating and recurring cycles of life, death, and rebirth. While good deeds and faithful adherence to their religions' tenets may result in a "better" next life, an outcome worth working toward, crowing about such accomplishments is inconsistent with the modesty and humility associated with any such desired transformational rebirth.

This reticence to discuss inner states, or to express undue pride in accomplishment, typically leads Gurkhas in interviews to discuss either the financial stability they bring their families, their pride in following in their fathers' footsteps (for the many generational Gurkha families), or their satisfaction in bringing honor to their families by earning admission into such a widely admired international organization, rather than focusing on how they feel they changed by surviving and succeeding in the crucible. But as valuable as the remittances that many of the young Gurkhas provide to their families at home may be, we suspect that their own eventual arrivals home to their loved ones' doorsteps, as respected members of a global elite, tested and proven through an excruciating crucible, may be just as emotionally priceless and precious to everyone involved, even if they do not wish to discuss it in those terms.

CHAPTER 6

Our Mothers: The Dahomey Amazons

"The military art has no mystery in it beyond others, which Women cannot attain to. A Woman is as capable as a Man of making herself, by means of a map, acquainted with the good and bad ways, the dangerous and safe passes, or the proper situations for encampment. And what should hinder her from making herself mistress of all the stratagems of war, of charging, retreating, surprising, laying ambushes, counterfeiting marches, feigning flights, giving false attacks, supporting real ones, animating the soldiery, and adding example to eloquence by being the first to mount a breach. Persuasion, heat, and example are the soul of victory: And Women can show as much eloquence, intrepidity, and warmth, where their honor is at stake, as is requisite to attack or defend a town."
—"Sophia, a Person of Quality"

"If the history of Africa was written by Africans and by women, I think we would find many unsung heroes."
—Sahle-Work Zewde

THE CITIZENS OF DAKAR, SENEGAL, are the last people in Eurasia and Africa to see the sun set each day, as their home city is located further west than any other continental location on those vast conjoined landmasses. Dakar has one of the most comfortable climates in West Africa, and the gloaming offers a lovely time to explore the city's streets and beaches in search of sights, souvenirs, or dinner spots featuring some of the most extraordinary fresh fish available anywhere, anytime, ideally biding the evening time until Dakar's musically rich late-night club scene kicks into high gear, in both Western-style venues and discos and smaller, though no less passionate, neighborhood bars. The regular experiences of residents and visitors alike (often to the surprise of the latter) are guided by a cultural concept known in Senegal as *teraanga*, a code of behavior that stresses openness, familiarity, warmth, and generosity, including the sharing of material possessions and property, with family, friends, and strangers alike.

Even though Senegal's modern borders, set by colonial powers, include numerous ethnic and linguistic groups, the country has been one of the most stable in West Africa's postcolonial period, most of its people bound at least in part to a spirit of community guided by *teraanga*. While the origin of Senegal's unique form of sharing and hospitality cannot be traced authoritatively, historians generally agree that its roots lie in the cultures of the vast and long-lived Ghana (or Wagadu), Mali, and Songhai empires, which sequentially dominated much of Western Africa (including modern-day Senegal and its environs) from about 300 to 1600 CE. The wealth and success of all three of those empires were anchored, by dint of fortunate geography, in trade, typically between Muslim Arab and Berber peoples to the north and other smaller kingdoms in the south, most of which espoused animist spiritual traditions. A willingness to trade goods, and with them ideas, fairly and openly across various cultural and spiritual traditions was a cornerstone to the economic success of the West African empires until the advent of the colonial age.

Somewhat remarkably, the spirit of *teraanga* continues to mitigate strife between the two great world religions (beyond enduring local animist traditions) most widely represented in modern Senegal's polyglot culture, even as Christians and Muslims elsewhere have often been unable to coexist peacefully for extended periods of time. During Easter season, Christian families in Senegal will often share a traditional dish called *ngalax* with their Muslim neighbors, who reciprocate during Eid al-Adha by sharing lamb dishes with their Christian cohorts. While most modern Senegalese people are Muslim, physical contact between men and women is not proscribed as it is in many other Muslim or Arab countries, perhaps in keeping with the ritualized meeting traditions of *teraanga*, where long handshakes, hugs, and heartfelt inquiries into the health and well-being of family members are integral to greetings both passing and planned.

Though illiteracy and genital mutilation rates among modern Senegal's women remain tragically high, particularly in rural regions, and women only represent approximately 10 percent of the formal workforce across the country, socioeconomic and cultural changes in recent decades are slowly increasing opportunities for women to thrive and lead within their communities. Many rural Senegalese women are often heavily involved in managing their communities' rice and millet mills, forestry programs, and regional health centers. Their urban counterparts are ever more involved in retail, professional, and manufacturing trades, and a thriving market in microloans, both domestic and international, has allowed many women to open their own businesses in Senegal's cities, often trading in textiles or in the food-related industries.

In early 2015, a striking series of large black-and-white portraits of nineteenth-century African women began to appear on the exterior walls of numerous woman-owned shops throughout Dakar and several nearby cities. The works were part of a series called *Amazone*, by acclaimed French street artist Yseult Digan, who creates under the pseudonym YZ (pronounced "eyes"). Widewalls, a prominent online marketplace supporting art galleries and collectors, describes Digan's work thusly: "Her art focuses on the problems that we face in the context of the modern metropolises that are able to eat on our humanities despite the fact they seemingly keep us together and connected. Although she employs a vast number of techniques in her projects, Yseult Digan is best known as a poster artist who creates her works on craft paper and puts them up on urban walls. These posters are usually very short-lived, a feature which puts an emphasis on the fast pace of urban lifestyle and the swift changes it brings."

"In 2014, I went to live with my family in Senegal for two years," explained Digan in a recent interview with us. "I already knew the country from having lived there when I was younger. When I start a new project there is always a reflection around the inhabitants, the habitat, and its heritage. I had already heard of Aline Sitoe Diatta, a young woman from Casamance who had fought for the rights of her family. Pulling the thread, I realized that there were many women who had taken up arms to defend their rights, especially the Amazons of Dahomey. This is how the project was born, as I wanted to portray the women who wrote the history of Africa. These women inspire me. Beyond that, I see that in Africa there is this strong culture of matriarchy and the place of women in African society."

So, who were "the Amazons of Dahomey" who so inspired YZ's stunning works in modern Senegal? Their story is anchored in what is now the Republic of Benin, which, like Senegal, was a part of French West Africa from the turn of the twentieth century until 1960. (Dakar was the administrative capital city of that vast colonial conurbation.) In precolonial times, the Kingdom of Dahomey arose among the region's Fon culture around 1600 CE, just as the Songhai Empire was crumbling to the north, along with its once-formidable trade routes. For the first century of its existence, Dahomey was a tributary state of the Oyo Empire, a Yoruba country centered in what is now northwestern Nigeria. But around 1700 CE, after conquering several key port cities on the Bight of Benin, Dahomey emerged as a key player in the region's economic and political structures, in large part fueled by its major role as a source of enslaved people to be traded within the Atlantic chattel slavery system.

The Kingdom of Dahomey was highly militaristic and almost constantly engaged in some form of warfare throughout its history, in some ways almost representing the opposite pole to Senegal's serene *teraanga* approach to coexistence. Most of the enslaved people sold to European traders in Dahomey were captured during wars and raids against neighboring communities, while other captured people became enslaved in Dahomey itself. The kingdom's calendar was anchored upon the monthlong "Annual Customs of Dahomey," a massive celebratory and spiritual festival in which the kingdom's citizens gathered to offer elaborate gifts and tribute (not necessarily voluntarily) to their king and his close counselors, to participate in various religious activities, and to watch military exercises and hear speeches from dignitaries regarding the kingdom's prospects and possible futures. One of the religious elements of the Annual Customs was the public execution of hundreds to thousands of enslaved people each year in ritualized human sacrifice ceremonies that stood as a regionally unique twist imposed by King Agaja (who ruled from 1718 to 1740) on the kingdom's heretofore mostly peaceful and matriarchal Vodun religion. (The Voodoo or Vodou religions of Louisiana, Haiti, and Brazil are generally syncretic blends of the traditional Vodun practiced in Dahomey and the Catholicism brought to the region by the French.)

By the mid-nineteenth century, Dahomey's fortunes began to decline as the British imposed naval blockades and anti-slavery patrols as part of its efforts to disrupt and later abolish the Atlantic slave trade. Dahomey also suffered in the 1850s and 1860s when a pair of invasions targeting Abeokuta, a city-state that had been founded specifically as a haven for escaped enslaved people and refugees displaced by Dahomey's regional aggressions, were rebuffed at great loss to the invaders. As France became a more active colonial power in the late nineteenth century, two rounds of Franco-Dahomean Wars (in 1890 and 1894) erupted, with the Dahomeans suffering approximately ten thousand casualties, more than five times the French losses. Dahomey's last king, Béhanzin, was ousted by the French following

his defeat in 1894, and Dahomey became a French protector-
ate until 1904, at which time it was reorganized politically as a
colony called French Dahomey, one of nine major component
territories of French West Africa.

Because of its tight involvement over a period of centuries in
the economic fortunes of the nations engaged in the Atlantic slave
trade, Dahomey was more frequently visited and written about
by Western European visitors than most other West African
nations. And, invariably, the feature of Dahomey's culture that
most fascinated its European visitors was the fact that for most of
the nineteenth century, Dahomey's army (and its related political
infrastructure) featured a formidable all-female contingent that
at its peak composed nearly one-third of the kingdom's military
personnel. With a limited cultural vocabulary to describe such a
formidable female force, the Europeans invariably defaulted to
dubbing them "Amazons," after the female warriors and hunters
who feature prominently in Greek mythology. While that anachronistic moniker has stuck with the women warriors of Dahomey
into modern times, they were known in their own tongue as
Mino, meaning "our mothers," or *Ahosi*, meaning "king's wives."
(For consistency's sake, we will use the former term for the dura-
tion of this chapter when speaking of the female warriors within
their own time and own culture.)

The roots of the *Mino* are generally traced to the reign of
Dahomey's third king, Houegbadja (he reigned from 1645 to
1685), who codified the kingdom's emerging cultural and political standards as a military state governed by a strong central
political authority. Houegbadja later established an all-female
cadre of elephant hunters, and his daughter, Queen Hangbe,
expanded on her father's innovation by establishing an all-
female palace bodyguard whose presence was first noted with
interest and recorded by European visitors to her court. Queen
Hangbe was succeeded by her brother, the aforementioned
King Agaja (who added human sacrifice to the core tenets of

Vodun), who deployed the successors to Hangbe's bodyguard and Houegbadja's elephant huntresses in battle for the first time, where they performed admirably and played a key role in the defeat of the neighboring Savi kingdom. The female palace guard remained an important part of Dahomean political culture thereafter.

In the early nineteenth century, King Ghezo elected to formalize the roles and increase the number and size of his female army units. Ghezo had come to power in 1818 following an internecine struggle with his older brother, King Adandozan, whom he eventually overthrew. The reasons given for Ghezo's decision to formalize the *Mino*'s role in his military vary depending on the historic sources consulted. Some perceive it as a shrewd decision to redeploy the formidable (though rarely required) skills necessary to defend the king at home onto the battlefields that Dahomey's warlike tendencies invariably produced in abundance. Others believe the decision was driven by the fact that Dahomey's penchants for unceasing warfare with its neighbors and for sacrificing captive men who could have served in its armed forces had led to a gender imbalance in the kingdom's population. A more nuanced modern interpretation comes from scholar and historian Edna G. Bay, who has written extensively and gloriously on Dahomey's culture and history: she asserts that King Ghezo needed to ensure the faithful support of his female palace guard, who had opposed his efforts to overthrow Adandozan, lest Ghezo himself fall to a usurper backed by the powerful female cabal at the heart of his military and government. He achieved this fealty from the *Mino* by raising the stature and status of the palace guards, making them a crucial part of his operational military tactics and strategy.

Whatever the reasons that motivated Ghezo may have been, his actions produced a formidable military force that served as a formal part of Dahomey's offensive and defensive capabilities until the kingdom was subsumed into French West Africa in 1904. Ghezo built his force by enlisting young women from throughout the kingdom and by conscripting women via raids on neighboring states. Through the remainder of Ghezo's reign (which ended in 1859), recruitment and enrollment campaigns for service with the *Mino* typically happened once every three years; his successor, King Glele, made the enlistment drives annual. During these drives, the king's representatives traveled throughout the kingdom, seeking the tallest, strongest, and most agile young women they could find, typically between the ages of twelve and fifteen, though records exist of girls as young as eight years old being enrolled. The king's recruiters would bring the fruits of their forays into the kingdom's villages and towns back to Abomey (Dahomey's capital city), where they were screened and examined by a council of advisors before being accepted into the training pipeline for service with the *Mino*.

While the recruits were forced to leave their villages and any semblances of "normal" Dahomean life upon their selection for service, the *Mino* were accorded significant privileges within Dahomey, living in five different cities in palaces from which men were banned; provided with tobacco, trade items, alcohol, and servants; and issued uniforms and arms comparable in quality to those that their male counterparts wore and carried. When the *Mino* ventured forth from the palace, servants were sent in front of them carrying bells to alert people to their presence, and the citizens were expected to step aside, avert their eyes, and bow to the passing columns of women warriors. The *Mino* were symbolically considered to all be the king's wives, and therefore off limits to any other men in the kingdom, a position that was further entrenched through an oath of celibacy, which the women were required to take. (The only exceptions to that oath were made when the king himself elected to take a member of the force as his own wife, in the non-symbolic sense of that word, or when he elected to "give" one of them in marriage for political reasons.) Of course, their cloistering and isolation from the kingdom's men did not mean that their lives were without emotional warmth and richness, as visiting English captain Sir Richard F. Burton wrote in 1864 that two-thirds of the *Mino* were "maidens with passions and love between each other."

The *Mino*'s training crucible was based on intense physical exercise, and on a goal of honing all latent aggressive character traits toward a single purpose: war. The training program consisted of drills and simulated large-scale military attacks, most notably on the twenty-seventh day of the Annual Customs of Dahomey gathering, when the *Mino* would stage a mock battle and slave raid to demonstrate their formidable skills. A report from 1861 by missionary Francesco Borghero describes three thousand *Mino* warriors marching onto the parade ground of Abomey, barefoot, bristling with knives, clubs, and three-foot-long razor-sharp blades capable of slicing a man in two. The warriors advanced on a series of fortifications intended to accurately represent the defenses around an enemy city: vast piles of acacia branches studded with two-inch-long, needle-sharp thorns. The *Mino* rushed the wall and scrambled to its top, seemingly impervious to the grievous injuries inflicted by the thorns. After a mimed sequence at the top of the wall simulating a fight with defenders, the soldiers fell back into the square, then climbed the bloody wall a second time, this time advancing to a series of structures where they captured simulated prisoners, marching them before the king for his approval. For their bravery and skill, the best of the warriors were awarded belts . . . made of acacia thorns, which they strapped around their waists, again never showing any signs of discomfort from the piercing wounds that decorated their bodies.

Suffering at the points of the acacia thorns was part of a regime designed to foster a stoic acceptance of pain as a central tenet of membership within this elite fighting and political unit. The *Mino* also underwent survival training, which involved being sent into the forests surrounding Abomey with negligible rations, and being expected to live, work, and thrive through hunger, discomfort, and thirst. Most alien to modern sensibilities was their "insensitivity training," posited on the theory that the only way to learn killing was to kill. New members of the *Mino* would be required to throw bound and gagged prisoners over the edges of a raised platform into the fevered crowd below, which would ensure that the victims were dispatched if the fall itself had not been sufficient to do the job. *Mino* trainees were also asked to execute prisoners in less ceremonial settings, typically with their formidable long blades.

Rites and rituals played important roles in the *Mino* training crucible as well, as the Vodun spirits were evoked and invoked through drumming, wrestling, singing, chanting, and dancing. Secret incantations that were purported to increase the women's strength were taught, recited, and repeated, and the *Mino* wore a variety of protective amulets and ornaments to make them impervious to injury in combat. More recognizably aligned with modern military training practices, the *Mino* also regularly performed drills and military parades, using their weapons and bodies in highly stylized and choreographed fashions designed to display precision, accuracy, and uniformity in their ranks.

While core elements of the training regimen for the *Mino* were largely standardized, there were distinct groups within the greater cohort who received specialized training and education on the arms, techniques, and skills required of their specific regiment's members. By their final years in the late nineteenth century, the *Mino* were organized into five regiments with varying skill sets and unique training requirements:

- Huntresses (*Gbeto*): Armed with long rifles and curved daggers.
- Riflewomen (*Gulohento*): Armed with long rifles and short swords; the *Gulohento* were the most numerous of the *Mino* and typically were the first into any fray, with specialized skills in close quarters and hand-to-hand combat.

- Archers (*Gohento*): Armed with daggers and hooked and poisoned arrows; as rifles replaced bows and arrows throughout the final years of the *Mino's* existence, the *Gohento's* role shifted toward battlefield support, the transport of weapons, and recovery of the wounded and dead.

- Reapers (*Nyekplohento*): The smallest, but most feared unit, armed with the terrifyingly long two-handed blades, which were intended to be a psychological weapon against their enemies just as much as they were a physical one.

- Gunners (*Agbarya*): Responsible for the army's heavy artillery, the pieces of which were mostly antiquated and not terribly accurate, but were very loud, and again widely used as a psychological intimidation element against their enemies.

By all historic accounts, the *Mino's* crucibles rendered them a truly formidable combat unit, and they enjoyed significant military success through most of King Ghezo's reign, their specialty being in predawn raids on enemy villages. The *Mino* experienced their first significant defeats in the previously referenced campaigns against Abeokuta, but those failures were less a product of their skills and commitment and more a product of their units being over-optimistically thrown into battle on the front lines against a huge (by local standards) city of fifty thousand people surrounded by immense and easily defended concentric mudbrick walls. The *Mino* fought two significant battles during the First Franco-Dahomean War, and only the sheer overwhelming firepower of the modern French rifles carried the day for the colonial interlopers, who took heavy losses in what proved to be a short-lived ceasefire.

The French learned a lesson before hostilities re-erupted in the Second Franco-Dahomean War three years later, bringing larger, better-armed forces to pursue their West African colonial aspirations. There were twenty-three battles between King Béhanzin's armies and the French forces, and the female troops were at the forefront in defending their kingdom in all of them, fighting heroically under increasingly parlous circumstances. The *Mino* were among the last units to surrender as their king was overthrown, and stories were passed down among the occupying French forces that many of the surviving women warriors disguised themselves, were taken into the French stockades with other female prisoners of war, cleverly seduced various prominent officers, then cut the throats of their victims as they slept in postcoital bliss.

To their credit after the cessation of active hostilities and passive acts of skullduggery, the French were generally full of praise for the valor that the *Mino* displayed in combat against them. While they did not approve of the Riflewomen's penchant for firing from the hip instead of from the shoulder, they were impressed by the accuracy the women could achieve from that posture, especially with older weaponry, and various firsthand accounts describe the *Mino* as outstandingly valorous, always ahead of the other troops, well trained for combat, very disciplined, remarkable for their courage and ferocity, and prodigiously brave. Despite those extraordinary traits, there was no place for women in the French Army that conquered Dahomey, nor in any other army in West Africa, either indigenous or colonial. And so, the *Mino* were disbanded and dispersed by 1904, returning to their home villages, or not, according to independent opportunity or whim.

The *Mino* largely disappeared from history at that point, and there are scant records documenting what life was like for these warrior women when they were no longer allowed to practice the skills that they had learned through their formative training crucibles and in the actual practice of war, nor to continue carrying a social and economic status equal to, if not superior to, most men in their country. From an actuarial standpoint, it is likely that at least a few of the final members of the *Mino* would have survived to see their country regain its independence from the French in 1960. We suspect it would have marked a bittersweet moment for them, knowing that they had been unable to pre-serve their kingdom's independence as young women, but that as old women, the cause they had fought for was finally proven a just one, with little credit or gratitude provided for the sacrifices they had made in that cause's name half a century earlier.

That sense of important stories being forgotten over time contributed to Yseult Digan's motivations as she implemented her *Amazone* project in Senegal, recognizing its tied colonial experiences with Dahomey. "I like to think that by highlight-ing strong, courageous, determined figures who take charge of their destiny, my art may inspire other women and change mentalities," she told us. "We need a referential universe on which to build, and I try to participate in curating its symbols. Traditional African societies have, since the dawn of time, given birth to ruthless warriors, women who are sometimes mytho-logical, sometimes real, at the antipodes of submission to the male model. Their power and feats have been transmitted from generation to generation via oral tradition, giving them a singu-lar nobility within the various African pantheons.

"The strength of women is sometimes to be physically or muscularly constrained, but to allow those constraints to lead to more ingenuity," she continued. "Women are resilient, deter-mined, and courageous, often much more so than men. We grow like that, with great resilience. Women will do everything to defend their own. There is also a belief in the commitment to and defense of our identity, of what we are deep within us. The women I featured in *Amazone* fought to keep their freedom, but the Europeans were afraid of that desire and did not under-stand it. They had this condescending settler spirit that made these women look like savages to them. So now I just want to show people the real women who have written the true story of Africa. We need women today to be proud of our roots, and to keep fighting for our rights, if we are to write the story of tomor-row together."

CHAPTER 7

Honor and Fidelity: The French Foreign Legion

"There are no foreign lands. It is the traveler only who is foreign."
—Robert Louis Stevenson

"Maybe I am not French, maybe I am from nowhere."
—Alain Prost

WITHIN HIS VAST, SUCCESSFUL, AND hugely influential catalog, Frank Sinatra's late-1958 single "French Foreign Legion" must be regarded as a minor entity, topping out at number sixty-one in the then-brand-new Hot 100 singles charts published by *Billboard* magazine. Set to a musical score by Guy Wood, Aaron Schroeder's lyrics as sung by Ol' Blue Eyes tell the tale of a heartsick (and clueless) American dandy attempting to blackmail his seemingly indifferent beloved, questioning her commitment, and demanding that she march down the aisle with him. And if she fails to meet his demands, well then: *"Au revoir, Cheri, it's the French Foreign Legion for me."*

While the gender politics of the song have not aged well, "French Foreign Legion" does accurately capture the midcentury American view of the unique multinational fighting force from which it takes its title and topic. The 1939 film *Beau Geste* (which essentially recreated with sound a silent film version of the story from 1926) was hugely influential in shaping this narrative, being a popular and enduring Hollywood entertainment, both in its time and in the years that followed, in some part because the story's protagonists were played by popular American actors, not Englishmen as per P. C. Wren's source novel of the same name.

With superstars Gary Cooper, Ray Milland, and Robert Preston atop the cinema marquees, a generation of American boys (and men) came to see the French Foreign Legion as the fantasy place and organization to run to when life at home was not going quite the way they might like it to be. Hollywood's version of the Legion offered great uniforms, high-caliber adventures, exotic locales, and strapping macho good times among an international cohort of men from mysterious backgrounds and with cloudy backstories, all producing great stories that the survivors of the adventures could tell, with embellishments, for the rest of their natural lives. What wasn't to love about that story arc for an ambitious young man looking to test his mettle and prove himself in the wide world beyond provincial small-town America?

Well, first and foremost, the fact that the percentage of survivors among the main cast of *Beau Geste* ran to about 20 percent. And the fact that the film's three Geste brothers were trained as legionnaires by the monstrous Sergeant Markoff (played by Brian Donlevy, who was nominated for an Academy Award for the role), who later assumed command of their unit, which was then utterly decimated in their primitive desert fort by Tuareg attackers. And, for those who looked to the stories behind the stories, the fact that this sort of decimation and high fatality rate was not only historically accurate, but was also a celebrated central aspect of legionnaire culture. Common public quotations by and about the French Foreign Legion capture this essence of "victory or death" consistently and concisely over the years. For example:

"You legionnaires are soldiers in order to die, and I am sending you where you can die."
—General François de Négrier, 1883

"The goal of a legionnaire is the supreme adventure of combat at the end of which is either victory or death."
—Colonel Pierre Jeanpierre, 1859

"We shall all know how to perish, following tradition."
—Lyric from "Le Boudin," the marching song of the
French Foreign Legion

So, who were (and are) the French Foreign Legion, really,
beyond the petulantly polite pictures painted by Frank Sinatra's
jilted man-child, and beyond the handsome, brave, and doomed
stars of *Beau Geste*? In its native French language, the corps' name,
Légion étrangère, more clearly reveals the nature of the order.
While English-speakers might focus on the "foreign" element of
the corps' name as a descriptor of the exotic places to which the
French unit deploys, the reality is that the "foreign" element in the
name refers to the soldiers themselves: the Legion was formed
by King Louis Philippe in 1831 specifically to allow non-French
foreign nationals to be incorporated into the French Army. That
nuance on the name perhaps becomes clearer when considering the usual English translations of Albert Camus's great novel
L'Étranger, which is most typically known as *The Stranger*, though
some English editions have dubbed it *The Outsider*. "Legion of
strangers" or "legion of outsiders" would be reasonably accurate
English translations for *Légion étrangère*, perhaps adding even
more of a sense of mystique had they found favor.

King Louis Philippe's primary goal in expanding his armed
forces through the admission of non-French service members
was to increase his military might as France's interests abroad
grew more aggressive; the royal ordinance that established the
Foreign Legion originally specified that its members could only
serve in combat outside of mainland France. The organization of
the Legion was also, probably not coincidentally, a way to herd
the growing numbers of dissolute young male immigrants in
and around Paris at the time toward a vocation that both took
them out of the view of polite urban society, and gave those with
potentially criminal backgrounds (or foregrounds) the opportunity to reinvent themselves productively, proving their met-

tle and reformation through service to the nation that deemed them worthy of the opportunity.

France's nascent colonial interests, especially in Africa, stood central in this initial drive to create a corps of "outsiders" and "strangers." The newly constituted Legion's first deployments were to Algeria, where its troops played a role in the establishment of the French Algerian colony, which was then ruled as an integral part of France until 1962; legionnaires were regularly barracked and deployed there throughout that 130-year French era in North Africa. In the decades that followed its initial Algerian engagements, various reorganizations and shifts in national interest and fortune led to an ebbing and flowing in Foreign Legion numbers and activities, though legionnaires were still engaged in active combat in Spain, Crimea, Italy, and Mexico between the 1830s and the 1860s.

It was during that foray in Mexico (known as either the Second French Intervention in Mexico or the Second Franco-Mexican War, depending on the origin of one's perspectives on the affair) that the French Foreign Legion's core, defining narrative story was crafted, at great expense to its participants. French armed forces arrived in Mexico via a naval landing in Veracruz in late 1861, joining Spain and the United Kingdom in a joint expeditionary force intended to force Mexican President Benito Juárez to honor his flagging foreign debt payments due to those three European nations. Suspicious of French motivations in Mexico (King Louis Philippe had already sent forces there in 1839 to secure French trade interests, in what came to be known as the First French Intervention in Mexico, or less glamorously: the Pastry War), the English eventually negotiated their own financial terms with Mexico and withdrew their forces, with the Spaniards following soon after. Flush with colonial fever, the French forces remained in Mexico to overturn the Mexican Republic and to install a monarchical government more aligned with French economic interests; in 1864, Maximilian von

Habsburg, an Austrian, was coronated with French backing as Emperor Maximilian I of Mexico.

During the campaigns preceding Maximilian's coronation, two battalions of legionnaires were deployed to Mexico, ostensibly to provide a nucleus around which a new Imperial Mexican Army could be established. On April 30, 1863, a company of sixty-five legionnaires (including three officers) commanded by Captain Jean Danjou was serving as a defensive escort for a supply convoy en route to the city of Puebla, then under siege by loyalist Mexican forces. Captain Danjou's unit was ambushed and attacked on the way by a Mexican force of some 2,200 infantry soldiers, supporting eight hundred heavy cavalry troops. The outgunned, outmanned, and outmatched legionnaires holed up defensively in a farm hacienda near the hamlet of Camarón, where sixty-two of the sixty-five men were killed, including Captain Danjou. When the Mexicans eventually penetrated the hacienda where the three survivors remained, they were presented to the Mexican commander, Colonel Francisco de Paula Milán, who declared, "These are not men, but devils!"

The three survivors were sent back to French lines as an honor guard for the body of Captain Danjou, and the legend of the "victory or death" code of the French Foreign Legion was codified in blood in perpetuity. To this day, April 30 is celebrated as Camerone Day (based on the French spelling of the Mexican village), the most important moment of the year for all former and currently active legionnaires. The Battle of Camarón also produced the most important and honored relic within the Foreign Legion's culture. Captain Jean Danjou had lost a hand in 1853 after his musket exploded, and he then designed his own wooden prosthetic, which allowed him to continue serving in the army through campaigns in the Crimean War and the Austro-Sardinian War, through low-grade campaigns in Morocco, and, ultimately, finally, in Mexico. Danjou's artificial hand was recovered from the carnage at Camarón and later returned to the

French. It remains to this day in the Foreign Legion Museum at the corps' headquarters in Aubagne, France, and it is paraded annually as part of the Camerone Day celebrations; being chosen to carry Danjou's hand is one of the highest honors to which a legionnaire can aspire.

The Legion's actions in Mexico were, eventually, all for naught strategically, as Emperor Napoleon III, facing the severe decline of his own fortunes at home, announced the unconditional withdrawal of all French troops from Mexico by 1867, conceding in part to pressure from the United States, which was once again focused on Mexico, Central America, and the Caribbean following its victory over its own rebel states in the Civil War. The French puppet empire was then rapidly defeated by the Mexican Republicans, and Emperor Maximilian I was executed on June 19, 1867. Soon thereafter, though, the Legion experienced another historic first, being deployed on mainland French soil as part of the Franco-Prussian War, as the corps' charter did note that its prohibition on actions within France itself were null and void in the event of a national invasion. (Never mind the fact that the French invaded Prussia's independent southern German allies first, before their Prussian antagonists under the leadership of Chancellor Otto von Bismarck counter-invaded France, far, far more effectively.)

Legionnaires were involved in the liberation of Orléans and strove valiantly (though unsuccessfully) to break the Siege of Paris through 1870 and 1871. Once Prussian victory in France was assured, Chancellor Bismarck proclaimed a new union of the various small Central European states (almost the entirety of German-speaking Europe, bar Austria) under the flag of the German Empire, and negotiated an armistice with the French. Bismarck's bargaining hand in the peace negotiations was strong, as the Prussians had captured Emperor Napoleon III after the Battle of Sedan, and he remained in German custody through March 1871, before his final exile in England, effectively ending

France's long monarchical era. In the revolutionary chaos that followed the Franco-Prussian War, the Paris Commune emerged briefly as the ruling government of France, and the Legion played a cornerstone role in its defeat and destruction, with the typically high levels of bloodshed and carnage (on both sides) that had already become a hallmark of the corps' activities and reputation.

The French Third Republic emerged from the wreckage of the Franco-Prussian War and the Paris Commune era, and continued to govern France until the Vichy government was established in 1940, following the fall of France during World War II. The Third Republic continued to keep the Foreign Legion busy, with service in the Tonkin Campaign, the Sino-French War, colonial expansion in Western Africa (including the Franco-Dahomean Wars discussed elsewhere in our chapter on the Dahomey Amazons), the Second Madagascar Expedition, the Mandingo Wars, and other minor global conflicts.

A paid appeal published in various French newspapers on August 1, 1914, as German military threats to France ramped up following the assassination of Archduke Franz Ferdinand in Sarajevo, presaged the next great opportunity for the Foreign Legion to serve in defense of mainland France. The text of the piece read,

The hour is grave.
Every man worthy of the name should act today, should forbid himself to remain inactive in the midst of the most formidable conflagration history has ever enregistered.
Any hesitation would be a crime.
No words, action.
Foreigners, friends of France, who during their sojourn in France have learned to love and cherish her as a second country, feel an imperious need to offer their arms.
Intellectuals, students, workmen, able-bodied men of all sorts—born elsewhere, domiciled here—we who found in

*France spiritual nourishment or material food, we group
ourselves together in a solid band of volunteers placed in
the service of the greatest France.*

By the end of August, volunteer units of Italians, Turks,
Russians, Belgians, Englishmen, Poles, Romanians, Armenians,
Syrians, Americans, and others had self-mobilized to defend
France from Germany and its allies. The French Ministry of War
authorized the rapid formation of "marching regiments" under
the auspices of the Foreign Legion to receive its unexpected surfeit
of volunteers, with a core of veteran legionnaires to be assigned to
train and mobilize the new recruits. The foreign volunteers began
their enrollment into the French Army on August 21, 1914, with a
ceremony at the Hôtel des Invalides in Paris's 7th arrondissement.
The travails of the American units (many members of which were
not actually American, but were English-speakers from abroad
who elected to self-identify as such for various personal reasons)
serving in the Foreign Legion during World War I are documented with exceptional detail and clarity in Colonel Paul Ayres
Rockwell's 1930 book, *American Fighters in the Foreign Legion,
1914–1918*, which also provides a clear overview of the training
that those "Americans" experienced. Rockwell's expertise on the
subject matter at hand was deep, as he and his brother Kiffin were
both members of the Foreign Legion during World War I. Paul
survived the war; Kiffin did not, having become a member of the
Lafayette Escadrille aviation squadron before he was shot down
and killed in his French Nieuport 17 fighter plane.

The new marching regiments' indoctrination began with
a series of physical examinations in Paris, after which the new
recruits were quickly shipped to training centers at Rouen,
Toulouse, Orléans, Blois, Bayonne, or Avignon. Early conditions
at those camps were lackluster and somewhat unstructured,
with severe shortages of military equipment and uniforms, and
few of the men capable of following the French orders given

by their officers due to a wide variety of language barriers. The recruits were generally divided into squads and sent into the countryside for what Rockwell deemed "brisk marches for exercise." Following a late morning meal, the squads would be set to work cleaning the grounds and barracks, assisting with food preparation, and engaging in the various other menial tasks that soldiers and sailors since antiquity have endured when there is nothing else that their superiors deem worthy of their attention. The afternoons were dedicated to drill and military instruction on the barracks' grounds, with evening liberty offered and typically taken by those with the financial resources to make it worthwhile to visit their nearby towns.

It was not until the Americans and their colleagues had been going through the loosely military motions for over a week that large groups of veteran legionnaires arrived from North Africa to formalize the training process. Drills became much more strenuous in the weeks that followed, and the new recruits were finally issued coarse fatigue uniforms, backpacks, rifles, and bayonets. Squads were reorganized to mingle veterans with new recruits, and the "brisk marches for exercise" transformed into "forced marches of many miles." Training exercises expanded to include target practice, digging trenches, advancing under fire, and tent-pitching, among other skills deemed essential for the would-be soldiers. Training that typically at the time would have unrolled over a six-month period was compressed into a mere six weeks, and on September 30, 1914, the first American units were shipped off to Camp de Mailly, near the Western Front. In the four terrible years that followed, approximately 4,100 legionnaires were killed on the Western Front and another roughly 1,200 were killed in other theaters of war. Those totals represented approximately 10 percent of all the men who served in the Legion between 1914 and 1918.

While the training experienced by the World War I–era legionnaires was chaotic and truncated due to the urgent nature of the needs of the French military, modern-day would-be members of the Foreign Legion pass through a much more structured crucible before being deemed fit for service. The initial portal for service remains the Foreign Legion information centers, located in various French cities; volunteers are required to appear in person at such centers to start the onboarding process, with no mailed-in forms, online applications, or phone solicitations allowed or accepted. The information centers receive candidates, provide them with the detailed descriptions of their actual likely daily duties, and discuss the terms of their potential contracts. Should volunteers exhibit sufficient interest and resolve, they are then processed at the Foreign Legion recruitment center in Paris, where they receive their initial medical clearance, have further discussion and screening regarding their intentions for military service, their goals, and their motivations, and then sign their provisional five-year-term enlistment papers.

Next stop: the recruitment and selection center at the Legion's headquarters in Aubagne, where recruits are given a variety of psychological and physical readiness tests, and where security interviews are conducted. At the end of this selection phase, recruits are confirmed for or denied the opportunity to serve and are even given new identities under the rule of *anonymat*, generally keeping only their initials, their years of birth, and their nationalities. After one year of service, a legionnaire may "reclaim" his old name through the "military regularization of the situation" process, though many legionnaires choose to spend the entirety of their careers under their assumed identities. Ostensibly, these assumed identities are to create a deep sense that joining the Legion marks an extreme point of transition from life before to life after, and to "even the playing field" for all recruits, regardless of their backgrounds. Practically, it is a modern relic of the days when service in the Legion was a way for those with criminal histories to unilaterally issue themselves a clean slate, though the modern Legion is diligent in screening and dismissing those candidates who apply with significant criminal records or who have deserted from other armed forces.

Those who are confirmed for service then advance to a roughly sixteen-week training course overseen by the 4th Foreign Regiment at various installations throughout France. After about five weeks at *La Ferme* ("the farm"), where the recruits train in drill, field, and military lifestyle aspects of service, the candidates embark on the *Marche Képi Blanc*, a thirty-one-mile, two-day forced march in full uniform with full marching gear; the *Képi Blanc* ceremony honors those who complete this phase of training. The next three weeks are focused on technical, practical barracks and field training, before the recruits are taken high into the French Pyrenees for mountain training at the Chalet de Formiguères. Then the hardened trainees are sent back to their barracks for another three weeks of technical, practical, and field training, followed by technical competency examinations, driver's training, and the *Raid Marche*, a seventy-five-mile final march, which must be completed within three days.

Throughout all these training periods, French language instruction is interspersed in both classroom and "practical usage" settings, as many recruits do not speak the language well, if at all; the only up-front language requirement for modern legionnaires is that they be able to read and write in their own native tongues. The training protocols are also deeply rooted in attempting to establish an *esprit de corps* among the recruits, building a single new community that supplants the many communities that spawned the legionnaires as individuals. Service in the Legion for a minimum of three years allows foreign nationals to apply for French citizenship, and the tradition of *Français par le sang versé* ("French by spilled blood") allows any soldier wounded during a battle for France to immediately apply for citizenship.

Those training travails successfully completed, and with that *esprit de corps* firmly established, recruits return to

Aubagne for a closing week and various ceremonial matters, after which they are assigned to their operational regiments. The modern Foreign Legion is composed of units representing various specialties, including infantry, cavalry, engineers, and airborne units. Nine of the current regiments at the time of this writing are based in mainland France, one is based in French Guiana, and one (the smallest operational unit in the modern French Army) is based on Mayotte, a small French island near Madagascar. Since the 1980s, when various low-level scandals created a sense among the Legion's leadership that its young candidates may often come to the Legion with less than an ideal set of innate moral principles and values, the Legion's binding *esprit de corps* has been further codified by the implementation of a Code of Honor, which is always recited in French, but translates into English thusly:

> **Article 1.** Legionnaire, you are a volunteer serving France with honor and loyalty.
> **Article 2.** Each legionnaire is your brother in arms whatever his nationality, his race, or his religion might be. You show him the same close solidarity that links the members of the same family.
> **Article 3.** Respect for traditions, devotion to your leaders, discipline, and comradeship are your strengths, courage and loyalty your virtues.
> **Article 4.** Proud of your status as legionnaire, you display this in your always impeccable uniform, your always dignified but modest behavior, and your clean living quarters.
> **Article 5.** An elite soldier, you train rigorously, you maintain your weapon as your most precious possession, and you take constant care of your physical form.
> **Article 6.** The mission is sacred, you carry it out until the end and, if necessary, in the field, at the risk of your life.

Article 7. In combat, you act without passion and without hate, you respect defeated enemies, and you never abandon your dead, your wounded, or your arms.

While many of world's armed forces would have written their codes in gender inclusive language, reflecting the growing role of women in the military, the Legion's Code of Honor is specifically "he/him" in its construction because the Legion remains a male-only fighting force. Women from the French Army or other branches of service may be attached to and deployed with Legion regiments in noncombat auxiliary and support roles (e.g., administrators, engineers, pilots, doctors, and other medical personnel), but they may not actually join the regiments as soldiers. Of course, hard and fast rules like that one are often either highlighted or undermined by their glaring exceptions, and the French Foreign Legion does indeed have one such notable anomaly in its storied history.

Susan Mary Gillian Travers was an English nurse who served as an ambulance driver for the French Red Cross during World War II, where she deployed with the French Expeditionary Corps to Finland. After France fell to the Germans, Travers returned to London and continued to serve, drive, and fight for the French cause as an auxiliary member of the 13th Demi-Brigade of the Foreign Legion under the Free French Forces, nominally commanded by General Charles de Gaulle. The 13th Demi-Brigade was later incorporated into the 1st Free French Brigade, and Travers was assigned to serve as driver to its commander, Colonel Marie-Pierre Kœnig, who, conveniently, also happened to be Travers's current romantic partner, despite his being married to another woman. The 1st Free French Brigade was posted to Bir Hakeim in Libya, eventually falling under attack by the German Panzer Army Africa and its Italian counterparts. While all English and French women had been ordered out of the area before the Battle of Gazala, Travers returned soon after the battle and spent two weeks in extremely hostile circumstances before eventually leading the convoy out as Bir Hakeim was evacuated; when she finally reached British lines, her car was found to be riddled with eleven bullet holes and with its shock absorbers and brakes destroyed and unserviceable.

Kœnig was transferred out of the North African theater and was reunited with his wife soon thereafter. Travers stayed behind to drive a self-propelled anti-tank gun with the Foreign Legion in the North African theater, then later served with them in the Italian Campaign and on the Western Front, where she was seriously wounded after driving over a land mine. After the end of World War II's hostilities in Europe, her military status within the Free French Forces was regularized into the true native French Army and she formally applied to enroll in the French Foreign Legion as an *adjudant-chef* (analogous to American chief warrant officer ranks). Her application was accepted, and she later went on to serve with distinction in French Indochina.

While Susan Travers remains a noble and inspirational anomaly in the Foreign Legion's history, the organization itself has continued to mobilize, serve, and fight in the postwar era much as it had for the century before, except that instead of fighting to build France's colonial empire, it was more often involved in the final spasms associated with the dismantling of the empire and the establishment of independent and free nations where the French had once ruled. Legionnaires played key roles in the First Indochina War and the Algerian War, both of which ended with France's withdrawal from their long-occupied territories, and they have since engaged in countless peacekeeping and stabilization roles throughout Africa, Asia, Oceania, and the Americas, most visibly (for the average American reader) in the Gulf War and the War in Afghanistan. The Foreign Legion remains a formidable force, with a particular mystique and appeal, and a truly unique and egalitarian culture that is exclusive enough to maintain very high standards, but inclusive enough to still allow young men from around the world to dream of running away to and with the Legion, an escape in pursuit of an oddly selfless sense of communal glory. While many nations have modeled military units around the models first framed by the French Foreign Legion, few if any have ever captured the multinational operational effectiveness that the Legion manages to offer to this day, spirits of honor and fidelity still in full effect, to both the very real nation and the very highly idealized romantic notions that are France for the non-French.

CHAPTER 8

Crouching Dragons and Divine Wind: Japan's Special Attack Units

"What joy, for fatherland to die! Death's darts e'en flying feet o'ertake, nor spare a recreant chivalry, a back that cowers, or loins that quake."
—Quintus Horatius Flaccus (Horace, translated by John Conington)

"I am a single human being. I am neither a good person nor a bad person. If I am not a great man, I am not a fool either. To the end I am a single human being. As a wanderer sent off on a trip who until the end longed for life, I want to end like a person as a human document and sanctified area."
—Heiichi Okabe

DECEMBER 7, 1941, REMAINS ONE of the most impactful days in United States history, posted and locked in the nation's collective cultural memory as "a date which will live in infamy" after President Franklin D. Roosevelt branded it as such during the opening lines of his address before a joint session of Congress, some twenty-four hours after the U.S. Navy base at Pearl Harbor was devastated during a surprise military strike by the Imperial Japanese Navy Air Service. (Less well remembered today is the fact that December 7, 1941, also involved related and coordinated Japanese attacks on British and American military assets in Hong Kong, the Philippines, Guam, Singapore, Malaya, and Wake Island.) The shock and scope of the aerial attack was profound: nearly 2,500 military and civilian personnel were killed at Pearl Harbor alone, and the Japanese air

assault destroyed or severely damaged numerous ships and aircraft, along with the infrastructure in place to build, house, fuel,
arm, and service those crucial defense assets.

Following President Roosevelt's terse six-minute-and-thirty-
second address (which was broadcast live, heard by over 80
percent of all households then owning radios, and is often
cited as one of the great political speeches of the twentieth
century), Congress wasted little time in declaring war against
the Japanese Empire. Four days later, Germany and Italy joined
Japan in declaring war on the United States, in keeping with the
spirit, if not the exact words, of the Tripartite Pact between the
Axis powers; Japan, Italy, and German were not technically obligated to declare war on each other's behalf under the terms of
the pact. The U.S. quickly reciprocated and declared war on Italy
and Germany, committing itself, its soldiers, Marines, pilots,
and sailors, and its vast natural and industrial resources to an
immense two-ocean, two-continent war, pursued under the ideals and images laid out in President Roosevelt's inspirational
"Day of Infamy" speech (as it has come to be known, though
those were not exactly Roosevelt's words), which effectively
neutered any widespread popular support among the American
citizenry for continued political neutrality or isolationism.

While television had not yet supplanted radio as the primary source of news and entertainment throughout World
War II's course, the increased portability and utility of still- and
motion-picture cameras, and their deployment for both commercial media and military reconnaissance purposes on the battlefields, seas, and airspaces in which combat occurred, left a
striking and rich visual tapestry of what the war looked like, in
real time, that paints the perspective of posterity. Some three
decades after the United States entered World War II, a twenty-
six-part BBC documentary called *The World at War* deftly wove
some of the most iconic frontline images of that great global
conflict into a single narrative, bound around a haunting score by

Mark Arnold-Forster and the elegant and emotive narration of Sir Laurence Olivier. Many viewers first encountered the visual horrors of the Holocaust through the series, which remains the most expensive documentary ever produced when production costs are adjusted for inflation. Since its original broadcast in the United Kingdom in late 1973 and early 1974, *The World at War* has been repeatedly aired, in whole or in part, across the English-speaking world and beyond; in 2007, it even received its first airing in Japan.

The World at War featured previously unseen governmental and military footage and images along with photographs and moving film stock that had been produced or cleared for newspaper or cinematic newsreels in close-to-real time with the events they documented. The period footage was supplemented with interviews featuring a wide variety of firsthand witnesses, including combatants, political officials, and civilians impacted by the war's course. The immense scope and breadth of the visual record of World War II, as well as the deep emotional impact that those images engender to this day, has created something of an iconic "look" to the conflict, which has been replicated countlessly in various films and television series set around, and in, the wartime period.

That standardization and cross-blending of footage from World War II and the many popular dramatic and documentary presentations of its course and narrative do occasionally produce inaccurate associations or suboptimal understanding of which images belong where and when. A simple case in point, returning to the Japanese attack on Pearl Harbor: if asked to explain what happened on December 7, 1941, a sizable number of casual students of history and war would likely include and invoke the word "kamikaze" in their descriptive responses, crediting Japan's notorious suicide pilots, in full or in part, for the carnage of that day. While there are numerous images, from Pearl Harbor and elsewhere, of Japanese aircraft flying near

American warships, often on "constant bearing, decreasing range" courses (i.e., collision is imminent), there are no records of any historic formal deployment of kamikaze pilots in the attack on Pearl Harbor. While there is, in fact, historic evidence that pilots in crippled aircraft with no chance of survival individually elected to fly their dying planes into ships or ground assets at or near Pearl Harbor, the pilots on that mission were trained and hopeful of returning home victorious and were not specifically sent on one-way suicide missions. In fact, the formal designation and deployment by Japan of kamikaze units (along with other types of suicide missions) did not actually occur until the final months of the war in the Pacific, as an act of desperation to turn the tide of what seemed to be an inevitable invasion of the Japanese home islands by Allied forces. (Of course, we know now that the deployment of atomic weapons at Hiroshima and Nagasaki brought the Empire of Japan to its knees in August 1945, precluding that expected invasion.)

In assessing the ways in which the Japanese Empire's military leadership evolved from the point where they were sending skilled and well-trained pilots to execute complex, round-trip sorties, to the point where they were conscripting suicide bombers, we must first quickly synopsize the evolution of the relationship between Japan and the United States as would-be imperial/colonial powers across the Pacific Ocean, the cultural cues that led Japan to embrace suicide missions, and the fortunes of the war between 1941 and 1945 that made such an embrace seem plausible and practical. Our assessment of the crucibles designed to vet and train would-be (or reluctant) kamikazes arises from these historic elements.

Japan has been nominally ruled by emperors for well over 2,500 years, with the (probably mythical) first emperor, Jimmu, having purportedly ascended to the throne around 660 BCE. The political power and influence of the Japanese emperors have waxed and waned across the millennia. Through the period when the future United States was being settled and exploited by European powers, then threw off the yoke of its colonial masters to establish a unique democratic republic, the political role of the Japanese emperors was at something of a ceremonial nadir, with their suggested and de facto functions being limited to writing poetry, creating and collecting art, or engaging in scholarly pursuits. True governmental and military power in Japan lay in the hands of the Tokugawa shogunate, a hereditary line of nobles who consolidated their control of the island nation around 1600 CE, following a century-and-a-half period of upheaval and war known to history as the *Sengoku Jidai*, or the Warring States Period in English.

Early European forays into Japan occurred near the end of the Warring States Period and in the early years of the Tokugawa shogunate. The pervasive tendency of the Dutch, Spanish, and Portuguese traders (and the missionaries who accompanied them) to attempt to convert the Japanese to Christianity and to engage in unfair or dishonest business practices led the Tokugawa shogunate to expel foreigners from their kingdom in 1639 and to severely limit which Japanese citizens could travel abroad. The isolationist political policy of *Sakoku* (meaning "locked country") remained in place for over two centuries, with the Japanese preserving only limited trade beyond their own lands via licenses issued to a small number of selected Chinese and Dutch merchants. The Dutch were authorized to maintain a trading outpost at the entrepôt of Dejima, housed on an artificial island originally built by the Portuguese off the coast near Nagasaki.

Fast-forward to the first half of the nineteenth century, when a now-independent United States of America was aggressively pursuing its own expansionist activities under the concept of "Manifest Destiny," which asserted that American institutions and the citizenry governed by them were inherently superior to any other people on the North American continent and beyond, giving the Americans a sacred right to expand from the

Atlantic to the Pacific coasts. Following the Mexican-American War, the United States acquired much of the modern American Southwest, including California, via the lopsided Treaty of Guadalupe Hidalgo, signed in 1848. The combination of its acquisition of a major Pacific coastline (including numerous valuable trading ports), the English-forced opening of Chinese ports to international trade, and the growth and expansion of the whaling industry led the U.S. to become increasingly active as a commercial, seagoing power in the Pacific. As sails gave way to steam-powered ships, the need for coaling stations across the Pacific Ocean emerged as a further political interest, and the deepwater ports and long coastlines of the Japanese islands made them a highly desirable target to merchants (and their financial backers) seeking supply stations, safe harbors, and launch points for rescue missions. The maltreatment of American sailors stranded in Japan after shipwrecks further fueled the desire to force the Japanese to admit American ships, as well as the commercial and military interests backing them.

By the time of the Mexican Cession of its northwestern territories, the Americans had already staged a variety of forays and sorties into Japanese waters by the U.S. Navy's Far Eastern squadron, homeported in Canton (Guangzhou), China, though the Tokugawa shogunate's representatives adamantly refused them the rights to come ashore. In 1851, President Millard Fillmore authorized a formal military and diplomatic mission to Japan to force the issue. Commodore Matthew Perry was selected to command the mission, and in July 1853, his small armada of four ships steamed into the harbor of Edo (now Tokyo), pointed their guns toward a nearby town, fired a variety of blanks, rebuffed efforts by boarding parties, and refused to treat with low-level administrators, claiming that Commodore Perry's possession of an order from President Fillmore accorded him the right and obligation to meet only with similarly senior personages in Japan. Following additional shows of force, and with the

Japanese administration impaired by the illness of reigning shō-
gun Tokugawa Ieyoshi, who died of heart failure soon thereafter, the Japanese agreed to accept President Fillmore's letter, and
Commodore Perry was authorized to land on Japanese shores.
With one proverbial foot in the door, the Americans applied
additional pressure and threats upon the Japanese ruling
class, eventually resulting in the signing of the Convention of
Kanagawa in March 1854, effectively ending the "locked country" era of *Sakoku*. Similar treaties opening Japanese ports and
markets to international commerce were soon signed with the
governments of Russia, France, the Netherlands, and the United
Kingdom; collectively, the pacts signed with the American and
European powers came to be known in Japan as the "unequal
treaties," as the commercial interlopers quickly leveraged their
terms to assume control over various Japanese assets and to
undercut domestic control of tariffs and other trade protections.

The sense of national shame that rose across Japan in the
aftermath of the unequal treaties diminished the standing and
power of the Tokugawa shogunate, directly contributing to the
Meiji Restoration in 1868, wherein the long ceremonial and
sidelined hereditary emperors of Japan regained political power
and control of the nation, first under Emperor Mutsuhito, posthumously honored as Meiji, in keeping with the Japanese tradition of assigning reflective names for their emperors after their
reigns had ended. With shrewd counsel from his non-Tokugawa
advisors, Meiji not only eschewed the *Sakoku* philosophy, but
essentially reversed it, seeking to blend traditional Eastern cultural values with an open embrace of various modern technological advances. Meiji's Charter Oath of 1868 proclaimed that,
in the newly reconstituted Empire of Japan, "Knowledge shall be
sought all over the world, and thereby the foundations of imperial rule shall be strengthened." Under Meiji, his son Yoshihito
(posthumously dubbed Taishō), and his grandson Hirohito (posthumously Shōwa), the Japanese embarked upon a remarkable

national reinvention, anchored in a vigorous embrace of industrialization, including within the military.

Another distinguishing characteristic of the Meiji Restoration was the legal and political drive to strengthen the emperor's control of the nation by weakening the traditional structures of the Japanese ruling classes, including members of the Tokugawa shogunate, the *daimyo* (feudal lords), and the samurai (hereditary military nobles). This was no small feat, as the samurai class alone included nearly two million members at the time of the Restoration, all of them eligible for stipends paid by the central government. By 1876, the samurai were compelled to convert the government stipends into bonds, and the government effectively replaced the samurai's traditional role in the defense of the home islands by implementing a mandatory conscription program. In 1877, the samurai rose against the emperor in the Satsuma Rebellion, which was quickly quelled by the new Imperial Japanese Army, eventually forcing the samurai to subsume themselves as fellow and regular citizens of the new imperial regime. The increasingly formidable Japanese armed forces fought and won the First Sino-Japanese War and then the Russo-Japanese War in the years just before and after the turn of the twentieth century, creating a legitimate sense of Imperial Japan having emerged from its shell as a regional power, with increasingly global aspirations. Japan then participated in World War I as an Allied nation, earning it recognition as a great power in the postwar years, while also allowing it to expand its sphere of influence and territorial holdings by seizing former German East Asian and Pacific territories and aggressively pursuing and expanding its territorial and mercantile interests in China.

While the formal dissolution of the samurai class achieved the desired results in cementing the hegemony of the emperors and their close counselors in the increasingly industrial, technological, and militarized Japanese nation, the former members of the heredity military cohort carried their values, beliefs, preferences, biases, and aspirations into many facets of Japanese life, business, and governance. The term *bushido* came to be applied to the code of conduct developed through the era of the Tokugawa shogunate to formalize samurai ethics and practices alike. *Bushido* was anchored in a blending of Buddhism's focus on peace and wisdom with the necessary violence associated with serving in military roles. Key tenets of *bushido* included the mastery of various martial arts, loyalty to one's leaders and lords, honesty, frugality, bravery, and a willingness to sacrifice one's mortal self honorably in service to a cause, mission, or value deemed more valuable and enduring than any individual's single, solitary life.

Between the Russo-Japanese War (1904–1905) and the Second Sino-Japanese War (which began in 1937, essentially launching the Asian components of World War II), *bushido*-based philosophies were increasingly adapted into training for military conscripts, with soldiers, pilots, and sailors being taught that war was a purifying crucible, and death in service to the emperor and the country was a duty to be proudly embraced, not a loss, nor an evil. As Japan rapidly modernized and Westernized, the embrace of *bushido* was couched as a necessary connection to traditional values, and the source of strength for those fighting on Japan's behalf. The willpower affirmed within the ancient codes of conduct led the country's military leaders to believe that their soldiers were collectively indomitable, as they did not fear death, while their various adversaries went into battle hoping to live, not to die gloriously. *Bushido* also taught that surrender under any circumstances was a cowardly act, bringing with it shame not only for those who did not fight to the death, but to their families and descendants as well. Soldiers were trained to die by suicide if captured, and conversely, Japanese treatment of captured enemy combatants became increasingly inhumane as their captives were considered worthy of nothing but contempt, regardless of how long, valiantly, or honorably they had fought against the Japanese. The routine murder of prisoners of war was largely excused in the Japanese military, as the prisoners were considered to have sacrificed any rights to dignity, respect, and release by surrendering to their foes.

Imperial Japan became increasingly belligerent and aggressively expansionist through the end of the 1930s and into the 1940s, especially during the Second Sino-Japanese War, often branded as "the Asian Holocaust," and through the invasion of French Indochina in September 1940. As popular and governmental opinion on ever-expanding military exploits (including attacks on the United States), and the consequences thereof, hung in the balance by 1941, Hideki Tojo was appointed in October of that year to serve as Japan's prime minister by Emperor Hirohito, after brokered negotiations with his advisory *jushin* (elder statesmen). Tojo was tasked with conducting a policy review on the nation's military goals and ambitions, and on November 2, 1941, he and his military chiefs of staff reported to the emperor that there were no valid and viable alternatives to Japanese imperial expansion through military means. Unfortunately, Japan lacked many of the natural resources required to fuel an international war machine, most especially oil. Following the Japanese occupation of French Indochina, the United States froze Japanese assets held in the American banking system, precluding Japanese oil purchases. The most readily accessible points of access for petroleum products were in the Dutch East Indies and British Malaya (both attacked on "the day of infamy"), but to negate likely American response to Japanese aggression in Southeast Asia, the United States military strength needed to be blunted. Hence, ultimately, the aerial bombing of Pearl Harbor and its naval assets.

While Pearl Harbor drew the United States and its allies into active war with Japan, the Imperial Army and Navy still made significant strides through military exploits across the Pacific basin. At its maximum extent in June 1942, Japan's occupied empire was one of the largest in global history, with more than 20 percent of the world's population under Japanese sway in parts of China, Indochina, Indonesia, Russia, the Philippines, and across the islands of Oceania. But as was the case for Germany in Europe, the overextension of resources across vast geographic swaths (compounded in Japan's case by the noncontiguous and isolated nature of its many island holdings) and the combined might of the formidable nations allied in opposition to Japanese expansionism resulted in the step-by-step recovery of captured territory and the eventual threat of invasion of the home islands by 1944. It was only at this point that the Japanese formally codified the policies and practices of the "Special Attack Units," a euphemism for suicide bombers, willing (or forced) to surrender their lives for the greater good of the Japanese Empire.

While aerial bombers represented the Special Attack Unit with the greatest notoriety (and the greatest success rate) in the telling of the tale of World War II, they were not the only suicide soldiers. The Japanese also developed and deployed the *Kaiten* ("Heaven-Shaker") and *Kairyū* ("Sea Dragon") manned torpedo and mini-submarine suicide vessels, deployed along with *Fukuryū* ("Crouching Dragon") frogmen, who were divers armed with mines on bamboo spikes, intended to be driven from below into the hulls of moored enemy ships, killing their deliverymen in the process. The "banzai charges" of futile human wave attacks, while not specifically tied to organized Special Attack Units, were also a form of military self-obliteration practiced and celebrated within the militarized interpretation of the *bushido* code; they were typically ordered when Japanese commanders perceived the tide of infantry battles turning irreparably against them. While kamikaze ("divine wind," historically used to describe a typhoon that wrecked Kublai Khan's fleet, saving Japan from a Mongol invasion) is the word most often used in Western narratives to describe Japan's aerial Special Attack Units, in their time and country, the suicide attack pilots were collectively known as *shinpū tokubetsu kōgeki tai* (abbreviated as *tokkōtai*), which translates as "divine wind special attack units"; for ease of narrative, we will continue to use the more familiar "kamikaze" throughout this text.

While there are a few historic examples of Japanese pilots crashing their planes into military targets in late 1943 and early 1944, there is no strong evidence that these were planned assaults by the organized Special Attack Units. The first inarguable and large-scale use of kamikaze strikes occurred at the Battle of Leyte Gulf in October 1944, when fifty-five Japanese suicide pilots hit twenty-seven American ships (including seven escort carriers), sinking six and inflicting damage of various degrees of severity upon the remainder. The dawn of the kamikaze era generated a high-stakes cat-and-mouse affair between Japanese and American pilots, soldiers, and sailors as the kamikaze pilots learned techniques to avoid American radar and antiaircraft fire, and the Americans countered through the development and deployment of new detection technologies and strategies for neutralizing incoming suicide attack planes. By war's end, over 3,800 kamikaze pilots paid the ultimate price for their service to Imperial Japan, with over seven thousand Allied naval personnel killed by their attacks.

There is a morbidly unique twist associated with assessing the crucibles through which otherwise standard military pilots became kamikazes. There were numerous pilots who completed their Special Attack Unit training, were formally deployed on suicide missions, but lived to tell their tales, either because they were shot down before they could strike their intended targets and rescued, or because weather or other navigational challenges prevented them from their intended goals, forcing them to return home alive. In postwar interviews with these would-be suicide bombers who survived, a recurring trend is that they do not accept that the term "kamikaze" (or its more temporally authentic Japanese variants) should be applied to them.

Essentially, there is but a single clearly defined crucible that makes a kamikaze a kamikaze: the act of self-destruction while piloting a flying bomb or heavily loaded plane into the military assets of the enemy. The divine wind only blew in one terminal direction, and it did not carry its would-be initiates homeward.

Beyond that crucial distinction of "in" versus "out" among the ranks of the kamikaze and their fellow Special Attack Unit soldiers and sailors, there were commonalities in the pipelines, technical training, and indoctrination tactics used to prepare young men to sacrifice their lives for their empire, which we may view as integral steps toward the final, fatal rite of initiation. The first waves of would-be kamikazes were culled, ostensibly as volunteers (though under severe pressure) from the pool of skilled pilots deep into their training pipelines. During the early years of World War II, pilots were expected to complete approximately five hundred hours of flight time to be declared competent for combat missions. By the time that desperation forced the hands of the Japanese military leadership, training flight averages for combat pilots had dropped to two hundred to three hundred hours, depending on whether the pilots were serving in the Japanese Army or Navy. The assignment to kamikaze duty was largely a terminal diversion from an extant training regimen.

Following the early converted combat pilots, there were two additional groups then recruited specifically for suicide missions. Approximately three-quarters of the remaining kamikazes were dubbed "boy pilots," having been drawn into the program, through coercion or naïve volunteerism, from the ranks of new conscripts or militarized youth indoctrination programs. The remaining cohort were known as the "student pilots," as they were university students whose early graduations were forced to allow them to be conscripted. While lack of resources and urgent war needs had already decreased the flight training hours required by conventional pilots, the kamikazes were provided even less training time, typically spending forty to fifty hours in the air over the course of a week or two. During these severely truncated training periods, the suicide pilots learned to take off, fly in formation, and attack their targets. Navigation skills, normally a fundament of flight training, were eschewed; Special Attack Corps officers instead deployed groups of conventionally trained veteran combat pilots to lead the boy and student pilots to their targets, using their honed skills at avoiding enemy radar and fire. Once targets were in sight, the kamikazes would be left to their own devices, with their escorts remaining in the attack zone only long enough to report to their superiors on the missions' successes or failures.

Beyond their limited flight training time, the boy and student pilots were also subjected to strenuous physical training and psychological indoctrination that typically ran over the course of one to two months. The physical brutality of the training regime, including extensive use of corporal punishment for offenses (real or fabricated), was intended to quickly instill the kamikazes with an idealized warrior's spirit, anchored in a routine of self-abnegation and an ability to press forward through physical and mental pain. The extant records of these tragic training arcs were typically left behind in the diaries of the student pilots, who were highly educated in a culture that valued written communication and who sought to rationalize, understand, and justify their decisions to die young for ideals and morals beyond their abilities to challenge or question.

There are several valuable English-language collections culled from these diaries, most notably and useful in our research being Emiko Ohnuki-Tierney's *Kamikaze Diaries: Reflections of Japanese Student Soldiers*. The texts within the diaries are tragic, poignant, and painful in equal measure, with one student reporting a desire to "live with 120 per cent intensity, rather than waiting for death. We read and read, trying to understand why we had to die in our early twenties. We felt the clock ticking away towards our death, every sound of the clock shortening our lives." Another harrowing text came from Kasugo Takeo, a draftee who was assigned to serve the kamikazes-in-training by tending to routine daily tasks in and about their barracks. Per Ohnuki-Tierney, Kasugo wrote of the night before one group's final flights:

> At the hall where their farewell parties were held, the young student officers drank cold sake the night before their flight. Some gulped the sake in one swallow; others kept gulping down [a large amount]. The whole place turned to mayhem. Some broke hanging light bulbs with their swords. Some lifted chairs to break the windows and tore white tablecloths. A mixture of military songs and curses filled the air. While some shouted in rage, others cried aloud. It was their last night of life. They thought of their parents, their faces and images, lovers' faces and their smiles, a sad farewell to their fiancées—all went through their minds like a running-horse lantern [a rapidly revolving lantern with many pictures on it]. Although they were supposedly ready to sacrifice their precious youth the next morning for imperial Japan and for the emperor, they were torn beyond what words can express—some putting their heads on the table, some writing their wills, some folding their hands in meditation, some leaving the hall, and some dancing in a frenzy while breaking flower vases. They all took off wearing the rising sun headband the next morning. But this scene of utter desperation has hardly been reported. I observed it with my own eyes, as I took care of their daily life, which consisted of incredibly strenuous training, coupled with cruel and torturous corporal punishment as a daily routine.

Another extraordinary document associated with the kamikazes' crushing training crucible was a "suicide manual" written in early 1945 by the commander of the Shimoshizu Air Unit. The manual provided detailed instructions for the ways in which pilots were to prepare, think, believe, and act from the moment their training began until the final seconds of their lives as they closed in at high speed on their military targets. There were various generic instructions in the manual associated with such idealized vagaries as attaining a high level of spiritual training, while pursuing and maintaining top physical conditioning. The manual also provided instructions on where and how the kamikazes were to strike their targets. Albert Axell and Hideaki Kase's *Kamikaze: Japan's Suicide Gods* contained this translation: "When diving and crashing on to a ship, aim for a point between the bridge tower and the smoke stack(s). Entering the stack is also effective. Avoid hitting the bridge tower or a gun turret. In the case of an aircraft carrier, aim at the elevators. Or if that is difficult, hit the flight deck at the ship's stern. For a low-altitude horizontal attack, aim at the middle of the vessel, slightly higher than the waterline. If that is difficult, in the case of an aircraft carrier, aim at the entrance to the aircraft hangar, or the bottom of the stack. For other vessels, aim close to the aft engine room."

Most chilling were the instructions and descriptions provided to prepare the suicide pilots for their final moments. Quoting again from Axell and Kase's translations, here are excerpted segments of the ways in which the officers behind the kamikaze program directed their charges to complete the one crucible that ultimately mattered within the regimen, the act of self-destruction that admitted them for the purposes of posterity into the rolls of the kamikazes:

Just before the crash: Your speed is at maximum. The plane tends to lift. But you can prevent this by pushing the elevator control forward sufficiently to allow for the increase in speed. Do your best. Push forward with all your might. You have lived for 20 years or more. You must exert your full might for the last time in your life. Exert supernatural strength. At the very moment of impact: do your best. Every deity and the spirits of your dead comrades are watching you intently. Just before the collision it is essential that you do not shut your eyes for a moment so as not to miss the target. Many have crashed into the targets with wide-open eyes. They will tell you what fun they had.

The moment of the crash: You are two or three meters from the target. You can see clearly the muzzles of the enemy's guns. You feel that you are suddenly floating in the air. At that moment, you see your mother's face. She is not smiling or crying. It is her usual face. All the happy memories. You won't precisely remember them but they are like a dream or a fantasy. You are relaxed . . . because of a succession of pleasant memories flashing through your mind, you feel that you smiled at the last moment. You may nod then, or wonder what happened. You may even hear a final sound like the breaking of crystal. Then you are no more.

Points to remember when making your last dive: Crashing bodily into a target is not easy. It causes the enemy great damage. Therefore, the enemy will exert every means to avoid a hit. Suddenly, you may become confused. You are liable to make an error. But hold on to the unshakeable conviction to the last moment that you will sink the enemy ship. Remember when diving into the enemy to shout at the top of your lungs: *"Hissatsu!"* ["Sink without fail!"]. At that moment, all the cherry blossoms at Yasukuni shrine in Tokyo will smile brightly at you.

Japan's Special Attack Units ultimately failed to provide any strategically significant slowing of the inexorable press by the

Allied forces to topple the Japanese war machine and the government that built and sent it forth across the Pacific Ocean, with
Imperial Japan surrendering unconditionally less than a year
after the first organized deployment of kamikaze pilots. Sadly,
the tenets and sentiments embodied in those harrowing "suicide
manual" texts have been adapted and adopted in the name of various ideologies, faiths, religions, and political positions since the
cessation of World War II's formal hostilities, with the actions of
subsequent suicide missions often egregiously directed at civilian rather than military targets, most notably on one of America's
other truly infamous dates: September 11, 2001.

The ephemeral concept of "cause more important than self"
may be swaddled in noble ideological garb and may in some circumstances result in valiant and valuable actions or changes.
And those willing to embark upon suicide missions may evidence an unusually high level of commitment to cause (noble or
otherwise) and may also endure formidably admirable training
crucibles in pursuit of their terminal goals. But, in the end, acts
of self-destruction in the sole name of destroying others is less
than a zero-sum game, and more a dire tragedy writ large, with
no happy outcomes for any of its players.

CHAPTER 9

An Offer You Can't Refuse: Mafia Made Men

*"There is no reason why good cannot triumph as often as evil.
The triumph of anything is a matter of organization. If there are
such things as angels, I hope that they are organized along the
lines of the Mafia."*
—Kurt Vonnegut Jr.

"Capitalism is the legitimate racket of the ruling class."
—Al Capone

A MERICAN LIFE IN THE LATE 1920s and early 1930s was
shaped by a unique confluence of social, economic, political, and technical trends that, collectively, spawned a particularly powerful and long-lasting creative moment in the nation's
cultural history. Silent films were being supplanted by "talkies,"
even as the October 1929 Wall Street crash unleashed the travails
of the Great Depression upon the American citizenry, and organized crime syndicates increasingly leveraged the racketeering
opportunities offered by the nation's constitutionally mandated
prohibition against the manufacture, sale, and consumption
of alcoholic beverages. The relative cultural libertinism of the
"Roaring Twenties" was increasingly reflected in the products of
Hollywood's emerging major studio system, despite the efforts
of former Republican National Committee chair and postmaster
general Will Hays, who had been engaged by the Motion Picture
Producers and Distributors of America in 1922 to self-police the
studios, largely as an effort to stave off potentially more intrusive
governmental regulation of the filmmaking industry.

Hays's efforts eventually resulted in the 1934 adoption of the Motion Picture Production Code (more widely known to history as the "Hays Code"), which provided a detailed set of industry guidelines that lasted largely unchanged until 1968, when the first version of the modern Motion Picture Association film rating system introduced its G, M, R, and X ratings for films to be released and screened in the United States, a self-policing approach later adopted by television and cable networks, and later still by video game manufacturers and distributors. The original Hays Code was anchored in a set of general principles designed to prohibit films from "lowering the moral standards" of audiences, to encourage the studios to depict "correct standards of life," and to preclude disrespect for the laws of the land by prohibiting scenes that communicated sympathy for those who violated said legal statutes. It was such a transformational moment in American cultural history that the period from about 1927 to 1934 has come to be known as "Pre-Code Hollywood," and some of the most critically and commercially successful films of the era remain surprisingly ribald, violent, and politically provocative, even to jaded twenty-first-century eyes.

The high-level focus in the Hays Code on banning films that offered sympathetic depictions of criminals can largely be laid at the feet of a trio of films released in 1931 and 1932: *Little Caesar*, *The Public Enemy*, and *Scarface*, all of which presented visceral and violent tales of the rises and falls of charismatic gangsters, launching the great careers of actors Edward G. Robinson, James Cagney, and Paul Muni in the process. All three films explored aspects of organized crime in America in lurid detail, were critically acclaimed and commercially successful, and spawned huge waves of backlash from the self-appointed forces of the rigid moral right (the Catholic Church in America played a key role in organizing outrage), who decried the films' perceived immorality and depravity. While the precursors to the Hays Code had been given due lip service since 1922, they were largely ignored by many Hollywood filmmakers through the late 1920s and early 1930s, but the organized hue and cry against *Little Caesar*, *The Public Enemy*, and *Scarface* (among other similarly scandalous films) provided a fulcrum for leveraging the formal adoption of the Hays Code in 1934, with its particular and peculiar prohibition against flattering depictions of criminals.

Organized crime films did not disappear between 1934 and 1968, of course, though the Hollywood studios typically worked their way around the Hays Code's constraints by ensuring that their bad guys got their comeuppance for their nefarious behavior, often in spectacularly gaudy fashions in the films' final acts. Think *Angels with Dirty Faces* (1938), *White Heat* (1949), *Touch of Evil* (1958), or television's *The Untouchables* (1959–1963). And, of course, foreign filmmakers were not bound by the Hays Code in creating their own visions of gangsters and mobs, though their American distribution was often limited to art house showings, in lieu of major national cinematic release campaigns. A seminal example: in 1962, director Alberto Lattuada released a black comedy called *Mafioso* in his native Italy; the film had its American debut nearly two years later. In the film, a white-collar professional from Milan returns to his childhood home in Sicily, where he is roped by unfortunate circumstances into performing a hit in New York City for the local Sicilian mob boss. He succeeds, he returns home, and he is haunted by his experiences, but otherwise suffers no obvious consequences for his work as a gunman for hire.

After the last vestiges of the Hays Code were abolished in the late 1960s, the gangster, mob, and crime genres exploded into the nation's cultural consciousness through some of the most acclaimed and commercially successful films in Hollywood's long history, most notably Francis Ford Coppola's *Godfather* series of films and the works of Martin Scorsese, who has returned again and again to organized crime tropes throughout his storied filmmaking career. Actors Al Pacino, Robert De Niro, Harvey Keitel,

Marlon Brando, and Joe Pesci also carved deep and bloody niches in the walls of the nation's cultural consciousness through their riveting work as charismatic mobster monsters, working with Scorsese, Coppola, and others. (Pacino returned to the idiom's roots with his over-the-top portrayal of Tony Montana in Brian De Palma's ultraviolent remake of *Scarface*, the original of which brought the hammer of the Hays Code down from on high.) Our modern era of bingeworthy and "must-see" cable and streaming television was then largely shaped and defined in the early twenty-first century by *The Sopranos*, an epic mob story told over eight years via eighty-six blood-soaked and profanity-laced episodes.

    While modern mob and gangster films cover a wide variety of criminal organizations (Mexican drug cartels have emerged in recent years as a topical favorite), the basic criminal paradigms presented in 1962's Italian import *Mafioso* endured as defining characteristics of the idiom. Where "Mafia" may have a specific definition (more on that below) as a cultural shorthand, it has become part and parcel of popular parlance as the catchall descriptor of organized crime, often with its roots in Sicily, and usually with its tentacles probing and penetrating deeply into a variety of businesses, industries, and illicit pursuits across urban America. Modern Mafia tales are typically set in the United States' larger, older cities, though Las Vegas certainly holds a place of (dis)honor in the filmed annals of organized crime, in large part due to Martin Scorsese's 1995 epic *Casino*. (De Niro and Pesci again play lead roles in that one.) Key to many of these films is the narrative wherein new recruits (willing or otherwise) rise through the organization's ranks, eventually earning the status of "made men," with its attendant benefits and (sometimes) risks, gloriously magnified through graphic on-screen violence, even when the filmmakers were not required to enthusiastically snuff their antiheroes as a matter of expected studio protocol.

    Because contemporary popular understanding of the Mafia and its practices are anchored so very deeply in film and tele-

vision, and because of the necessarily secretive nature of organized crime syndicates, it is hard to discern how much of said
understanding is fictional and how much is real. We looked to
Las Vegas to help us discern the truth behind the fiction, aided
and abetted by Geoff Schumacher, vice president of exhibits and
programs at the National Museum of Organized Crime and Law
Enforcement, better known to visitors as "The Mob Museum."

"The word 'Mafia' is not actually a synonym for organized
crime," Schumacher explained in an interview. "It is a *type* of
organized crime. So, you can be an organized crime group, or a
'mob,' if you will, without being in the Mafia. The Mafia is specifically related to Italians and Italian American individuals whose
traditions date back at least to the mid-1800s, and some people
say it dates back much further than that. The Mafia specifically
is the idea of a secret society. The idea, in Sicily, was that there
were hundreds of years of different conquerors of Sicily, everybody from religious conquerors to fascist conquerors, all kinds
of different individuals and groups who came in and controlled
the island. The Sicilians themselves were constantly victimized
by these groups, and they ended up supporting each other by
finding ways, surreptitiously, to advance their own interests and
to quietly retaliate against their invaders. The Mafia was about
Sicilians helping themselves, and not relying on the government
to help because the government was often the problem. When
Italians started immigrating to the United States in large numbers in the 1870s and 1880s, some of those individuals brought
with them this concept of 'the Mafia,' or *La Cosa Nostra* as it
is often described in the States. It is ultimately a secret society
that has traditions and expectations attached to membership,
and if you are part of the Mafia, then you are typically involved
in organized crime activities, through which you are supporting
the other members of your organization in a variety of ways."

The quintessential manifestation of the American Mafia
emerged in the early 1930s, following the bloody Castellammarese

War, a fifteen-month-long power struggle among New York City's Italian mob organizations, largely allied with either Joe "The Boss" Masseria or Salvatore Maranzano, and further divided generationally between the "Mustache Petes" (who hewed to "Old World" ways and refused to do business with non-Italians) and the "Young Turks" (often American born and raised, with more openness to dealing with non-Italian parties, especially Irish and Jewish criminal organizations). After numerous casualties of increasingly senior persons on both sides of the conflict, several of Masseria's key lieutenants struck a backroom deal with Maranzano to have their own leader murdered if Maranzano would then agree to end the Castellammarese War.

On April 15, 1931, Masseria was shot to death while playing cards at a Coney Island restaurant, and Maranzano reorganized New York City's Mafia under the "Five Families" rubric. The modern Bonanno, Colombo, Gambino, Genovese, and Lucchese crime families are the inheritors of Maranzano's organizational structure, which divided New York City and various other northeastern cities into specific territories under control of each of the families. Each of the families was led by a boss (also known as a don), with an underboss and a consigliere as the other key members of the leadership team. A group of ranking family members known as capos oversaw groups of soldiers known as "made men," typically required to be Italian Americans. Below the made men were associates, who could be of any ethnic background and who committed crimes under the direction and protection of the made men, sharing a portion of their ill-gotten gains with their direct made-men supervisors.

Maranzano declared himself the *capo di tutti capi* (boss of all the bosses), though his reign as such was to be short-lived: on September 10, 1931, he was shot and stabbed to death in his Manhattan office. Maranzano's passing allowed the Young Turks to wrest control of the Five Families from the Mustache Petes, with Charles "Lucky" Luciano establishing the Commission, a ruling committee that included the bosses of the Five Families, as well as representatives from the Chicago, Philadelphia, Detroit, and Buffalo Mafia organizations at varied times in its history. Luciano is considered to be the father of the modern Mafia accordingly, and the Commission reputedly still exists today in deep secrecy, though clearly documented meetings have been sparse since the 1980s. Salvatore Vitale, onetime underboss of the Bonanno crime family, now living anonymously under the witness protection program, reported in 2003 as part of a deal to cooperate with federal law enforcement agencies that the Commission had, in fact, met as recently as early 2000, with a key outcome being the restoration of the requirement that both parents be of direct Italian descent in order for an associate to become a made man.

"If you are a made man in the Mafia, you have officially and completely joined the group and committed to all of the basic tenets of being in the Mafia," explained Schumacher. "And there is really nothing like that outside of the Italian American Mafia. In other words, if you are in an Irish gang, or an Eastern European Jewish group in the Lower East Side in New York, you really do not have anything like an initiation ceremony that makes you into a made man. It is definitely unique to the Italian American tradition, and it is very much a select group. You can only be invited to be part of it. You cannot apply for membership, like we do for so many things in the world. And you are not likely to be invited unless you have paid your dues in different ways, to earn that right to be invited. Ultimately, a made man is someone who has declared total loyalty to the Mafia family. That is a big thing to do because what total loyalty means, in the Mafia world, is that you are loyal to the Mafia boss, and that loyalty exceeds the loyalty you might have to, say, your wife or to your children. You know, if your mother is on her deathbed in the hospital and the boss needs you to come right away to do something for him, then you pick up and leave your dying mother and go, to take care of whatever business the boss has. That's the level of loyalty that they expect of a made man."

The "invite only" aspect of earning status as a made man makes the Mafia different from many of the other elite organizations discussed in this book, which allow open pools of applicants to earn their way into the ranks of the elites by completing the prescribed set of crucibles. But, of course, given the criminal nature of the Mafia, it remains intuitively obvious that such invitations would only be extended to those with a demonstrated willingness to engage in appropriate criminal activity, perhaps limiting the candidate pools, and building in certain selection biases for those who do find themselves under consideration for a criminal promotion.

"There have been changes over the years, depending on the location in the country, and depending on the whims of the different Mafia dons, in the expectations or requirements to earn an invitation to become a made man," explained Schumacher. "The most commonly expressed requirement is that you must have killed someone on behalf of the organization, though that may or may not always be the case. I'm sure that was true for some people who became made men over the decades, but I don't think that it is absolutely required of everyone who became a made man. Often, the most important thing in the Mafia families is making money. So, if you're really good as 'an earner,' as they say, you might get away with becoming a made man without killing somebody. They're actually very inconsistent on that front across the different families. And I will go one step further with that and say that there have been a lot of rumors about different periods of time when a person could just buy themselves into becoming a made man by paying a certain price, say one hundred thousand dollars, directly to the organization."

And what happens once the invitation is extended? "It's not like there's a set script that is followed to the letter across the country, or across different families, but the general practice is that when you are invited to become a made man, there will be a small ceremony, perhaps in someone's house, or in the back room of a restaurant," Schumacher answered. "The idea is that you are going to come and there will be a group of men there who are, generally, the leadership of the family's other made men, the people who run that particular crime family, and then there is a ceremony in which you pledge your undying allegiance to the group. Again, the practice differs depending on the situation, but one of the typical ceremonial acts is that there is a pricking of the finger, so that blood is drawn, symbolizing that you are willing to spill blood to become part of this group. Or they will present you with a particular face card from a deck, which may be seen as having some mystical value due to the purported image of a saint on it, and it will be symbolically burnt while you recite your undying allegiance to the group.

"Once the ceremony is complete, being a made man provides a lot of privileges within the organization, one of which is that you are not going to be killed without the express permission of the boss," said Schumacher. "Because if any murder occurs without the boss knowing, there are going to be consequences because it is supposed to be the boss who is making those kinds of decisions. You could be a pretty big screw-up as a made man and you are not going to be killed, you know? You may be the black sheep of the crime family, but you are still a made man. And if you are invited to become a made man, that there's some feeling among the leadership of the group that you are a capable person. That you are someone who can make money for the group, that you are a tough guy and you can take care of problems for the group. That you're not an idiot. And that means you have opportunities to advance up the ladder within the family.

"Who's eligible to become the next underboss? Who's eligible to become a capo? Who's eligible to maybe even become the boss someday? And the answer to all those questions is that it is going to be a made man," Schumacher continued. "So, it's an elevation of your stature within the family and it also presents opportunities for you. And once you are a made man, unless you do something really horrible like snitch to the police or something where they would then get rid of you, then you're in. Permanently. Of course, I am sure there are a lot of examples, as in other parts of life, where you have a family business and you're giving a job to Uncle Bill because he's your family, but he's not really contributing a whole lot, so you just do it out of loyalty. You don't want to see the guy end up homeless or something. There is definitely dead weight in the ranks of the made men, and I'm sure that's difficult for some people to deal with. But if you start doing really great work, you'll keep moving up, just like corporate America, right?"

Since our ostensible purpose in researching and sharing the crucibles deployed by elite organizations, even criminal ones, is to glean a deeper understanding of what works, what does not, and why, we asked Schumacher to elaborate on that comparison to corporate America, or other similar organizations within the nation's legal sphere of operations. "Well, I think that if you are a smart boss, then you are going to allow people to innovate and to try new things, and I think that is certainly true in our mainstream business world. A good leader is going to allow his innovative people to try new things," he replied. "And another thing centers on the fact that a boss in the Mafia makes decisions that are absolute, but the smart Mafia boss is someone who, much like Abraham Lincoln, has people around him who are going to tell him the truth, or who are going to provide different points of view, after which he will make a reasoned decision. I think there have been many cases of that, where you had mob bosses who would listen to the people around them and learn from them. And then there are others who would not listen, and they ended up typically not doing very well as bosses.

"One of my favorite parts of mob history is studying the guys who were the innovators and who were very, very clever in the ways that they figured out how to make money. Illegally, you know, but they were smart," Schumacher continued. "And their smarts were related to how they committed crimes without getting caught. And how many ways there were to make a lot of money without being caught. A classic example of this would be a guy named Murray Humphreys. Murray Humphreys was like a lieutenant to Al Capone in Chicago; he was with Capone in the late '20s and early '30s, and he continued with the Chicago outfit into the early '60s. But Murray Humphreys was a brain, and he one time famously said to Al Capone, 'Hey, we're making a lot of money with this bootleg whiskey and bootleg beer, but only a certain percentage of the American people are imbibing, not everybody is drinking bootleg liquor. But think about it, Al: What is the refreshment that 100 percent of the American people drink?' And, while it is probably not true today, at that time, that refreshment was milk. So, Murray Humphreys's idea was: *We need to get into the milk business.* And then, in fact, they did just that. They bought a dairy and they got involved with milk as a money-making venture. So, here's a guy who's thinking very cleverly, working for a boss who gave him the freedom to do that. There's a lesson there, certainly."

As we wrapped up our conversation with Schumacher, we noted that there is a certain antiquated quaintness to these Mafia tales, which seems out-of-kilter in a modern world where digital surveillance, data harvesting, and monitoring are constant factors of our online existences, and where the casual, occasional neighborhood shakedown by the local mob associates seems laughably anachronistic. But Schumacher assured us that the history of the Mafia is a current and ongoing one, and that the loose network of criminal organizations continues to evolve and adapt to meet its own needs in these, our modern times.

"The traditional Mafia in America absolutely still exists in certain areas in New York, Philadelphia, Chicago, Detroit, and maybe in New Jersey," Schumacher concluded. "But the truth is that the Mafia is a far smaller enterprise than it was in the past. The RICO [Racketeer Influenced and Corrupt Organizations] Act of 1970 led to countless cases being brought against them over the years, and to intense federal surveillance. But the Mafia still exists, and they still function in a similar way to the ways that they did in the past. They keep a lower profile these days, unlike, say, John Gotti, who was just so defiant about his activities, which really made the feds want to nail him. So, he ended up paying for it, just like Al Capone did. By being so public you draw media attention to yourself, and you draw police attention to yourself. Not a good idea. In recent years, my understanding from talking to law enforcement people and people still 'in the life,' as they say, is that the Mafia still exists, that they still have made men, that they still have the Commission, and that they dictate policy for a lot of the country when it comes to organized crime activities. But in the end, I do not think that anything about them is quite as dramatic these days as what we saw at the peak of the mob in America, which was really during the 1940s, '50s, and '60s."

Hollywood does not seem to have gotten the memo on that reduced level of drama. And so long as the ticket-buying and television-watching public retains its obsessions for charismatic hitmen and troubled dons, and the women who love them, we doubt very much that they ever will.

CHAPTER 10

Great Tiger Sharks Swimming on Land: The Hawaiian Koa

"The way to lose any earthly kingdom is to be inflexible, intolerant, and prejudicial. Another way is to be too flexible, tolerant of too many wrongs, and without judgment at all. It is a razor's edge. It is the width of a blade of pili grass."
—Queen Lili'uokalani

"Here's to old warriors calling. Here's to old battles won. Here's to Hawai'i's victory. Here's to each valiant one."
—"Co-Ed Fight Song," University of Hawai'i at Mānoa

THE *ACACIA KOA* ("KOA TREE") is gloriously large and fast-growing and is endemic to the major islands of the Hawaiian archipelago, where its ability to convert nonreactive atmospheric nitrogen into usable compounds allows it to root, grow, and thrive in the youngest volcanic soils surrounding the island chain's active volcanoes. The ancient Hawaiian people used the koa tree's wood to craft outrigger canoes, surfboards, furniture, and artistic objects, while in modern times it has earned a niche as a desirable tone-wood for high-end ukuleles and guitars.

As the native koa forests have been dramatically depleted in the twentieth and twenty-first centuries through cattle grazing, habitat destruction, and over-logging, objects crafted from the tree's richly textured, red-hued wood have gained the luster and cachet that always accompany the scarcity of exotic goods. Few koa trees grow large and straight enough anymore for traditional outrigger canoes to be carved from their boles, and modern

163

surfboard manufacturers have generally eschewed the increasingly scarce and expensive koa and wiliwili (another endemic Hawaiian tree) woods, opting instead for mass-produced models of polyurethane foam, fiberglass, and polyester resin.

As a result of these evolving manufacturing processes, there are ever fewer koa wood objects being produced today that would have been recognized, respected, and resonant in traditional pre-twentieth-century Hawaiian culture. Even koa wood ukuleles miss the mark there, since that seemingly timeless and emblematic Hawaiian musical instrument was not actually introduced to the islands and adopted by the islanders until the 1880s, after Portuguese sailors and immigrants had arrived with their *braguinhas*, small guitar-like instruments, also known as *machetes*.

So, if precolonial-era native Hawaiians were transported to the modern-day American state of Hawai'i and set loose to explore the many craft markets (traditional local and tourist-oriented alike) found throughout the inhabited islands of the chain, what contemporary koa wood objects would most likely catch their eyes and attention as recognizable symbols across time and space? Perhaps not surprisingly, given human nature across time and space, the answer to that question would be: *weapons*.

One of your authors (Eric) visited the Big Island as we were in the early phases of researching this book, and he was awed, amazed, and appalled in equal measure by some of the fearsome tools of human harm on sale from stalls closely adjacent to ones selling lei garlands, aloha shirts, macadamia nuts, ukuleles, puka shell necklaces, and other mostly benign modern-day manifestations of Hawaiian culture.

There were koa wood melee weapons in those market stalls, for close-in, hand-to-hand combat. Some were designed for stabbing at the torso, some for tripping or disabling the legs of an opponent, facilitating an easier final dispatch to follow. The stabbing instruments lay on tables alongside a variety of long spears displayed vertically, many of them specifically designed so that their points would break off after penetrating the flesh of their targets, to maximize the damage they inflicted. There were various slings and throwing weapons designed to increase the possible range of carnage achieved by those who wielded them. Perhaps most visually terrifying were the *lei o manō* ("shark's lei"), which were slashing weapons with koa wood hearts, surrounded on their business ends with arrays of jagged, razor-sharp shark's teeth embedded into the grain of the wood. As is the case for sharks themselves, the teeth were also designed to break off, continuing to cut and shred even when the motive force of jaw or handheld weapon was no longer applied.

We certainly hope that modern makers and purchasers of these weapons see them as exquisite works of art, destined for peaceful display, but there is no question that historically, these weapons were used skillfully and formidably in combat situations, often by the Hawaiian caste of warriors who bore the same name as the tree from which their fearsome tools were manufactured: the Koa.

Many public and popular sources assert that the tree was named for the elite fighting force because the tree's great strength made it the warrior of the Hawaiian woodlands. Other sources correctly observe that the koa tree's name is derived from a Proto-Austronesian word with related derivatives spanning the Oceanic basin, and which means "ironwood," in recognition of the hard, dense wood that can be milled from the heart of the tree. While definitive answers are few on such historic linguistic connections, there's no argument that the mighty kings of the Hawaiian forest and the mighty warriors who served Hawai'i's monarchs are culturally closely associated, one with the other.

Brook Kapūkuniahi Parker is a modern-day expert in and aficionado of both Koa (warriors) and koa (wood). He is a direct descendant of both John Palmer Parker, founder of the Parker Ranch on Hawai'i's Big Island (one of the oldest and largest ranches in the United States) and of King Kamehameha the

Great, the warrior chieftain who, through battle and statecraft, united the archipelago's eight main islands into the Kingdom of Hawai'i between 1782 and 1810, ably aided and abetted by his faithful Koa. John Palmer Parker, originally from Newton, Massachusetts, became a trusted confidant of Kamehameha the Great, eventually marrying the king's granddaughter, launching one of Hawai'i's most prominent dynasties over the course of the islands' independent kingdom era and through its assimilation into the United States near the turn of the twentieth century.

Brook Kapūkuniahi Parker is an exceptional artist, specializing in *kū*, the masculine paintings of warriors in battle scenes and kings; his striking renditions hang in many public spaces and private collections across the state of Hawai'i and beyond, and he has illustrated numerous publications, most notably an audaciously powerful edition of *Ruling Chiefs of Hawai'i*, commissioned by Kamehameha Publishing. He is also a popular historian and lecturer and a skilled artisan of Hawai'ian weaponry and crafts.

Parker's passion for his place and his people was thrilling in its intensity during an interview with us, as was the unique perspective that his artisan's eye brings to his telling and interpretation of his native island's extraordinary history, and his commitment to celebrating and respecting the memories of the ancestors who crafted it. That visceral personal connection with his ancestors imbues his artwork with an exceptional sense of presence and personality, his painted warriors not mere two-dimensional "any man" ciphers of the Koa and their kings, but instead vivid individuals, leaping from the canvas, typically in the throes of the most rigorous moments associated with their roles as warriors.

"If the ancestors help to inspire you to do great things with your life, and to use the talents that you have, and you celebrate them for that, then that's really wonderful," Parker explained. "But, then, you also need to remember that they are not you. They are themselves. So, I think a better perspective when we talk about the ancestors is to remember that someday we will be face-to-face with those guys. I will meet the ancestors on the other side. And I will have an accountability report for them. What did I do with their names and memories? Did I teach my children the same love and respect they taught theirs? Did I teach that to others? I know that I do not want to have a negative accountability report when I meet them. They are all important to me. I am Hawaiian, yes, but I am Chinese, too. I'm Scottish. I've got English in me. It's all important. I live in Hawai'i, so, yeah, I probably do concentrate my activities on my Hawaiian ancestors more. But they're all great, great people, the ones I knew intimately, and the ones I didn't. I want them to be proud when I meet them."

While the details of human settlement of Hawai'i remain murky, current consensus is that Polynesian long-distance navigators may have sporadically visited the islands between 400 and 1100 CE, with a larger and more systematic wave of settlement occurring circa 1220–1265 CE. Regardless of the settlement date, the uniformity and Eastern Polynesian culture and language is indicative of close cross-communication between distant islands, and of a rapid period of settlement in the Hawaiian archipelago once large-scale immigration began. Those spiritual, political, and social connections would have influenced the emergence of warrior, priestly, and kingly classes in Hawai'i that were deeply influenced by the traditions in the islands from which the early Hawaiians sprang. Not to mention the ways in which they viewed the need for and execution of warfare.

The specific origin stories of the Koa culture, and those of its warrior forebears, were largely passed down through oral tradition across generations, richly flavored with mystical and mythological details before the more literal and documentarian-minded Europeans arrived, with Captain James Cook's landing on the island of Kaua'i in 1778 as the first drip from the floodgates of immigration and emigration that followed. Cook was killed on

Hawai'i's Big Island a mere year later, but the young and wise warrior who would one day become Kamehameha the Great witnessed the English captain's demise, and was then quick to embrace, adapt, and apply European weaponry, battlefield tactics, and political strategies to the arsenal of his military resources, arguably a difference-making factor in his unification of Hawai'i.

"In Polynesia as a whole, you only have so many natural resources," Brook Kapūkuniahi Parker explained. "Whenever there were any inter-island disputes or troubles, it was always over the fact that one island's rulers were not good stewards of those resources. So, one ruler would go over and kick over the other ruler's stewardship. It was never about ownership because the Akua, or the gods, they owned everything. How are you going to charge somebody to use the sun, or to use the water? Those things do not belong to you. You are just a steward over those things, and good rulers help their people that way, by being good stewards. And the good rulers—we don't really call them kings, we call them *ali'i nui*—surrounded themselves with experts, with people they could trust. And a lot of those people in their inner circles, they served dual purposes as military advisors and also as religious advisors. They wore two hats: they were very connected to the Akua but were also great leaders of men."

One of the distinguishing caste-specific traits that emerged among the early Hawaiian *ali'i nui*, along with the members of their royal families, their guardsmen, and the professional warriors who advanced their political interests, was the use of a martial art form known as *Kapu Ku'ialua*, often shortened to "Lua" in modern English parlance. Lua was a combat art dedicated to strikes, throws, bone breaking, pressure point manipulation, and joint locks; in its broader philosophical manifestations, it also came to define approaches to battlefield and ocean warfare strategies, and Kamehameha the Great adapted it further to incorporate the firearms he acquired from his European allies after Captain Cook's arrival and demise.

Lua's full historic name combined two elements of the culture from which it emerged. *Ku'ialua* translates to "two hits" in English, focusing on the tactile, close combat aspects of the discipline. *Kapu* means "forbidden," a word used to codify a host of taboo behaviors, violations of which typically came with a death sentence for the offender. Interestingly, while the rigid *kapu* system inexorably dominated and defined daily life and gender roles through a slew of prohibited actions and behaviors, there was an out provided to the all-too-easily-earned death sentences: if a violator of *kapu* was able to elude the authorities and make their way to a *pu'uhonua*, a place of refuge, then no harm could befall the offender. While a large National Historical Park called *Pu'uhonua o Hōnaunau* on Hawai'i's Big Island is a well-preserved place of refuge, traditional accounts indicate that the *ali'i nui* could declare various *heiau* (sacred spaces) as refuges as well, not only for violators of *kapu* but also for the families of combatant forces, who would be guaranteed safe return to their homes following the cessation of hostilities, no matter the outcome of the war or battle that displaced them.

Lua, then, was the "forbidden two hits," a martial art restricted to the Hawaiian society's elites, most notably the *ali'i nui* and the Koa. While commoners could serve as artillerymen in combat and would be introduced to the basic elements of Lua, full training in the art was closely protected and restricted, and teaching or practicing it outside of its assigned castes was, itself, a punishable violation of *kapu*. To maximize the advantages that Lua training gave them, the Koa would also remove all their body hair and coat themselves with coconut oil to avoid being grasped and grappled on the battlefield. While spectacular ceremonial headdresses and capes were often worn onto battlefields to convey majesty and strike fear, the Koa would fight nearly nude beneath them, wearing only snug loincloths, thereby explaining the meaning of the traditional word for masters of the Lua form, *ōlohe*, which translates into English as "hairless."

Parker further explained that *ōlohe* status as he addressed his forebear, King Kamehameha the Great. "Kamehameha himself was a special category of warrior called *niuhi*. They went through rigorous, rigorous training, sometimes even since they were little, before they could be considered *ōlohe*," Parker said. "And the way that I look at that word, *ōlohe*, I think about our *kahunas*, who are masters at their skills, like somebody with a PhD today. There were different types of *kahunas*, ones who took care of the agriculture and the aquaculture, ones who could read the stars. The *ōlohe* were the *kahunas* of war. These guys were trained in bone-breaking and in the arts of war. But not only that, they also knew how to heal. So, Lua has a dual meaning, like yin and yang. You could break it, and then you could fix it. And they had a special Lua school in Hawai'i. You had to be invited to attend, and it was hard, hard work."

Selective processes for admission into an elite society followed by rigorous training phases are, unsurprisingly, common factors in most of the stories covered in this book. But the final crucible for admission into the highest levels of the Koa caste remains one of the most awe-inspiring and terrifying that we have encountered throughout our research into such rites of passage.

"When a warrior was about to graduate from the Lua school, they would keep him up all night to tire him out," Parker explained. "Then, early in the morning, they would take him out in a double-hulled canoe, and they would chum the waters with an unfortunate enemy soldier or criminal, or with a rotten pig if no fellows were available, to get it all bloody and oily so the big tiger sharks would come. Now, a lot of times these tiger sharks were longer than a sixteen-foot canoe. They were just *huge*. And the warrior's graduation ceremony would require him to jump in the water and kill that tiger shark with his bare hands. If he was a skilled Lua guy, then he would be able to kill that giant tiger shark with his bare hands. Then he would get help hauling the carcass up onto the canoe, and once he did that, and completed the deed, he would eat the shark's left eyeball right there on the canoe. He would also take out the right eyeball and take it home to show what he had done. And then he would become one of the *niuhi*: a great tiger shark that is now swimming on land. He is a devourer of men in battle. And Kamehameha was a *niuhi*. His specialty was picking men up and breaking their backs. Nice and close."

For all the brutality associated with the Koa and their deployment of Lua, the practice was rooted in a deeply spiritual, honor-bound tradition. In the same way that offenders against *kapu* could find refuge and earn forgiveness by finding their ways to a *pu'uhonua*, so too could widespread battlefield carnage be avoided by one-on-one contests before the combatants between the most accomplished warriors of the opposing forces. Victory in such an intimate engagement could then serve as an acceptable proxy to judge the outcomes of a major battle without the loss of lives associated with such a mass engagement, though such symbolic battles were, of course, subject to the mutual concurrence of the opposing *ali'i nui*, which was no foregone conclusion.

Another spiritual element of Koa culture was a deep embrace of the concept of mana, a spiritual energy derived from the life force of ancient ancestors, and said to course through the veins of Hawai'i's lava rocks just as blood flows through the human body. The Koa engaged in combat not only for personal, political, or professional reasons, but also to obtain mana, believing that brave actions and victories in battle increased their own mana, with equal and offsetting reductions in the mana of their defeated enemies. Loss of mana was associated with loss of societal status, and the most tragic turn of events for the Koa would be to be reduced to the commoner or slave castes by ignoble or unsuccessful performance on the battlefield. Fights to the death were logical under such a paradigm, if not necessarily conducive to the peaceful perpetuation of a society.

While Kamehameha the Great is venerated to this day as one of the most accomplished warriors and military commanders in Hawaiian history, his greatest and most lasting achievements may, in fact, be anchored in his political acts following the unification of the Kingdom of Hawai'i. As *ali'i nui* of the entire archipelago, the king worked hard to create a kingdom that could, and did, outlive him, promoting international trade, establishing sound taxation policies to fund the instruments of state, and standardizing and codifying the islands' legal structures and systems.

His most resonant political act may have been the implementation of *Kānāwai Māmalahoe*, or the "Law of the Splintered Paddle." Its eloquently stated central precept, "Let every elderly person, woman and child lie by the roadside in safety," was a cornerstone in the transition of Hawaiian culture from centuries of aggressive warlike behavior to one anchored in a fundamental respect for human dignity. Kamehameha's great law has been reaffirmed in modern Hawai'i's state constitution, and it has long been cited as a model for international human rights statutes regarding the treatment of civilians in or near warzones.

Following Kamehameha the Great's death in 1819, his islands were further transformed by the 'Ai Noa, a period of taboo-breaking that soon led to the formal abolition of *kapu* and its many rules and regulations, along with the frequent death sentences that accompanied violations of the same. The king's son, Kamehameha II, ceremonially and finally marked the cessation of the old order when he ate a meal of dogmeat with and served by his mother, Keōpūolani, and other women of her retinue, all strictly forbidden behaviors before that time. (To be historically accurate and fair, this "feast" and its fallout were driven more by the formidable Keōpūolani and her women than it was by Kamehameha II himself, who essentially just acceded to and ratified a change beyond his power to control.)

The ascent of Christian missionaries during Kamehameha II's brief reign (he died of measles, to which he had no native immunity, during a state visit to England in 1824) further eroded and displaced the traditional warrior cultures that had defined Hawai'i and the rest of Eastern Polynesia for centuries. The detrimental impact of European missionary practices on traditional Hawaiian culture notwithstanding, there's little doubt that the modern perception of Hawai'i as a peaceful island paradise, tailor-made for tourism, would not have been possible without the eradication of *kapu* and the caste structure that empowered the most violent attributes of the Koa and their *ali'i nui*.

The *Kapu Ku'ialua* martial arts of the Koa and their *ali'i nui* masters also fell from prominence as a secret art of the elite class, though Kamehameha II did establish three Lua schools to protect the art from extinction. Elements of that martial craft persevere to this day, long after the Kingdom of Hawai'i was annexed into the United States in 1893. Lua concepts are still taught (not necessarily faithfully or accurately) in various modern martial arts disciplines, perhaps most notably American Kenpo, which was established and championed by Edmund Kealoha Parker, the uncle of our ebullient artist and interviewee Brook Kapūkuniahi Parker. Ed Parker also maintained a healthy side career training Hollywood stuntmen and celebrities; he awarded Elvis Presley a first-degree black belt in Kenpo and was later one of Elvis's personal bodyguards.

While records of such matters are not necessarily as clear and transparent as historians might like, we do remain comfortably certain that Elvis did not have to kill a tiger shark and eat its left eyeball to earn his belt. So, score one for the original Koa and their king.

CHAPTER 11

Fiercely and Faithfully: The Swiss Guard

"Heaven offers nothing that a mercenary soul can desire."
—C. S. Lewis

"The Lord gets His best soldiers out of the highlands of affliction."
—Charles Spurgeon

W E ARE RESEARCHING AND WRITING this chapter of *Crucibles* during particularly tense geopolitical times, with hot conflicts in Ukraine and Gaza, attacks on Red Sea shipping by Houthi militants in Yemen, dire hints from resurgent Middle Eastern and Central Asian terrorist organizations, and economic and political posturing related to China, Mexico, Taiwan, NATO, North Korea, and other international flash points potentially threatening to draw the United States and other great and regional powers into what could become another catastrophic global war. Although technological advancements since the cessation of World War II and its Cold War sequels have significantly increased nations' abilities to fight battles and wars—or to inflict damage on their enemies—from control centers far from actual physical flash points, significant escalation in any or all of the currently simmering regional contexts would lead to the deployment and use of large numbers of military personnel in closer combat situations.

While the percentage of U.S. citizens with current or prior military service has declined relatively steadily since the end of the Cold War, and while the challenges faced by military recruiters have become a commonly reported news item across the contemporary media and political spectrums, the United

States still maintains one of the largest (by number of personnel) active-duty military forces in the world, with over 1.3 million soldiers, sailors, pilots, Marines, and others currently on duty. That number of active-duty personnel is only exceeded by India (approximately 1.4 million active-duty members) and China (about 2.2 million). North Korea, Russia, and Malaysia are the other nations currently enrolling over one million active-duty members of their various armed services.

But those active-duty personnel statistics do not tell the full story of the world's militaries, as many nations also maintain various reserve units (i.e., trained members of the military who drill occasionally around their civilian lives, and are ready for full-time call-up as required to address all variety of hazards to a nation's well-being) or paramilitary organizations (i.e., personnel trained to protect their homelands from threats foreign and domestic, without actually being conscripted, enlisted, or serving as officers in their respective armed services) supplementing their active-duty military units. When active, reserve, and paramilitary force numbers are aggregated, the United States drops to ninth place in the global military personnel table with about 2.1 million members. North Korea (7.8 million members) and South Korea (6.8 million members) top the aggregated rankings, with Vietnam, India, China, Russia, Ukraine, and Brazil filling the slots between the Koreas and the United States. Another six nations count over one million military personnel when all active, reserve, and paramilitary units are included.

World Population Review (an independent nonprofit organization that works to provide current and accessible demographic and statistical data for a variety of global metrics) identifies 171 nations globally with reportable and trackable military personnel figures; the figures cited above are from their 2024 dataset. The information presented in their public reports provides some fascinating perspectives about the different ways that nations support their military interests (e.g., the United States has no formal paramilitary units, while other nations consider vast swaths of their populations to fall within that cohort), how important those interests are to the nations' political leaders, how much of their gross domestic products are applied to these military interests, and the need for ostensibly nonbelligerent nations to support strong militaries for no reason other than because they are inconveniently located near various geographic choke points and geopolitical hot spots around the world.

Of course, part of the fun of playing with datasets like those offered by World Population Review is exploring the extreme points within them, so a long scroll to the very bottom of the "Military Size by Country" column reveals the world's smallest military unit: the 135-man-strong armed forces of Vatican City, the world's smallest country, geographically and by population. The 135 Vatican soldiers are listed in the "reserve unit" column, and while their absolute numbers are small, the population of Vatican City is also the world's smallest, so when assessing the total military size of various armed forces per one thousand citizens of the nations they serve, Vatican City is the third most militarized sovereign state in the world, following only Israel and North Korea. Oddly impressive on one hand, and curiously anachronistic on the other, with this unique fighting force serving the needs of a national enclave buried deep in the heart of bustling modern Rome, Italy, both a national capital and a global tourism hub. Those elements of anachronistic exceptionalism are magnified when delving into the history of Vatican City, and discovering that its armed forces are cited by the Guinness World Records as the world's oldest standing army, having been formally organized in 1506, with some related roots dating back at least a century before that time.

So, while the great powers of the world and their massive armies teeter at the edge of various potential apocalyptic abysses, let us reflect instead on a different sort of military, an inarguably elite unit with an equally unique history and mission. This tiny army's formal name is the *Pontificia Cohors Helvetiorum* though they are generally known in English as the Swiss Guard. Their official website describes their roles thusly: "The Pontifical Swiss Guard are the constant watchmen of the [Catholic Pope] and his residence. They guard the official entrances to the Vatican City, run access checks, and are available to the many international visitors to the Vatican. The Swiss Guard keep watch at papal audiences and church ceremonies where the pontiff is present. This surveillance is done in both traditional uniform and in civilian clothes. Higher officers accompany the pontiff on his travels abroad. The Swiss Guard provide a military guard of honor at official visits from presidents, prime ministers, and ambassadors. The guard of honor is also present at masses, audiences, and entrances to the Vatican City." The Swiss Guard are also tasked with protecting the Sacred College of Cardinals (the body of all cardinals within the Catholic Church) when the Holy See is vacant between papal administrations.

The current population of Vatican City includes about 820 souls, 135 of them the Swiss Guards, and about 40 of them wives and children of same. (For centuries, the guards were required to be single and celibate. They still must be single when they join the Guard, but after turning twenty-five years old, they may marry with approval after five years of service, a more humane and lenient policy only adopted under the current reign of Pope Francis; interim policies had restricted marriage only to those who had achieved certain senior rank within the Guard.) Vatican City has no birthright citizenship because there is no hospital within its confines, so citizenship is a right bestowed by the pope, granted only to cardinals living within the Vatican's confines or nearby Rome, diplomats of the Holy See deployed abroad, and persons resident in Vatican City specifically because of their official positions. Members of the Swiss Guard do carry Vatican and Holy See passports, but they are also all, by definition, history, and requirements, native citizens of Switzerland.

While the term "mercenary" is fraught with negative implications associated with soldiers of fortune or hired guns willing to fight and kill for any masters, no matter how unsavory, in return for adequate remuneration, the Swiss Guard are, indeed, mercenaries at bottom line: born, raised, and trained under one flag, then traveling abroad where they are paid to fight under another.

While modern Switzerland is a developed Western nation colloquially known abroad for its spectacular Alpine scenery, chocolates, watches, pocketknives, and secretive banking practices, its largest international claim to fame once centered around its ability and willingness to provide mercenaries to serve under a variety of European states and powers. The Old Swiss Confederacy was a union of urban and rural communes (called "cantons") loosely organized in the Alpine region in the early thirteenth century under nominal rule-from-afar by the Holy Roman Empire. The Swiss cantons developed formal militias into which young men were conscripted, and within which they were trained to fight in mass formations using fearsome halberds, spears, and pikes. The Swiss militias were fierce, effective, and readily deployed, often to protect Swiss interests from the Holy Roman Empire's predatory Austrian Habsburg regime. Following significant upset victories over Austrian forces at the battles of Morgarten (1315) and Laupen (1339), the Swiss cantons and their soldiers embarked upon various forays into the Italian Peninsula. In the Burgundian Wars (1474–1477), they soundly defeated what were then considered Europe's most formidable armies (from the Duchy of Burgundy and the Duchy of Savoy), sealing their reputation as a formidably elite fighting force.

Following the Burgundian Wars, the Swiss soldiers' reputations for ruthless battlefield successes soon made them highly attractive to foreign powers seeking to solidify and secure their own military strength. Conveniently, the cantons of the Old Swiss Confederacy made it quite easy for foreign powers to employ their soldiers, as entire trained and organized units (along with their necessary weaponry) could be acquired under contract and deployed en masse to serve their new masters-of-convenience, sparing the states that engaged them the expenses and difficulties associated with recruiting and training individual soldiers, while also significantly enhancing Swiss economic and political strength.

One notable noble who sought the support of Swiss mercenaries was Giuliano della Rovere, who was elected to the papacy by the Sacred College of Cardinals in November 1503, taking the pontifical name of Pope Julius II. While his reign lasted just short of a decade, Julius is regarded to this day as one of the most consequential and influential men to lead the Catholic Church over the course of its convoluted history. Among his many accomplishments were launching the rebuilding of St. Peter's Basilica, establishing the Vatican Museums, commissioning Michelangelo's monumental work in the Sistine Chapel, and launching the Catholicization of the Americas by establishing the first bishoprics in the New World. Julius was also a master statesman and warrior in his own right, known as the "Fearsome Pope," and identified by no less an authority than Niccolò Machiavelli as a role model and ideal for the world's would-be princes.

Julius's political acumen was a crucial skill in the face of sweeping dynastic struggles across Europe in the late fifteenth and early sixteenth centuries that have been labeled for posterity as the Italian Wars. The Italian Peninsula at the time was composed of a collection of small states of political and economic interest to the French House of Valois, the Austrian Habsburgs and their constellation of allies and subjects within the Holy Roman Empire, and the Spanish, then ruled by the joint monarchs Ferdinand and Isabella, who had united most of the Iberian Peninsula's states alongside their holdings in Naples, Sicily, and Sardinia. The Ottoman Empire and England also dabbled in extraterritorial skullduggery in the Italian Peninsula, and the region's various statelets often switched alliances between the various continental powers. Smack in the middle of this tapestry of political chaos and intrigue were the Papal States, the territories over which the pope maintained sovereignty from his seat of power in Rome.

Julius's predecessor once-removed (the pope immediately before him, Pius III, ruled for just twenty-six days before dying of sepsis from a leg wound), Pope Alexander VI of the powerful Borgia family, had striven mightily to expand the breadth of, and his control over, the Papal States. That aggressive pursuit of territory continued under Julius II, often with the pope leading combat campaigns himself. Julius's warrior spirit was inspired and shaped, in part, by his exposure to the formidable Swiss mercenaries, both from his time serving as the bishop of Lausanne in Switzerland from 1472 to 1476, and as an observer and a participant in various campaigns of the Italian Wars in which the fierce Swiss fighters were engaged. Upon his election to the papacy in 1503, Julius requested that the Federal Diet of Switzerland (the governing legislative council that bound the federated cantons together) provide him with an entourage of Swiss mercenaries to serve as his personal guard. Their employment was underwritten by German business owners who saw Julius as being beneficial to their own interests in the Italian Peninsula. The first 150 soldiers so assigned arrived in Rome on January 22, 1506, under the command of Kaspar von Silenen; Julius later dubbed them the "Defenders of the Church's Freedom."

While the date of the original Swiss Guards' arrival in Rome is cited and remembered as the foundational point of the military unit, current initiates are always sworn in to service on May 6, commemorating an even more formative point in their early history: the Sack of Rome in 1527. Pope Julius II had died in 1513 and was followed in short order by popes Leo X (a member of the Medici family), Adrian VI (a Dutchman, and the last non-Italian to head the Church until Poland's John Paul II was elected 455 years later), and Clement VII (another Medici). The fortunes of the various continental powers continued to ebb and flow across the Italian Peninsula throughout these popes' reigns, and their Swiss mercenaries were occasionally deployed in their traditional combat roles. In 1522, French interests in Italy were routed at the Battle of Bicocca by the joint forces of the Holy Roman Empire and Spain. In the aftermath of France's defeat, the opportunistic Clement VII laid claim to Milan, severed his allegiance to the Spanish, and joined the Holy League of Cognac, along with France, Milan, Florence, and Venice. England's King Henry VIII also withdrew his support of Spain and the Holy Roman Empire at this point in the international chess match; both of those political entities were ruled by Emperor Charles V, who also ruled Austria, the Netherlands, and Burgundy.

England's withdrawal of support for Emperor Charles V left the multi-crowned monarch with insufficient funds to pay his troops, leading to a revolt in March 1527, with his soldiers seeking to take matters of remuneration into their own hands through the time-honored practices of sack, siege, and seize. Following a stalemate at Florence, the frustrated troops (most of them incidentally Lutheran, not Catholic) turned southward and set upon Rome. They arrived on May 6, 1527. Aided by a thick ground fog and by the absence of organized military resistance in the capital of the papacy, Charles V's hungry and ambitious marauders fell upon the city with zealous and catastrophic abandon, searching for the pope for some combination of ransom and revenge purposes.

Pope Clement's Swiss Guard then consisted of 189 members. Forty-two of the guardsmen were able to extract Clement from the Vatican via a secret exit passage. The other 147 members of Clement's Swiss Guard were killed, standing alone against some twenty thousand attackers, protecting their pontiff to the end. Rome itself fell to its invaders within a day, after which the rampaging mercenaries set off on a wild spree of pillage, murder, rape, and property crime. Tens of thousands of people were killed or injured, and an estimated 90 percent of Rome's artworks and collections were destroyed or stolen. Pope Clement took refuge in Rome's ancient Castel Sant'Angelo fortress for over six months and was eventually forced to pay a sizeable ransom and to yield significant portions of the Papal States to Emperor Charles V's Holy Roman Empire to secure his freedom.

The annihilated Pontifical Swiss Guard was not restored until 1548, under the reign of Pope Clement's successor, Pope Paul III. As the Italian Wars wound to their close, the Swiss Guard evolved from its aggressive combat mission into a more ceremonial and personal protective role for the pontiff. Beyond a few brief periods in the eighteenth and nineteenth centuries when the Guard was dissolved, then reinstated soon thereafter, the successors of the original Swiss mercenaries have served the popes in a variety of roles for over five hundred years. For much of the late nineteenth and early twentieth centuries, their role reached its operational nadir, with the Guard's members largely being recruited from families of Swiss descent resident in Rome, rather than from Switzerland itself, and with their training and duties being rendered minimal and ceremonial.

Jules Repond, the unit's commander from 1910 to 1921, is largely to be credited with the Swiss Guard's modern resurgence, operational structures, and recruiting policies, along with the unit's distinctive look. Repond designed their "gala uniforms" himself, featuring the blue, red, and yellow traditional colors of the Medici dynasty and cut to resemble garments worn by subjects in Raphael's Vatican frescoes. (It is an oft-quoted myth that Michelangelo was responsible for the guards' sartorial splendor; he was not.) The guards also add a variety of ceremonial gloves, helmets, hats, armor, and traditional halberds for special events throughout the Vatican official calendar. The Lateran Treaty of 1929 between Italy and the Holy See further codified the roles of the Swiss Guard (along with the Palatine Guard and Noble Guard, which were dissolved in 1970) and their relationship with the papal Gendarmerie Corps, a more traditional police force responsible for criminal investigations, public order, traffic control, and other related civic matters in and around the Catholic capital. The assassination attempt on Pope John Paul II in 1981 and threats made against Vatican City by the Islamic State in the early years of the twenty-first century resulted in an increased focus on nonceremonial training and duties by the members of the Guard, whose numbers were increased from 110 to 135 by Pope Francis in 2018. The Swiss Army now ensures that the members of the Pontifical Guard are provided with and trained to deploy a variety of automatic rifles, handguns, and personal protective gear, and senior members of the Guard travel abroad with Pope Francis, serving in similar roles to the U.S. Secret Service under its presidential protective mission.

Switzerland's long history and tradition of providing mercenary service to various continental powers wound down in the nineteenth century, first after the famous Swiss neutrality was formalized in the nation's 1848 constitution, and then when said constitution was amended in 1874 to specifically ban the recruitment of Swiss citizens by foreign governments. The sole exception to those rules were and remain the Pontifical Swiss Guard, the last relic of Switzerland's once formidable power as an exporter of elite soldiers. This change in no way undercut the Swiss commitment to military service, training, and success—it just internalized those features. Per World Population Review's 2024 military rankings, Switzerland's armed forces currently include about 20,000 active military personnel and about 196,000 reserve personnel, for a total of roughly 216,000 total service members, ranking forty-seventh in the world's hierarchy of force levels, and twentieth in the standings of total military personnel as a percentage of total population. The primary focus of the modern Swiss military is on defensive needs, with no engagement on behalf of foreign powers or other offensive forays, though Switzerland does support and participate in various peacekeeping missions abroad.

Switzerland maintains its force levels through a mandatory conscription program for all physically qualified males above the age of nineteen, though men and women alike can volunteer for military service at eighteen years of age. About one in five conscripts are deemed unfit for service; they are still required to support the nation's defense by paying an additional annual income tax until their thirty-seventh birthdays. Recruit basic training runs about eighteen weeks, with additional time required for those training for specific special forces. In keeping with the Swiss approach to maintaining a ready guard, service members are required to maintain their personal military equipment (including weapons) at their homes or in nearby community armories, facilitating rapid response to any emergent defensive requirements. Military members remain available for call-up and service until the age of forty-nine.

Switzerland's military indoctrination program provides the first crucible for would-be Swiss Guards, all of whom are required to have completed basic training with the Swiss Armed Forces. Applicants for the "Pope's Army" must also be Swiss citizens, between the ages of nineteen and thirty, at least five feet eight inches tall, unmarried, practicing Catholics, and male. (A current project to build a new barracks for the Swiss Guard at the Vatican will upgrade the facility to move from communal living quarters to single apartments, ostensibly to open Guard service to women, subject to the pope's approval; the project is scheduled to be complete in 2026, and various Vatican and Guard spokespersons have indicated a willingness to remove the gender barrier for Guard service at some unspecified point in the future.) Would-be guardsmen must receive affirmation from their parish priests as to their faithful participation in the life of the Catholic Church, have a certificate of good conduct from the Swiss military, and possess a high school diploma or comparable professional certification or degree.

Candidate applications are painstakingly reviewed by the command staff of the Guard, with finalists being brought to the

Vatican for interviews with the commander of the Pontifical Swiss Guard. Two hundred to three hundred applicants apply in most years for thirty to forty billets opened through attrition, completion of contracted terms, or retirements. In a 2017 interview with the *Catholic News Agency*, current commander (since 2015) Christoph Graf stressed the importance of the spiritual component of the Swiss Guard's mission in the review and screening process. "If someone in the interview only talks about security and does not know who they are giving security for, for me he is not a candidate," Graf noted to reporters before the 2017 Swiss Guard swearing-in ceremony. "For me, a candidate must have a foundation in the faith, be a practicing Catholic, who goes to Mass and prays. If a young man knows nothing of the faith, I do not know what he is looking for here." Commander Graf also explained that members of the Guard must fill a missionary purpose and must commit to protecting the pope "with weapons, but also with faith, with prayer."

Applicants accepted for service into the Swiss Guard must commit to at least a two-year active term before enrolling in a two-month-long training program. The first month of Guard training takes place in Switzerland, where the candidates are taught principles of self-defense, firearms use, first aid, firefighting, law of armed conflict, and psychological profiling by members of their home cantons' police forces. The second month of training takes place in the Vatican, where candidates are indoctrinated into the detailed lay-of-the-land of the microstate and the people within it, while also learning formal formation drills, use of the traditional halberd, and the rites, rules, and expectations associated with being vigilant, protective, public-facing representatives of the Holy See. Candidates may also receive language training if they are not fluent in the various tongues widely used within the Vatican's confines. The guardsmen's uniforms are then individually tailor-fit to the incoming unit members; when their service time ends, all of their own bespoke uniforms are destroyed.

The May 6 swearing-in ceremony for Swiss Guard members, remembering and honoring those who defended Pope Clement VII during the Sack of Rome, is preceded by a Mass and a group meeting with the pontiff. (Pope Francis reportedly maintains relaxed, first-name relationships with many members of his Guard, and is notoriously reluctant to accept all their requests regarding his personal safety, eschewing armored vehicles for a modest Fiat 500, riding with windows down, and often breaking from script, spontaneously leaving his planned and screened routes to engage with his followers.) The oath of service is delivered and received in the apostolic palace's Cortile (Courtyard) di San Damaso and is typically attended by representatives of the Swiss government, military, and church leadership.

During the swearing-in ceremony, the new guards are called forward individually to approach the unit's flag-bearer, grasping the unit's standard with their left hands and raising their right hands with three fingers open, symbolizing the Holy Trinity. They take their sacred oath in the native language of their home cantons (which may be German, Italian, French, or Romansh). The English translation of the current oath reads: "I swear I will faithfully, loyally, and honorably serve the Supreme Pontiff Francis and his legitimate successors, and also dedicate myself to them with all my strength, sacrificing, if necessary, also my life to defend them. I assume this same commitment with regard to the Sacred College of Cardinals whenever the See is vacant. Furthermore, I promise to the Commanding Captain and my other superiors respect, fidelity, and obedience. This I swear! May God and our Holy Patrons assist me!" Following the oath-taking ceremony, new guardsmen, with their parents, each receive a private audience with the pope, where they are offered His Holiness's personal blessings.

The guardsmen only earn about $18,500 per year (tax free) for their service, though they receive free room and board, and children of Guard members receive free private education. A staff of five Albertine nuns from Poland prepare meals for the Guard in the unit's canteen, with popular Swiss and Italian dishes regularly on their menu. The unit's members typically work for six straight days at a time, followed by three days of rest and relaxation, with thirty days of annual vacation available to allow them to travel home to Switzerland or elsewhere. Life within their tiny enclave is surprisingly rich, in quaint ways, with some guardsmen joining the Swiss Guard Band, and others playing for FC Guardia in the eight-team Vatican City Championship, the top-tier football (that is, for Americans, soccer) association within Vatican City; their guards' team was founded in 1924, but they have never won a league championship, alas.

While their pay is modest, their duties often dull and monotonous (which is the desired status, as any moments of extreme terror or sudden action would be indicative of something having gone catastrophically wrong, in dangerous ways), and their current visibility to the world at large often restricted to tourists giggling at their gala uniforms in social media posts, interviews with contemporary and former members of the Swiss Guard often find their subjects reflecting with extreme pleasure and pride about their service, roles, and responsibilities. While the denizens of larger nations, or the members of larger armies, may scoff at the quaint and anachronistic historicity of the Swiss Guard, its members understand and embrace their work as a true vocation: protecting the person of the singular leader of global Catholicism, with the church currently counting nearly 1.4 billion members around the world. They see their calling as a noble one, and they gladly live their lives in accordance with their unit's historical motto: *Acriter et Fideliter.*

"Fiercely and Faithfully," indeed.

CHAPTER 12

Doctor, Doctor: The White Coat Ceremony and Beyond

"This is the way physicians mend or end us, / Secundum artem: but although we sneer / In health, when ill, we call them to attend us, / Without the least propensity to jeer."
—George Gordon, Lord Byron

"In the name of Hippocrates, doctors have invented the most exquisite form of torture ever known to man: survival."
—Luis Buñuel

THE SURVIVAL INSTINCT IS ONE of the most deeply rooted elements in human cognition and behavior, standing as the baseline foundation for self-preservation, atop which virtually all other higher order processes, actions, and thoughts reside. Acts of self-harm are categorized as aberrant symptoms of mental illness accordingly, and reckless daredevils who take needless life-threatening risks are often viewed with disdain or derision by those more appropriately attuned to their own innate survival instincts. Of course, there are also diagnosable mental conditions and atypical social behaviors at the opposite end of that spectrum, where the instinctual individual fight-or-flight responses to dangerous stimuli are activated in situations that are not objectively threatening, making benign situations seem far more menacing than they may actually be, often paralyzing or isolating those experiencing such disordered acute stress responses on a regular and routine basis. As social animals with an equally strong built-in urge to propagate the species and pass on our genetic material, we are often able to expand the reach of our own survival instincts and fight-or-flight responses to include our offspring and families, and may automatically and reflexively place ourselves in harm's way to protect those who carry our genes or who, through ties of matrimony, adoption, or other partnerships, may be integrally and intimately connected into our own senses of self.

The related drives for self-preservation and perpetuation of the species are ancient evolutionary responses that, through the "survival of the fittest" gristmill over countless millennia, have ostensibly prepared us to thrive both individually and communally as human beings. But evolution is an exceptionally slow process, and the world in which we reside is becoming ever-more complex with even greater rapidity, leading to an emergent cohort of situations where our brains' abilities to accurately assess and process stimuli are not necessarily in correct alignment with the factual realities within which we find ourselves. Nobel Prize–winning psychologist Daniel Kahneman studied and wrote at length about what he dubbed "cognitive biases," which may cause us to process stimuli, remember information, solve problems, and make decisions in ways that are not necessarily the most accurate nor conducive to producing the best long-term outcomes, but which, by virtue of being efficient in terms of response time and energy consumption, are "good enough" to enhance the likelihood of individual and societal survival.

Among many other ramifications, both positive and negative in impact, Kahneman's cognitive biases contribute to the ways in which modern human beings are extremely ineffective at accurately assessing risk. We find tornadoes, sharks, lightning, plane travel, and obscure diseases highly anxiety-inducing, even though routine rainstorms, mosquitoes, automobile travel, influenza, and heat waves are objectively more lethal on a per capita statistical basis than the higher-profile modes of mortality cited in the first list. Our ancient forebears could readily see the threat posed by, say, a large predatory animal, and could choose to vanquish the threat by fighting (perhaps earning sustenance in the process) or to distance themselves from the threat by fleeing. But we cannot see coronaviruses, sense tectonic plates preparing to shift, anticipate turbulent air, or smell carbon monoxide, so our innate rapid response systems to those potentially legitimate threats are out of alignment with the dangers they realistically pose. Conversely, our brains are routinely bombarded with shocking global content from our myriad of modern electronic communications platforms and devices, and those who create, curate, and disseminate said content want to further their own purposes, be they profit or provocation, and so are often incentivized to show us the things to which we respond most viscerally, leading us to believe that rare, isolated, uncommon, or unusual events are constant and imminent threats to our well-being.

Given the collaborative ways in which human beings organize themselves into cultures and communities, our cognitive biases and the related functional flaws in risk assessment skills do carry one regular and beneficial side effect, namely that we routinely, unthinkingly place our own individual survival in the hands of others, mostly unknown to us on any personal basis. We pack ourselves like sardines in airplanes' economy-class seats, our survival wholly dependent upon the skill and professionalism of the pilots seated before us, unseen, and only occasionally heard. We drive our cars on an almost autonomous basis, muscle memory and habit guiding us along busy roadways from point A to point B, our survival entirely dependent on the social contracts and customs that keep cars moving from point B to point A predictably on the other side of the dividing line, though nothing is physically stopping every such passing car from turning into a head-on collision. Every time we cross a bridge, or ascend a tall building in an elevator, we are trusting the skill and accuracy of the architects, engineers, and construction crews who brought those infrastructure edifices into being. We bring highly flammable chemicals into our homes and burn them in ways that can produce lethal gaseous byproducts, trusting wholly in the work done by installation contractors as we go about our everyday business in the most personal of spaces. If we began to actively, collectively consider that our well-being and survival at any point in time hinges entirely on the compliant behavior of countless unseen agents before and around us on a routine and regular basis, and not on anything that we can do or control, then we would likely quickly and wholly find ourselves unable to function in any modern society, civilization, or setting.

Perhaps the most literal example of the ways in which we willingly place our lives in the hands of others can be found in our relationships with medical professionals, in both routine and emergency care situations. We allow them to touch and see us in ways otherwise restricted to our most intimate relations, for starters. We also acquiesce to treatments, medications, and procedures that would have sent our ancient ancestors fleeing in terror, trusting that short-term discomfort or inconvenience may allow us to live better, healthier lives in the long-term. We allow them to scrape, poke, pierce, and cut our bodies to collect samples that are processed in distant laboratories, and then we adjust behaviors or agree to procedures or medications based on the results of those laboratory analyses. And in the most extreme cases, we allow our doctors and their professional associates to put us in states of suspended animation, as close to death as any of us will ever actually find ourselves before our final curtains fall, and then we allow them to open us up, laying hands (in gloves) on the very physical essences of ourselves—our beating hearts, our worrying brains, our yards of guts and viscera.

Key to this willingness to cede individual autonomy to healthcare professionals is our collective understanding of the formidable crucibles through which contemporary healthcare providers must pass. For physicians in the United States, the combined academic and experiential time required to achieve full board certification in a chosen field of medicine can approach two decades from beginning to end. While social media alarmists can always find outlier examples of malefic or incompetent behaviors, the vast majority of practicing medical professionals are extensively trained, highly ethical, and deeply qualified as caregivers, healers, diagnosticians, or researchers. Or sometimes any and all of the above, at the same time. But, interestingly, once again, our cognitive biases about our relationships with our doctors can result in twisted outcomes: very few of us will ever fly our own airplanes, or install our own natural gas pipes, or build our own bridges and skyscrapers, trusting in the expertise of those who do such things for us, but we are almost all more than willing to consult Doctor Google or Nurse Wiki to evaluate our health situations and solutions, and then to argue their findings with our own known and real-world healthcare professionals.

"That is absolutely a significant factor for medical professionals today," said Dr. Todd L. Wagner, DO, in an interview with us. "I have seen the evolution of it because I came into the medical field around the time when the internet was first catching on. It can certainly be a little frustrating at times, as it can require you to spend much more time discussing things with the patients, which is tough when it seems like we always have less and less time available to talk to patients. It's not bad to have patients be somewhat educated about their own situations and care, but they obviously need to understand the sources of the information they're bringing to their doctors. There's some really good stuff out there, for sure. But then there's lots of not-so-good stuff too. I understand that people are going to have that spectrum of information available to them, and I do think we as a profession have to evolve to address that. I've read articles positing that information in the medical community turns over about every two years now. That's how fast the pace of information is, and personally, I think that's a good thing because it keeps us on our toes. I do admit it can be a bit of a struggle when you're trying to treat people who have a lot of inaccurate information in front of them. But that's the nature of the beast today, so we must get smarter as a community in how we deal with it."

Dr. Wagner was a classmate of ours at the United States Naval Academy in Annapolis, so in addition to enduring the crucibles associated with earning board certification as a United States medical professional, he also endured the Plebe Year crucibles discussed in the prologue and epilogue to this book. He began his Navy career as a surface warfare officer before being accepted into Michigan State University's medical school while still on active duty. Upon the completion of his training, he joined the Navy's Medical Corps and served there until retiring as a captain in 2019; his active-duty time included two wartime deployments to Iraq as the preventive medicine officer for the multinational forces engaged there. As formidable as his professional training was, he was spared one common thorn in the side of aspiring physicians in not having to go deep into debt to finance his medical school years, as the Navy covered those costs in exchange for his subsequent service in the Medical Corps.

"I did what they called the Health Professions Scholarship Program so that really tipped the return on investment [ROI] for me, since the Navy picked up the tab," Dr. Wagner explained. "But still, you don't make a lot of real money for quite a few years, frankly, in medicine, until you get past your residency and such, so for most folks, that ROI doesn't fully kick in for a while. There are a lot of people who go into a lot of debt, so I always say to people who are looking to go into medicine, never, ever do it just for money. I mean, the money is obviously good, but frankly we have a lot of, say, investment bankers who make a heck of a lot more money than physicians do. And we work a lot of long hours, so the effective hourly rate is not that great sometimes as a physician. But frankly, I think it must be more about the service and what you do for other people if you are going to be successful in medicine, and not about the money. You may *get* money in your early years as a doctor, but you are not going to be *making* money, given what it costs you to get there."

There are obviously sizable monetary costs associated with becoming a doctor in the United States, but those can typically be financed, kicking the actual paying-the-bills burden from today to tomorrow, while the actual time costs associated with the training pipeline are among the most formidable of any profession, ever: years and years' worth of "right here, right now, today," chockablock with strenuous academic and practical training requirements. The process begins with a standard four-year collegiate degree, ideally with a variety of prerequisite courses completed, as required by most medical schools as part of their own academic programs. As with most elite postgraduate academic programs, medical schools are looking for more than just test scores, so that meaningful extracurricular or relevant volunteer activities are close to mandatory as well.

After achieving a bachelor's degree, prospective doctors must take, and ace, the Medical College Admission Test (MCAT). For the 2024 MCAT testing year, the total estimated "seated time" for the test was about seven hours and thirty minutes, with 230 questions covering chemical and physical foundations of biological systems; biological and biochemical foundations of living systems; psychological, social, and biological foundations of behavior; and critical analysis and reasoning skills. Upon successfully completing the MCAT with solid scores, prospective doctors are encouraged to apply to multiple medical schools, ideally seeking those with specialties aligning most closely with students' desired career goals, and with median MCAT scores matching those achieved by the students. Applicants must also decide whether they want to focus on research-oriented academic institutions or on medical schools that focus on primary care aspects of the healing professions, as well as decide which type of medical degrees they want: medical doctor (MD) or doctor of osteopathic medicine (DO).

The vetting process for admissions is extremely competitive, with the interview components playing a key role in schools' decisions on best-fit students for each year's academic cohort. The rigorous up-front aspects of the admissions process may be judged effective by the relatively high rates of matriculation from medical schools: the Association of American Medical Colleges (AAMC) reports that 81–84 percent of admitted students over the past two decades have completed their studies in four years, with the number rising to 96 percent who graduate after six years in medical school. More students who drop out of the medical school programs do so for nonacademic reasons than for an inability to complete the requisite course work, though again, this is largely a function of higher dropout and drop-off rates earlier in the process.

"Much of attrition comes at the beginning of the premed cycle," Dr. Wagner confirmed. "Although there are typically a fairly large number of premed students in a variety of majors at most universities, many quickly realize that the path, even in the premedical school portion, is long and somewhat arduous. Though not specifically constrained by a particular major, the vast majority of all medical schools require [prerequisite courses such as] biology, inorganic chemistry, organic chemistry, physics, and others. This course load requires the premed student to start these classes very early in their college career, and as they progress, many realize that they don't want it badly enough to complete these courses. Additionally, the rigor of preparing for the MCAT and also fulfilling the other requirements of medical schools to work in the medical field in patient care, volunteering, or research activities also dissuade many from pursuing, as they realize these requirements will need largely to be completed by the time they apply for medical school."

Following their acceptance and enrollment into a four-year medical school, students must prepare to take the first two of three portions of either the allopathic or osteopathic national medical licensing exams. The former, for MD candidates, is known as the United States Medical Licensing Examination (USMLE); the latter, for DO candidates, is the Comprehensive Osteopathic Medical Licensing Examination of the United States (COMLEX-USA). DO students may also elect to take the USMLE.

When he reached that step in his training process, Dr. Wagner chose the osteopathic path. "It was interesting to have gotten my DO at Michigan State, where we had both a DO and MD school, and all of us literally went the first two years together, and then we sort of branched off," he recalled. "The thinking of the DO community is generally in a broad-brush view to take a more holistic view of the body, recognizing that everything works in unison. It isn't that MDs don't believe that, but the DO community has more focus on that approach, and part of our armamentaria is to utilize osteopathic manipulative techniques to align the spine, manipulate the spine, manipulate other bones in the body, to be able to kind of make the body function as a whole. We also take a more holistic view of combining things like diet and exercise as part of our overall approach to good health. And again, it's not that MDs don't believe in that either, but it's just that the osteopathic community has always been anchored in that particularly holistic view of healthcare."

After passing the first two sections of the USMLE or COMLEX-USA, medical students apply for their residencies, typically through the National Resident Matching Program. Students who successfully complete their studies and graduate with medical degrees are technically and officially doctors at that point, though the medical residency is typically required to practice independently in the doctor's chosen healthcare community. Medical residencies take place at hospitals or academic centers, are intended to provide hands-on experience and technical training, and can range from three to seven years in length, depending on the areas of specialization. New doctors typically take the final portions of the USMLE or COMLEX-USA in the early days of their residencies. Upon successfully completing the exams, they are eligible for their general medical licenses, which allow them to practice without direct supervision by other doctors.

As highly competitive as medical school applications are, the residency phase of the process can move into the realm of the actively savage, as extremely qualified candidates vie for a relatively small number of matches and placements. "It's not the medical schools that are the issue right now in terms of feeding the medical pipeline, it's residency training programs, because there aren't enough of them," explained Dr. Wagner. "So, we have got a lot of people who get through medical school, but then cannot find a match for a residency. The reason for that is primarily that residency programs don't pay, from the hospitals' perspective. Like it or not, training is considered an overhead expense and a lot of them don't want to be involved with that or to take on that expense. So, there are some gaps there in those training slots. Personally, I would say that the first year of work-ing as a resident was probably the most difficult because new residents are expected to know a lot more than they really do because they are just starting out. You are just churning hours in that first year, doing a lot of what they call step work; you are the gofer on the floor, gathering information, rounding on patients, and the upper-level residents often just kind of lean on you. You are the frontline caregiver in many cases, and it is very intimi-dating at times because you just do not have a lot of additional knowledge or experience, so you're just working your tail off to stay afloat, all the time. That was the most difficult portion of the process for me, I would say."

Completing the medical residency is the final step toward achieving one of the twenty-four American Board of Medical Specialties (ABMS) certifications for demonstrated knowledge in a particular medical specialty, though there are some special-ties that can require up to an additional three years in a medical fellowship at a hospital or academic center specializing in that particular field of expertise. Board certification is, essentially, the completion point of the long and arduous crucible associated with becoming a licensed, independently practicing MD or DO in the United States, though it's less fraught with ceremonial or community-building rites and rituals than might be expected, in part because doctors have already been practicing as residents for years before they are certified, in part because the cohorts they started their crucible with in medical school have largely scattered to the winds, and in part because the ABMS is a centralized credentialing agency without the ability or interest to individually fete its recipients across the country. It is a monumental professional transition for each doctor receiving their board certification, obviously, but not one typically cloaked in any shared, formal, institutional rituals or ceremonies.

Which is not to say that such institutional rituals or ceremonies do not exist for doctors-in-the-making, it is just that the medical community typically experiences them in a somewhat atypical timeframe when compared to most other crucible-linked ceremonial transitions. The most common current formal ritual among medical professionals in training in the United States is the White Coat Ceremony, a tradition that has also expanded to a variety of global medical schools in recent years. Prior to the twentieth century, physicians and nurses (who were often Catholic nuns) typically wore black garb, but the emergence of modern preventive medicine and antiseptic surgery (Joseph Lister standing as a pioneering advocate for both) led doctors to adopt the white laboratory coat as their emblematic garb, communicating both cleanliness and their connection to scientific inquiry and process, in lieu of the quackery and mysticism that had often shaped and defined their profession through the preceding centuries.

While the symbolism of the doctor's white coat dates to the late nineteenth and early twentieth centuries, the actual ceremonial donning of same is of a much more recent vintage, with Dr. Arnold P. Gold generally given credit for introducing the tradition at Columbia University College of Physicians and Surgeons in 1993. Most contemporary White Coat Ceremonies occur early in the medical school process, typically after a first examination break. Students are presented with, and don for the first time, short white laboratory coats, often while taking the Hippocratic Oath, the ancient guide for medical conduct, as part of the ceremony. Prior to the 1990s, most medical schools did not have the students take the Hippocratic or Osteopathic Oath until they had completed their studies and received their degrees. White Coat Ceremonies are intended to be public affirmations of the long path upon which students are embarking, and families, friends, and other loved ones are invited and encouraged to attend.

"I loved my White Coat Ceremony, I really enjoyed it," remembered Dr. Wagner. "They vary a bit from school to school, still. Some do it at the very beginning, when you start medical school (that's when we did it at Michigan State), other ones do it when you're starting clinical training, in the second and third year, when you're moving from the didactic to the clinical world. The school typically provides you with the short white coat, and, depending on how fancy they want to be, sometimes they will embroider your name and stuff on there. Some just give you a plain old white lab coat and let you figure it all out. You can have your family or friends put the coat on you for the first time, so there are good photo ops and memories associated with that. When the ceremonies were first conceived, it was almost exclusively the physicians who wore white coats in hospitals. You had the medical students in short white coats; you had residents in medium-length coats; and then you had the attending staff physicians in long coats, and those were pretty much the only people that wore those in the hospital. But that has totally changed over the course of my career, sort of analogous to the ways that the internet has changed our practice. Now you can have everybody from a phlebotomist, who has maybe a few months of training,

all the way up to a neurosurgeon, who has about seventeen years
of training, all wearing a white coat. Other communities like
pharmacists and physical therapists are adopting the tradition
too, so things are evolving with the times, and I know that some
of the older stalwarts are not very happy about that."

Grumpy stalwarts notwithstanding, White Coat Ceremonies
and traditions are indeed changing across the healthcare universe, with many hospitals directing that such symbols no longer be worn outside of laboratory or research settings, either
because of the public displays of perhaps distasteful hierar-
chical structures they present, or because patients find them
off-putting and frightening, or because the coats themselves
are increasingly seen as vectors for the transmission of infec-
tion between patients. It may be that, sooner rather than later,
doctors' white coats will go the way of naval officers' swords, or
academics' professorial robes—items presented as part of ceremonial traditions that immediately go into the proverbial coat
closet, being removed only for subsequent ceremonial purposes,
and not for anything having to do with the actual day-to-day
work being done by the professionals possessing them.

For many of the rites of passage discussed in this book, the
ceremonial aspects of the crucibles are inextricably linked to the
actual performative aspects of the test(s) required to enter an elite
society. For our doctors and other medical professionals, that is
not particularly the case, as the academic, residency, and fellowship requirements of earning board certification remain pro-
foundly competitive and difficult, regardless of when and whether
those passing through the professional medical crucible receive
some form of ceremonial garb to mark some defined transition
point. Our doctors will not be less skilled or committed without
their white coats or the ceremonial presentation of them.

That said, rituals do remain important community-building components of crucibles, and the physical ability to wear
a white coat is one of the tangible, visible things that separates

our trained medical professionals from the incorporeal Doctor
Google and Nurse Wiki, and that may be enough in and of itself
to keep the tradition alive.

CHAPTER 13

The Poor Widow's Sons: American Freemasonry

"To enlarge the sphere of social happiness is worthy of the benevolent design of a Masonic institution; and it is most fervently to be wished, that the conduct of every member of the fraternity, as well as those publications, that discover the principles which actuate them, may tend to convince mankind that the grand object of Masonry is to promote the happiness of the human race."
—George Washington

"Secrecy has been well termed the soul of all great designs. Perhaps more has been effected by concealing our own intentions, than by discovering those of our enemy."
—Charles Caleb Colton

IN THIS BOOK'S EARLIER CHAPTER concerning the Knights Templar, we obliquely alluded to elite and esoteric societies that have been perceived historically and in contemporary narratives to wield undue economic and political power through connections and controls largely hidden from public view. The Knights Templar and the Illuminati were historically grounded organizations whose mythologies and legends have morphed over the centuries, with various ahistorical modern bodies claiming or perceived to be knowledge-carrying descendants of their mystical forebears. The noxious *Protocols of the Elders of Zion*, first published in Russia in 1903, has become the textbook tome of modern antisemitism, positing an alleged plot for global domination by a secret cabal of Jewish religious and business figures. In the contemporary United States, the myth of the

"Deep State" fills a similar niche, with nefarious unelected figures allegedly pulling the strings from the hidden halls of power in Washington, DC, working to shape policy and to keep the nation's "sheeple" in thrall, in pursuit of widely varying and conspiracy-laden goals and objectives, depending on who is doing the telling. Extreme versions of the Deep State myth go so far as to incorporate such elements as chemtrails, Flat Earth theory, Reptilian control of humanity, and a grand conspiracy to hide the fact that the U.S. government is in possession of alien technology and life-forms. The very real Trilateral Commission, a cooperative international nongovernmental development organization founded in 1973, has also taken on a contemporary sheen of conspiracy chic, for its alleged behind-the-scenes efforts to create a single world government, at the expenses of and on the backs of its global citizenry.

High in the pantheon of organizations perceived as bearing such secretive and undue power, throughout centuries of both American and European history, are the grouping of myriad loosely connected fraternal organizations known collectively as the Freemasons. First emerging in the late fourteenth century (not coincidentally within living memory of the demise of the Knights Templar), the earliest Masonic organizations were, in fact, guilds of actual working stonemasons, with their lodges sharing certain commonalities with modern labor unions, guiding the ways in which skilled "labor" (the masons) interacted with "management" (typically governmental bodies or churches possessing the political and economic wherewithal to commission stone construction). The initial, literal bodies of masons then came to accept nonworking lay members from other professions, and eventually such "speculative" nonworking masons established their own lodges, embracing useful fraternal facets curried from earlier incarnations, without requiring any actual personal or professional experience with the real work of masonry.

In 1717, the Grand Lodge in London was established, an organization from which most modern Masonic organizations can trace their philosophical heritage, if not their actual organizational roots. British Freemasons then carried their fraternal interests abroad to their various global colonial holdings, with the Provincial Grand Lodge of Pennsylvania, New Jersey, and New York emerging in 1730 as the first major Masonic organization in the American colonies, and various regionally based Provincial Grand Lodges established in the following decades. Following the American Revolution, the Anglocentric Provincial Grand Lodges were dissolved, with a variety of regional independent Grand Lodges emerging to take their places. While historical details are scant and inconsistent, as many as one-third of the signatories to the Declaration of Independence have been considered to have been members of Masonic lodges, and the Constitution and its Bill of Rights have been said to bear the heavy stamp of the Masons' "civil religion," which sought a society anchored in individual self-governance, empowered by limited state authorities, economic free enterprise, and the passionate embrace of personal liberties and freedoms.

The earliest organized working stonemasons considered their knowledge of the artistic, design, and technical constraints and opportunities presented in stone construction work to be their most precious collective asset, with secrecy surrounding those skills being a foundational and paramount concern, thereby precluding unskilled tradespeople from being able to poach their expertise to the detriment of their collective reputations and earning capabilities. The early guilds developed and embraced a variety of symbols and practices designed to allow members to quickly recognize their brethren and their works, and to preclude unskilled or untrained craftsmen from participating in their projects. As Freemasonry evolved into a fraternal body populated by speculative rather than literal stonemasons, many of those secret symbols endured as defining organizational marks, allowing members to communicate their presence and actions quickly, to some extent unencumbered by linguistic barriers within a growing global body of lodges.

The strong Masonic presence among the nation's founders purportedly led to the incorporation of such arcane symbols as the Square and Compasses, the letter G (possibly for "Geometry," possibly for "God,"), and the Eye of Providence atop its pyramid in the United States' early iconography, though the causation versus correlation aspects of using such symbols may not, in fact, be as linear as it seems after the fact, as other organizations and artists used similar symbols at the time, most especially the Eye of Providence. That said, perception often trumps reality, and the belief that the nation's early symbols are heavily culled from Freemasonry, and indicative of possibly undue Masonic influence, is widely held and persistent.

Of more testable historical accuracy is the Anti-Masonic movement in the United States of the early nineteenth century, emerging just as the nation's founders were largely shuffling out of political power and beyond this mortal coil. The inciting event of what eventually became the single-issue Anti-Masonic (political) Party was the disappearance of William Morgan in western New York. Born in Virginia, Morgan emigrated with his family around 1820 to Canada, where he claimed to have become a highly ranked Master Mason. Following the destruction of his brewery in a fire, Morgan relocated to Rochester and then Batavia, New York, where he attempted (in vain) to join various local lodges, before eventually working to establish new ones that would have him. His efforts were rebuffed due to claims of bad character, evidenced by his alleged habitual drunkenness and gambling. Incensed by these rejections, Morgan crafted a tome called *Illustrations of Masonry*, which threatened to reveal the Masons' secrets and practices in full and strident detail.

In September 1826, Morgan was arrested and jailed for theft and default on his debts. After being bailed out by newspaper publisher David Cade Miller (who was a financial backer and stood to profit from the publication of *Illustrations of Masonry*), Morgan was again arrested for allegedly failing to pay a tavern bill. Morgan was released from jail under mysterious circumstances during the jailer's absence, left for Fort Niagara, New York, with his wife, and promptly disappeared. In October 1827, a body washed ashore on Lake Ontario, and it was identified and buried as Morgan, despite disputed claims of its identity by the heirs of other missing persons. The subsequent conviction of several individuals (all of them Freemasons) for Morgan's kidnapping, conspiracy, and murder, coupled with Miller's publication of *Illustrations of Masonry*, which became a bestselling book, fueled a strong Anti-Masonic sentiment that galvanized New York's Thurlow Weed into organizing the Anti-Masonic Party, both in opposition to Freemasonry and to the presidency of Andrew Jackson (himself a Mason).

While Masonic opposition formed the crux of the new party's organizational initiative, it quickly expanded to embrace a more generic anti-elitist sentiment (built on the sense that Freemasons were using their supposedly formidable powers and connections to maintain their positions within the young nation's elite), in some ways mirroring the rhetoric of the modern Tea Party and Freedom Caucus on the right, and the Occupy and 99% platforms on the left. The Anti-Masonic Party fielded William Wirt as its presidential candidate in 1832, and though he managed to secure Vermont's electoral votes, he finished a distant fourth behind the reelected Andrew Jackson, Henry Clay of the National Republican Party, and John Lloyd of the Nullifiers, a South Carolina–based party formed by Andrew Jackson's first vice president, John C. Calhoun, that espoused slavery, states' rights, and small government. As outrage associated with William Morgan's disappearance and presumed murder abated over time, the formative impetus of the Anti-Masonic Party dwindled, and its members were largely absorbed into the nascent Whig Party by the late 1830s. While their active influence proved to be short-lived, the Anti-Masonic Party did fundamentally alter the nation's political processes by holding the first presidential nominating convention, a practice quickly adopted by other, more successful political parties.

Membership in Masonic orders plummeted during the period of Anti-Masonic fervor, though it began to steadily rise again in the mid-nineteenth century, peaking at over four million members in the late 1950s and early 1960s, followed by an equally steady decline through present time; the Masonic Service Association of North America estimates that there are about 875,000 Freemasons in the United States at the time of this writing. Which, though it may be small by historic levels, does distinguish American Freemasonry from other inaccurate modern understandings of such elite and esoteric societies as the Illuminati, Knights Templar, Deep State, and Trilateral, if for no other reasons than because the Masons are verifiably real, are anchored as the heirs to a documented history, and maintain a national presence with at least 1,500 members in every state, with a highwater mark of over 76,000 currently recognized Freemasons in Pennsylvania.

What are the motivations and experiences of these modern American Freemasons in an era when many such historic, in-person fraternal organizations are experiencing dwindling membership, largely supplanted by the counterintuitive aching loneliness that has often come with global digital connectivity? We turned once again to one of our accomplished Naval Academy classmates to answer this question and to discuss the crucibles associated with attaining membership in contemporary American Masonic lodges. Kendall Linn is a thirty-third degree Mason of the Ionic Lodge, based in Duluth, Minnesota. After earning his nurse practitioner's degree and license, Linn founded Stepping Stones, a group home consortium for vulnerable adults with traumatic brain injuries; he managed that compassionate care organization for over twenty years before recently selling the business.

Given the Masons' reputation for secrecy, we had some trepidation about what we could ask Linn, and what he could answer, but we were delighted to find him a warm and open source of information about the organization that holds a deep and abiding place in his life. "Quite frankly, there really are no secrets anymore," he noted with a laugh. "I was reading Dan Brown's book about the Masons, on sabbatical in Albuquerque while my parents were, uh, exiting this life. I got that book to read, so that makes it about twelve years ago, and I read the first three pages sitting out by the pool and I just started laughing and I told my sister, 'Well, anything they think was a secret before, certainly isn't now.' Because he described most of the rituals in the very beginning pages.

"And he got a lot of it right and so close, though he missed the overall meaning and purpose. First off, there are a lot of very wealthy Masons, yes, but there are also a lot of very poor Masons. And as far as the Masons getting together to meet, to plan to take over the world, and world dominance, you should come to one of our lodge meetings to see how many brothers cannot stay awake during the meeting, so they definitely cannot stay awake for like a huge project like that! But I think, ultimately, it is just because of the Masons' ability to keep secrets, their devotion to one another, and their belief in a higher cause that they get greatly seized upon with movies like *National Treasure*, or with Dan Brown's books. The Masonic lodge gets almost a dark reputation, and all sorts of conspiracy theories mull around because of the secrecy, but what we always say is that we are a society with secrets, not a secret society."

As is most often the case, Linn's introduction to Freemasonry came via an invitation from one of the organization's members. "While you can apply to join a lodge, usually you are asked to join by an existing brother," Linn explained. "I was asked by a dear friend who was a Vietnam vet Marine survivor, a Purple Heart recipient, who I was working closely with through various charities and with the VFW [Veterans of Foreign Wars] here when I first moved to Duluth. We had a very strong bond, and my friend the Marine asked me if I wanted to join because he knew how involved I was with charity work and with my church, St. Paul's Episcopal. I said yes, I would be interested in seeing what they did. At first, I just went down and I would do a lot of the cooking for the meals, and then finally they asked me if I did want to officially join. And I knew enough of the guys, and I loved what I saw, so I accepted.

"At that point, it went to a petition, which involved a term that most people do not realize comes from the Masonic lodge, and that is 'blackball,'" continued Linn. "That term and tradition came from the days before everybody could write. They would cast their vote with black or white marbles because not everybody in the lodge had a command of the language so that they could write down names or read the names on ballots. The names would be called out and a marble would be dropped in a box. And this also traces back in history to when Masons were being persecuted and killed, along with why we came up with so many secret rituals to identify a fellow Mason. If anybody in the lodge got a feeling that somebody was trying to infiltrate the community or was not being honest about their intentions and was going to destroy their lodge, they would blackball them and could do so without explanation or fear. All it takes is for one member of the lodge to say no to a prospective applicant, and that is the end of it forever, you cannot reapply to that lodge. If you move somewhere else or find another lodge, you may reapply to them, but you must be honest and let them know you have been blackballed at another lodge. That is very rare, though."

Once his petition stage was passed without blackballing, Linn was asked to participate in three separate interviews with three different members of the lodge, none of whom he knew.

The goal of this step in the process was to assess the applicant's moral character and to enhance the applicant's understanding of the lodge, what it means, and what it does. If the interview reports are favorable, then the applicant is invited into the lodge to formally begin the process of admission.

"When you first come in, you're an apprentice Mason, and that is the first degree, which is very easy," Linn explained. "You then start your education in the craft, which I know sounds very mystical, but it is mainly the history of Masons, how Masons serve each other, and how Masons serve the world. Then you go up to your second degree, which is intensifying in the history of the Masons and the Masonic secrets. Then you get to something that is called the third degree, and that's when you truly become a Freemason. That's another Masonic phrase that has become part of everyday parlance, by the way, 'being given the third degree.' Or 'meeting on the level,' or 'being square with someone.' Those phrases are all part of the Masonic rite. But anyway, the third degree is really something to see. Or well, I guess I should say, no, it's *not* something to see for most people. The third degree is where you are formally accepted into what is called the Blue Lodge, and it is a very arduous procedure, one that's often ridiculed or parodied by everybody about, you know, whether we're sacrificing goats or whatever."

So, what, then, does the legendary third degree entail, if not the visions evoked by popular culture and rituals crafted from thin air by presumptuous outsiders? "Well, it's mainly just horrific memorization work about the history of the Masons, and you use that memorization to act out the killing of Hiram Abiff," responded Linn. "Hiram Abiff was the first Master Mason, in charge of the building of King Solomon's temple. He would pray to God, had a great relationship with God, and was guided in the building of the temple by the word of God. Three of the lower masons were jealous of his standing with the king and in the community, so one day after work, they trapped him and started beating him to have him give up the secrets of Freemasonry, eventually killing him. The lower masons then fled and escaped to other lands but were found and brought back and tortured to death for the killing of Hiram Abiff, the king's favorite mason. They finally found Hiram's hidden body, retrieved the skeleton, and placed it in a place of honor in King Solomon's temple. And that is the entire basis for the beginning of the Masons. It has to do with keeping secrets, serving God, serving man, and complete loyalty to brothers.

"Going through the third degree was probably one of the most intense experiences of my life just because of the memorization and reliving the murder of Hiram Abiff, and his killers being brought back to justice," Linn continued. "And once you are beyond the third degree, most Masons continue their craft forward. I'm up to the thirty-third degree now, which is the highest you can rise in my lodge. And beyond all those degrees, every brother is expected to fulfill a position; for instance, as the Worshipful Master, who is the one in charge of the lodge for a year. You start in a lower position as a Steward and work your way up through the five positions to be the Worshipful Master. Once your year is over, you are reduced to nothing and you can never climb back up the arc. That keeps it all very democratic."

That concept of a democratic organization touches on another widely held belief about the Masons, namely that they are *nondemocratic*, with a variety of stipulations about who may, or more importantly *may not*, become members within the organization. Linn explained the limitations on membership thusly: "The primary reason that we are seen as exclusive is probably because there are no female Masons in most rites. It's a brotherhood. It's a fraternal organization. It is a gentlemen's club, and I doubt that rule will ever be broken. Women can come to meetings with us, they're our wives, they're our sisters, they can be included in everything except for private lodge meetings. Women who are married to Masons do have something called Eastern Star that is their own form of Masonry that they practice, and it's a part of the lodge, too. It's just not part of the male lodge. And the other thing is that to be a Mason you must believe in a supreme power, another power, or God. My particular lodge is a very big and spiffy one, and we are made up of about, I would say, 70 percent Christian, 20 percent Jewish, and 10 percent other faiths, which includes some mystic faiths, not witchcraft or anything like that, but Druid-type attitudes, a belief in a higher power with that higher power being Mother Earth. But most of it is Judeo-Christian.

"I've been a Mason for over twenty years and it's a very important part of my life; I'm also a very devoted Episcopalian, very active with my church, and they kind of support each other," Linn continued. "So that is another myth, that the Masonic lodge is a replacement for organized religion. They are not mutually exclusive. They are more beneficial to each other. And it is nice to belong to a brotherhood. This is a little bit personal, but I am a very openly gay man. While I have kept in touch with many of our Naval Academy buddies, there is not a full level of acceptance in our military brotherhood, but there is that level of that acceptance within the Masons, for who and what I am. They do not make any differentiation because of those kinds of personal traits. It is a very strong brotherhood, and I could turn to any one of them, or call on brothers in any city at any lodge, and I would have a family there. When I am traveling, I always travel with my Masonic pin on, or my ring. Most Masons do. There actually is a secret handshake that only Masons know, another thing that often gets made fun of. But if a Mason is traveling and runs into any kind of trouble, they can say, 'Will no one help the poor widow's son?' and any Mason is obligated to immediately rush to the aid of that person. 'The widow's son' refers to Hiram Abiff because his mother was a widow. And I have heard that utilized several times, and been involved in aiding someone in a bad situation. So, there is another interesting, beneficial part of the culture and community."

While long-term numerical trends have shown a steady decline in the numbers of active Freemasons in the United States since the 1960s, Linn has been heartened to see a growing number of younger members applying and joining, thereby ensuring the continuance of his own lodge and the Freemasonry as a whole. "The Masonic lodge was dying out there for a while, just all old men," he explained. "But then with everything that started going on in the world in the past twenty years or so, really since September 11, 2001, I guess, there has been a resurgence of youth in the Masonic lodge. Because so many young people were missing something in their lives, a sense of direction beyond work, a sense of brotherhood, a sense of family, or a sense of positive vibes and beliefs. You know, the world was feeling so dark, and people went in and found the light of brotherhood, which sounds very hocus-pocus, I know, but it comes from a loving place. There is a level of benevolence within the community that people outside really are not aware of. I am highly involved in charity work, but what I do outside is nothing compared to what goes on with the Masons, who offer an astounding level of support for the community and for each other. There is just so much Masonry involved in everyday life. And the huge and growing lack of such community experience in the world at large is, I think, driving a great influx of youth into Masonry."

While Freemasonry has unquestionably been a force for good in the life of Kendall Linn and countless other modern American Masons, the fact remains that our popular culture tends to perceive and paint the organization in sinister hues. We closed our conversation with Linn by asking why he thinks this is the case, and how he feels about it. "I think that Masons, and this is just my personal opinion, are perceived in a negative manner now because of our beliefs, not because of our brotherhood," he concluded. "But to be quite fair and honest about that: religion in general, church, faith, and a belief in God, especially a Christian God or Jewish God, have all become very passé in a lot of corridors. We are existing like a Catholic church or an Episcopal church or a Baptist church or a synagogue in a world that does not want to have anything to do with us or anything else religious. I have personally experienced people who would see something that I posted about a Masonic brother online and they would just *attack* me, for no reason, and the fearmongering they would direct toward what they saw as an exclusive Christian group was hard to take. 'How stupid is that?' and 'How evil of you!' and so on. So, I personally think there is a kind of reverse hatred, or a reverse prejudice, against Masons today. But despite that, we still get together to have fun, there's laughter, we do good work, and we support each other. The overall experience has exceeded all my wildest expectations, by far."

While the actual details of the modern rituals associated with achieving membership and seniority within Masonic organizations may not be as physically extreme as other crucibles discussed in this book, the role that those rituals play in creating organizational culture and cohesion are crucial to the sustenance and strength of such organizations on a macro basis. As with the White Coat Ceremonies for doctors and related medical professionals, the rituals are touch points in ongoing processes, representing points of passage, acknowledging work gone by, but also presaging work yet to come. While White Coat Ceremonies are generally public events that allow those outside of the medical training pipeline a peek into the machinery that produces medical professionals, Masonic ceremonies are private events, but anchored in the belief that those who complete them will manifest organizational desires and goals in the public lives they lead outside of their Masonic halls and temples.

Kendall Linn's description of the Masons as "a society with secrets, not a secret society" touches on the ways in which rites and rituals shape the self-defined workings within modern Masonic orders, while eschewing the often-conspiratorial views of those outside of the organization as to their motivations and modes of operation. Given the long-held and deep-seated Anti-Masonic sentiments that have echoed throughout European and North American history, the reflective and private aspects of Masonic practices, even if they are not as nefarious or noxious as outsiders might claim, may stand as the most vital building block of cultural cohesion among diverse individuals who have largely self-selected to serve, often in the face of overt or discreet hostility from those not so inclined. And given that cultural hostility, the most challenging hurdle associated with becoming a high-level Mason must, on some plane, be in making the decision to seek membership, ideally based on sound and informed self-reflection about what the individual aspirant will get out of, and contribute to, the body at large.

While Masons may not have to wrestle tiger sharks or climb barriers built from acacia thorns or give up their worldly, material property, their commitments to their chosen paths are no less meaningful, and the rubrics used by the organization to separate those deserving from those not are no less valid and valuable than those anchored primarily in physical suffering, even if those who endure the latter might have more outrageously entertaining stories to recall in their days of dotage.

CONCLUSION

Elites Everywhere: Crucibles in Context

"Life is the only art that we are required to practice without preparation, and without being allowed the preliminary trials, the failures, and the botches that are essential for training."
—Lewis Mumford

"Extinction is the rule. Survival is the exception."
—Carl Sagan

IN CHOOSING THE RITES OF passage documented in the preceding chapters of this book (including our own Plebe Summer experiences at the Naval Academy), we have purposefully focused on the "extremity" aspect of human crucibles, seeking to find examples that were unique, unusual, exemplary, or over-the-top difficult, while also documenting a variety of historical periods, cultures, and ultimate outcomes. Some of our covered crucibles died with the cultures or ages that spawned them, while others continue apace to this day, and will do so for most reasonably foreseeable futures. Some of our crucibles resulted in noble outcomes at their back ends, ostensibly advancing the well-being of the cultures that spawned them, while others resulted in criminality, violence, destruction, or death. Another element that we sought in our studied crucibles was the concept of purposefulness, where the tests, trials, rituals, and rites were intentionally and formally structured, for specific purposes, with set outcomes desired.

Of course, the formal structures associated with such extreme rites of passage did not generally emerge full-cloth from nothing, and for many organizations and entities, they were just as evolutionary as the skills required to turn accidental metal-melting into purposeful metalworking deep in humanity's ancient history. Early incarnations of human crucibles may have been just as accidental as threads of shiny metal emerging from stones around a hearth, as a small group of people defined some sense of commonality between themselves via their abilities to do, say, or be something that their neighbors could not generally replicate, nor perhaps even had an interest in doing so. Other early incarnations could have been trial-and-error based, as organizations and individuals actively sought to achieve something new and unprecedented, but did not quite know how to get there or what steps would be required to prepare their initiates for their desired service and purpose.

In these modern digital days, many of the rites of passage required by various organizations are primarily shaped by shared service providers who offer standardized services online (e.g., job banks, volunteer boards, professional certification sites, etc.), allowing those who buy their services to select from a preexisting menu of steps that they want their applicants to complete, essentially outsourcing those early steps of the portal process. And at bottom line, all the human crucibles discussed in this text are manifestations of such simple portal processes, just gussied up a bit, with steps to get from A to B, including challenges that limit who may embark upon and complete that journey toward belonging. Such portal processes are extremely widespread when you remove the elements of extremity, or even the elements of purposefulness.

While most people wouldn't evoke "trial by fire" when applying for any type of job, there are portal processes that they must complete nevertheless: identify a desirable job for which one is qualified, write a CV, write a cover letter, submit required paperwork, participate in interviews, have your references checked, receive an offer, negotiate said offer's terms, accept a position, perhaps relocate, start said job, receive training to do the job, eventually becoming an integral part of the employing organization. Similar portal processes, rigorous or otherwise, may apply to joining fraternal organizations, volunteering for charitable organizations, or receiving credentials to fill a wide variety of professional responsibilities, from the most white-collar (e.g., lawyers taking the LSAT, applying for law school, graduating from same, passing the bar exam, being admitted to the bar, joining a law firm as an associate, or taking their legal skills in-house with a corporation or business) to the most craft- and trades-based vocations (e.g., would-be electricians graduating from high school or trade school, accruing thousands of hours of hands-on apprentice experience and hundreds of hours of classroom time, taking business and trade examinations, applying for licensure, joining a union, perhaps hanging a solo shingle, perhaps joining a contracting firm).

Neither of those two representative professional tracks described in the preceding paragraph are the least bit easy, but neither of them would likely or regularly be described as a "crucible" either, in part because their elements take place over long-ish periods of time, in part because they may occur in different places under different supervisory situations, and in part because they feed professional conduits that are absolutely essential to the smooth working of our modern world, but which are not themselves seen as particularly unique and unusual communities due to the large numbers of practitioners in each of those fields, covering an equally large range of quality and skill sets. It is a great and worthy accomplishment to complete either of those portals and to achieve either of those professional certifications, absolutely, and then to successfully make one's way in either of those professional fields, but general members of the public are not necessarily going to have the same sort of "Wow!" reaction to meeting a lawyer or an electrician as they might to meeting an astronaut or a monk or a brain surgeon in twenty-first-century America, just due to the relative rarity of those latter fields in the circles through which most of us move.

While portal processes are widespread and essential, the most notable ones, perhaps meriting the "crucible" appellation, are typically going to be defined not only by the challenges associated with completing them, but also by the rarity of or esteem in which their end communities are held at large. If we accept that portal processes can and should reflect the organizations implementing them, then it is highly likely that "ordinary" organizations will have "ordinary" portal processes, and "extreme" or "elite" organizations will be more likely to have "extreme" or "elite" crucibles. Obviously, what defines "ordinary" versus "extreme" versus "elite" lies to some extent in the eyes of beholders on the outside looking in, but also in the ways that organizations view themselves, some perhaps accurately, some with a level of self-delusion. Crafting an extreme crucible-style intake process for a job that does not confer financial, social, political, or reputational acclaim is a recipe for failure, simply because few applicants will find the destination worth the arduous journey, effectively choking the pipeline shut. Similarly, small, highly specialized organizations which cast their nets too widely, funneling aspiring members into easily accomplished portal processes, will either end up with a huge cohort of disgruntled applicants left without available billets to fill, or with a diluted organization that is increasingly ineffective at doing what it intends to do because it has not acquired an internal cohort capable or motivated enough to preserve whatever elite stature it once held.

Portal processes, be they mild and simple checklists or extreme and complex crucibles, must ultimately reflect the existing and desired characters of the organizations that deploy them. It is important to note, though, that both portal processes and organizations themselves must evolve over time, to meet both their own internal needs, and to respond to external pressures placed on them by their surrounding environments. Ideally, organizations will periodically conduct self-assessments of the pipelines through which their would-be members must pass, and consciously, purposefully adjust, adapt, amend, or abolish elements that do not serve their intended purposes. All too often, though, organizations hew to "we've always done it this way" approaches to their recruiting, vetting, and training practices, falling awry of shifting values and practices adopted by the corporate, political, military, professional, or social worlds around them, eventually being forced to alter their characters and practices suddenly and fundamentally via the imposition of external forces, not necessarily to the benefit of their former statures and continued successes.

On a general, macro basis, then, organizations must deftly balance their onboarding trials and tests with the benefits that those who complete them will receive, and with the benefits that the organization will receive from its newest members. They must also ensure that the trials realistically assess that which needs to be tested to fulfill each organization's mission; undue physical trials for an organization that requires no strenuous physical activity of its members is pointless (and usually illegal under current federal labor law), just as undue, or overly broad, academic testing for roles based primarily on specific physical or technical skills may be equally pointless. While tests and trials may emerge organically over the life of the organization, becoming customary, traditional, or expected ritual acts locally established at the actual site(s) of the crucible(s), often by those tasked with administering them, at some point, organizations must assume positive central control over such processes, documenting them, assuring they are in alignment with organizational needs and societal expectations, and setting criteria to monitor their efficacy, to evaluate those responsible for their success, and to adapt and evolve them when and if necessary.

Failure to secure such centralized implementation and evaluation functions creates compartmentalized environments where abuses (e.g., hazing, racial profiling, abuse, gender bias,

sexual violence, etc.) may grow and flourish, inevitably impact-
ing both the quantity and quality of applicants, and the organization's standing and reputation, should such abuses become
widely known outside of the organization. Which, in an era of
cellphone cameras, anonymous online posting, and heightened
awareness of assaults and affronts on various legally protected
classes, is all but certain to occur, sooner or later. It is also crucial that the control and regulation of such portal processes is
cross-departmental, involving multiple leadership sectors and
functionalities within the organization as part and parcel of
the organization's culture, practice, and reputation, rather than
being dumped into the "human resources" bucket (however that
manifests itself across various entities) as some sort of statutory
or regulatory checklist item.

In our introduction to this book, we noted that we intended
to explore a variety of crucibles over time and space, hoping to
glean perspectives and insights about the commonalities and differences between our test cases, ideally establishing rubrics that
modern organizations may deploy to build their own crucibles,
or to monitor and amend (when necessary) existing portal processes. As we researched and wrote the chapters preceding this
one, we found ourselves evaluating our test cases for each one's
single, simple, core takeaway that captured the essence of the narrative via lessons that other modern organizations may find helpful in establishing, evaluating, and maintaining their own portal
processes. We summarize these takeaways as follows:

Naval Academy Plebe Summer/Year: *Design your crucibles
to potentially open more than one door.* While those of us who
completed the Plebe Year training process (we will return to that
narrative in the epilogue following this chapter) were considered
adequately vetted for the remainder of our time in Annapolis,
and then for our subsequent military service, we also went on to
do many other things, using the skills we developed through our
crucible experiences. We (Eric and Jim) became writers (among

many other things), and while writing this book, we were able to interview other Naval Academy classmates or alumni from other classes who went on to become doctors, astronauts, commanders of military recruit depots, or Freemasons. The training we received at Annapolis was valuable for the purposes the Naval Academy intended, but it opened so many other doors for so many of its graduates, all of which rebound to the benefit and reputation of the Naval Academy itself.

Marine Corps Recruit Depot Parris Island: *Put your best people in charge of the crucible pipeline, and reward them for their efforts.* While recruiting duty is viewed as either an onerous necessity or a career-killing side step among most branches of the American armed services, the U.S. Marine Corps (rightly) considers it to be one of the most important functions in maintaining the stature, reputation, and capabilities of the Corps as an elite fighting force. The Marines celebrate the recruiting role accordingly, and success in the recruiting function is considered both a feather in the cap and an essential professional step in the idealized path of the most successful career Marines. Equally important, stressing the importance of recruiting among existing Marines makes them more passionate about, and better at, bringing in high-quality recruits than are likely to be landed by unwilling, disengaged, bored, or reluctant recruiting offices and staffs.

Shaolin Monks: *Create living history through your crucibles.* While few, if any, contemporary Western organizations can trace their histories back as far as the Shaolin Monastery can, any organization can create a sense of "links in the chain" (as we refer to it in Naval Academy circles) or "the long gray line" (as our West Point counterparts describe the concept) among its new recruits, anchoring them as living, working paragons carrying on the good works done before them, either in recent or ancient history. While teaching new recruits "we've always done it this way" is not generally an effective training gambit, teaching them *why* current practices exist, and anchoring said practices in the lives, accomplishments, and stories of those who came before them is a highly beneficial approach to cultivating *esprit de corps* and making an organization's members feel that they are part of something bigger, deeper, longer, and older than they and their own works will ever be. Such an approach also encourages current members of the organization to take active, productive interest in those who follow them, often keeping them publicly engaged, enthused, and supportive long after their actual work or service time comes to its close.

Astronauts: *Let those who complete your crucibles do what they have been trained to do.* While the front-end processes for recruiting American astronauts are stringent, resulting in only very small numbers of applicants earning their way into the program, the percentage of qualified astronauts who fly space missions after completing the training pipeline is quite high, with the baseline presumption being "everybody flies." While it may take many years for a newly qualified astronaut to receive assignment to their first flight mission, the expectation is in place that it will come, which increases willingness to provide ground and other support for missions preceding theirs, as they know that in time, they will need and benefit from such return support from their colleagues. Forcing candidates through onerous crucibles, then not giving them the opportunities to do the very thing that drew them to the organization in the first place is a recipe for internal dissent, defections, and organizational anomie.

Knights Templar: *Control the spin and messaging about your crucibles.* While the Templars' crucibles were not terrifically onerous compared to some of the other case studies covered in this book, their business and political practices made them highly secretive about their rites and rituals, benign as they might have been. The absence of messaging about the realities of their crucibles allowed their enemies to craft a (false) public narrative about wicked, evil, filthy, and Satanic aspects of their (purported) practices, and that false telling of their own tale directly contributed to the political and religious will required to completely topple the Templar organization. By the time that the Templar leaders were denying the accusations against them (at least until false confessions were tortured out of them), it was too late to set the record straight in the chattering society of the times about what was, or was not, truly required to become a member of the order.

Gurkhas: *Allow your crucibles to uplift your people.* In desperately poor Nepal, joining the Gurkhas is a signature path toward allowing its unit members and their families to escape poverty, while serving a goal generally seen to be admirable among the populace. Many of the young people who strive to join the units are from small, isolated, rural communities and are given the opportunity to experience urban Nepal during the crucible process, and then often to travel and see the world at large during their service times, in ways and places that they never could have attained otherwise. The pride associated with completing a challenging crucible, and ensuring your family's security for years to come as a result, is immense, and it translates into respect, affection, and even love for the organization that provided its members with such opportunities.

Dahomey Amazons: *Be open to innovative solutions for your recruiting difficulties.* The Kingdom of Dahomey's warlike tendencies and aggression toward (and from) most of its neighbors eventually resulted in a shortage of young men able and willing to serve in its armed forces. By allowing, encouraging, and empowering women to serve in its elite military units, Dahomey's leaders significantly expanded the pool of available recruits for its own state purposes (nefarious though they often might have been), rather than unilaterally and thoughtlessly closing the door to a vast cohort of interested and capable aspirants willing to fight on the kingdom's behalf, and to earn and carry the esteem and acclaim that such service brought with it.

Yes, it was a highly unusual approach in its time and in the eyes of the cultures surrounding it, but it was indeed effective, allowing Dahomey to flourish as a regional military power until the dawn of the colonial era in West Africa.

French Foreign Legion: *Let your crucibles create mystique in service of a common good.* The Foreign Legion arose from the French government and its allies abroad, framing threats to its territorial integrity and well-being as idealized, existential perils, not just against one nation and its people, but against the very underpinning concepts of freedom, liberty, and equality, atop which the state was symbolically built. Recruitment activities celebrated these ideals, while also creating the sense that the world's citizenry (or at least the male half of it) had the opportunity to defend these basic principles, often in exotic settings far removed from the cities and rural regions across Europe and the Americas from which the recruits were largely drawn. While on one hand, the French Foreign Legion was just a regular military unit that disregarded the typical citizenry requirements associated with enlistment, on the other hand, it came to possess a level of glamour and accomplishment that made it ever more attractive to young people seeking to make a difference in the greater world around them. While France may have had (and may still have) uncertainty about how the governments of its allies would respond to threats against it, the act of recruiting, training, and deploying its legionnaires made its own singular causes into far-reaching global ones, to the benefit of both its military prowess and its place in the pantheon of democratic powers.

Japan's Special Attack Units: *Do not kill those who complete your crucibles.* This seems obvious, but we mean it both literally and figuratively; when the grueling crucible phase of an in-boarding process is complete, there should be some normalization of expectations and roles that does not involve the utter, absolute, and continuous consumption of the lives of those who have passed through the portal process. We noted in our core text that the ultimate crucible associated with being called a "kamikaze" was that you had to die while destroying enemy military assets, but in a figurative sense, allowing those who complete their in-boarding crucibles to then be morally, mentally, psychologically, or physically ground into dust by the work that follows their accession is counterproductive to needs, except in obviously unavoidable cases of wartime casualties, workplace accidents, unforeseen emergency actions, etc. Japan's Special Attack Units hewed to the ancient *bushido* code of the samurai, which taught them that dying for the empire was both noble and necessary. Today, the concept of "corporate *bushido*" is widespread among Japanese businesses, and while the "salarymen" (a gender-neutral term that includes women) working under its rubrics do not fatally fly their desks into enemy boardrooms, they do often literally work themselves to death on behalf of their corporate overlords, to the ultimate detriment of all involved.

Mafia Made Men: *Craft your crucibles to cultivate organizational loyalty.* While we certainly do not celebrate, nor even condone, the criminal enterprises of the Mafia and other gang- or mob-related organizations, we do note that the concept of organizational loyalty embedded in their crucibles can be a valuable one, in moderation, and with respect to conventional expectations for workplace professionalism and the checks and balances we deploy to balance and align individual ethics within various organizational cultures. While the ways in which the Mafia may define loyalty expectations for its made men are often unethical and illegal, there is a more ethically grounded concept in modern governance theory called the "duty of loyalty," often touted as a cornerstone principle (along with the related "duty of care" and "duty of obedience") in contemporary nonprofit and corporate board orientations. Most simply, the duty of loyalty means that those within the organization place the good of the organization above their own competing personal interests, and shape their professional actions accordingly.

More specifically, the duty of loyalty prohibits organizational members from engaging in any activities that may result in any of the following situations, or the appearances thereof:

- Conflicts of interest, where a member has a personal or professional interest in a proposed transaction;
- Self-dealing, where transactions between the organization and its "disqualified persons," such as a spouse, parent, or child of a board member could directly or indirectly lead to conflicts of interest;
- Misuse of assets, including theft, embezzlement, excessive compensation or rent, and/or personal use of the assets, facilities, or services of the organization; and
- Using a position of trust to personally take advantage of an opportunity presented to the organization.

This does not mean that organizational members must undertake immoral actions when directed to do so (unless they're members in good standing of some criminal enterprise), since loyalty to the organization may, at times, involve standing up and being heard when given illegal orders; taking such stands may ultimately be to the long-term benefit of the organization, even though it might also be to the short-term detriment of the individual fearlessly pursuing the duty of loyalty. Training on the concepts of loyalty, obedience, and care during the crucible process will advance the interests of the organization at large, with lasting long-term benefit. While the purposes for which the Mafia demands such ethical loyalty are ignoble, the ability to inculcate new organizational members into the rationale for prioritizing organizational cohesion and success in noble fashions are a reasonable extrapolation from otherwise problematic cultural practices.

Hawai'i's Koa: *Embrace and integrate meaningful cultural symbolism into your crucibles.* While killing a tiger shark and eating its eyeball certainly demonstrated a would-be Koa's strength, bravery, and fortitude, it also had strong symbolic meaning, designating those who completed the task as "great tiger sharks swimming on land." Koa weaponry, battle tactics, dress, and behavior were also deeply anchored in symbols resonant with the Hawaiian people of their era, communicating important community themes and concepts instantly, without words. While the Koa no longer exist as a military force, many of the cultural concepts integral to their training and service are preserved in a variety of modern martial arts and performance traditions, knowledge of which carries their legacy and impact into modern times and creates a shared sense of history and community among those who practice these skills today. Words are potent in the moment, but symbols resonate long after the words are forgotten. Indoctrinating would-be applicants into the subtle language of cultural symbolism is a deeply efficient way to empower them to act publicly and memorably on the organization's behalf.

Swiss Guard: *Develop crucibles around the traits that most make your organization unique.* Yes, the Swiss Guard is the world's smallest army, representing the country with the smallest land area and population in the world. And, yes, the guardsmen are often seen in harlequin-styled uniforms evoking some likely fanciful belief in what fancy Renaissance people wore on a day-to-day basis. But being small means, by definition, that you are also exclusive, and unusual, and special as such. While the Swiss Guard has a far more limited scope of responsibility and action than most military units the world around, the guardsmen understand and embrace the fact that the person they protect is viewed as God's primary emissary on Earth within a faith claiming over two billion members. They also know that while their fighting skills are infrequently called upon in modern times, when needed, they are ready, and they have the brave examples of their forebears, especially during the Sack of Rome, to inspire and shape their behavior and beliefs about the lasting, singular importance of their work, and the tested worthiness required to serve within their unit.

White Coat Ceremonies: *Embrace and share your core rites of passage with those outside of your organizational circle.* While the modern White Coat Ceremony does not mark the completion of the process required to become an MD or a DO (or any other coat-donning medical profession), nor does participation in the ceremony in any way guarantee or forecast that such completion will come, it is a valuable community-building ritual, both for those in the portal process and for the family members and friends who will support them through their studies and beyond. That public opportunity to celebrate the medical professions and the practitioners within formalizes and anchors the commitment to the process by its aspirants, and the act of making that commitment in public, before the eyes of others, can be a valuable motivator and incentive during the challenging months and years to come before they earn their terminal degrees and begin their actual medical practices.

Freemasons: *Balance inward- and outward-looking facets within your crucibles.* Our expert insider Masonic interviewee noted that the Masons are less of a secret society and more of a society of secrets in their modern American manifestations. The secretive aspects of their practices are certainly part and parcel of both their portal processes for admission and their practices among initiates, but they are also fervent and dogmatic about the importance of the service components of their mission, working together not only to benefit their own organizations, but also to advance purposes they see as valuable and worthy in the communities in which they live, love, work, and play. Integrating such inward- and outward-looking aspects of organizational culture into the acquisition crucible process effectively prepares initiates to understand that once they are on the inside, they are not bunkered in isolation from the world around them, but are instead committed to making that world a better place through the merged power of their members' skills and commitment to service.

Having gleaned those key lessons learned from each of our case studies, we now return to the list of questions that guided our research, and which we posed to Dr. Marcus Hedahl in the introduction to this book. Our brief answers to each of these questions, aggregating the cumulative knowledge gleaned from researching and writing this book, are as follows:

What are the key purposes, both internally (i.e., for an elite organization itself) and externally (i.e., for the society served by the elite organization) of grueling, crucible-style training and indoctrination rites of passage? Elite organizations depend on crucibles to ensure that they in-board only those candidates with the aptitude, expertise, and skill to advance their organizations' missions effectively. While all organizations deploy portal processes of some form for recruiting new members, the barriers to participation are higher, and the probability of completing the pipeline is lower for the most exclusive, elite organizations.

Well-designed crucibles also create deeply ingrained senses of community, demonstrating a shared experience among the successful few and creating commonality between new and long-standing employees, as well as connectivity with those who preceded and those who will follow the current team. Effective crucibles also serve an outward-looking public relations function, demonstrating to the community at large that those bestowed with certain rights, responsibilities, and duties are deemed qualified to perform said duties, as vetted by those who came before them, and who bear actual real-world experience with the same.

In considering multiple types of crucibles, are there universal threads that can be potentially codified to define the tools and approaches used by elite organizations in choosing and training their members? We would tout the list of takeaways linked to specific chapters above as a solid codified set of guidelines for how organizations may establish, maintain, document,

modify, or (occasionally) eliminate crucibles or other portal processes. The most important universal thread that emerged in our
studies of representative crucibles is the important role they play
in creating and sustaining organizational culture, which itself is a
key component of the broad academic and professional pursuits
collectively known as organization development (OD). In assessing how crucibles can be best deployed across various organizational structures, leaders and managers could be well-served by
considering the core texts of the modern OD movement (which
we briefly summarize below), then assessing how the codified
takeaways from our representative crucible stories could fit
within an OD framework to enhance the organization's performance, outputs, outcomes, and successes.

The seminal tome on modern OD, *Organization
Development: Behavioral Science Interventions for Organization
Improvement*, by Wendell L. French and Cecil H. Bell Jr., was
first published in 1978, and defined OD as "a long-term effort,
led and supported by top management, to improve an organization's visioning, empowerment, learning and problem-solving
processes, through an ongoing, collaborative, management of
organizational culture—with special emphasis on the culture
of intact work teams and other team configurations—using
the consultant-facilitator role and the theory and technology
of applied behavioral science, including action research." The
term "action research" was coined by Kurt Lewin in his influential 1940s works on group dynamics and social psychology; it is
essentially an iterative, feedback-intensive process of steps, each
of which includes elements of "planning, action, and fact-find-
ing about the result of the action." French and Bell also built on
the work of management theorist Chris Argyris, especially his
books *Personality and Organization* (1957) and *Interpersonal
Competence and Organizational Effectiveness* (1962).

One of the more influential and useful works of the past
quarter century in OD circles was Peter M. Senge's *The Fifth*

Discipline: The Art and Practice of the Learning Organization (1990). Senge expanded on concepts first developed by French, Bell, Lewin, and Argyris, ultimately framing and celebrating the concept of "learning organizations," which he defined thusly:

- They embrace personal mastery, which requires a commitment by individuals in the organization to the process of learning;
- They challenge ingrained mental models and assumptions held by individuals and the organization as a whole;
- They build a shared vision to create a common culture and identity, and provide the energy needed to pursue personal mastery;
- They practice team learning, wherein individual learning is shared, thereby expanding access to knowledge and expertise across the entire organization;
- They embrace systems thinking, an overarching strategic process that unites the other four elements into a practical, useful whole.

Crucibles and other portal processes can and should be designed and managed to meet each of those five elements: testing personal mastery, challenging assumptions, building culture, expanding expertise, and representing a purposeful strategic process. The successful achievement of those elements as part of culture crafting would be the most important universal thread tugged in various ways over the course of this text.

Similarly, are there any universally problematic threads that can be potentially codified to express ways in which such elite organizations may harm themselves or their societies? The most problematic aspects of the crucibles we studied always hinge around either the illegality or immorality of an organization's mission, or on the ways in which stringent physical testing can often cross the blurry barrier between the challenging and the abusive. Optimal crucibles may push candidates to various physical, psychological, emotional, and mental extremes, but they should not be unduly dangerous, nor inflict permanent damage to those on their receiving ends.

To our collective cultural credit, modern American academic, corporate, business, and fraternal organizations have largely become acutely attuned to identifying and stamping out practices and behaviors that demean or degrade the fundamental humanity of those passing through their various crucibles, and anti-hazing and anti-bullying initiatives are common in K–12 and higher educational circles. There is still work to be done on this front, of course, but we know from first-hand experience that many of the things done with and to us in 1982 as Plebes at the Naval Academy would not fly in Annapolis today. (We will discuss that further in the epilogue to this book, when we return to telling the story of our own crucible experiences at the Naval Academy.) This is not to imply that the crop of students passing through America's service academies today are having an inferior experience to our own, since today's students are tasked with myriad tests and tasks that were not on the training radar screen in our time. Ideally, though, there is less abuse and more focus on fair and safe training today, in all areas of academic and professional attainment.

Are there differences between elite organizations that make their crucibles widely and publicly known versus those that conduct their indoctrinations in a more secretive fashion? And is that a matter of marketing their "eliteness" to the greater society, or a matter of bolstering the elites within the organization, separate from the expectations or understanding of the greater society? While secrecy may have been a cornerstone principle for various organizations and their crucibles historically, the reality in modern America is that it is awfully hard to keep secrets in the internet era, with omnipresent cellphone cameras and countless public portals and outlets available to current and former employees and the applicants who wished to join them, all of whom may have less-than-charitable agendas driving their actions, to widely share information and practices that were once closely held.

We see little benefit to hewing to overly secretive practices related to portal processes at this point in our cultural and vocational history accordingly, and we note that the organizations that are often most widely touted or criticized for their secrecy are often fantastic constructions of myth and conspiracy-making, and not real-world examples of effective and efficient modern entities. "Deep State," anybody?

Are crucible approaches a dying phenomenon in modern times, or are they becoming more common and widespread in modern times? Portal processes are ubiquitous and are becoming ever more standardized in the internet era, with popular websites and applications being acquired or contracted by a variety of governmental, corporate, charitable, and academic organizations to streamline the personnel acquisition process, and to create documentation that those processes were conducted without bias and in accordance with applicable labor laws.

There are obviously countless organizations that preserve and maintain a variety of onerous crucibles (we have written about several of them in the preceding pages), but our sense is that there are not a lot of organizations today developing elaborate, ornate, and secretive new processes for in-boarding new recruits, in large part because the changing workplace and academic expectations of the Millennial and "Zoomer" generations (who now outnumber the old Gen X and Boomer cohorts in the modern working world) are out of line with heavily test-based and exclusive policies and practices. The post-COVID world, where more and more people work either entirely from home or in hybrid work models, further degraded the efficacy of extreme, in-place, on-site training pipelines, outside of obvious exceptions of necessity, such as military or police service, or credentialing processes for technically, legally, financially, or academically rigorous disciplines and pursuits.

How well do such crucibles really work? Are they simply a form of self-indulgent and ritualized sadomasochism, or are they valuable to creating meaningful elite organizations within any given society? Crucibles still certainly have value, even if their absolute numbers may be declining. They remain valuable for transmitting cultures and creating cohesion within organizations, for demonstrating "the right stuff" to those outside of the organizations, and for culling applicants for limited positions in high-desirability fields.

While the White Coat Ceremony, to cite but one example, may be an entirely symbolic ritual, the long and rigorous processes surrounding it provide us with lingering sense that our doctors are properly trained and qualified before they start cutting on us, or prescribing drugs and other treatments that might be fatal if administered incorrectly. Yes, most of us will consult Doctor Google as a first line of defense today, but when we do finally reach the point of visiting our physicians, we are generally glad for the crucibles that have allowed them to hang their shingles and practice on our collective behalf. We place our lives and well-being into the hands of others (e.g., pilots, doctors, architects, engineers, financial advisors, military, and police personnel, etc.) far more often than we likely actively consider in real time, and so long as that is the case, there will be a role for rigorous crucibles in sustaining our faith in those professionals' skills, even if we do not understand or know about the actual steps and processes involved within the generative crucibles.

Are there selection biases to be considered in evaluating crucibles—i.e., are crucibles that funnel willing volunteers into the elite organizations fundamentally different from those that conscript members? Volunteer organizations are always going to engender more internal loyalty and affection than organizations that depend on forced conscription. Yes, there may be selection biases that work to the disadvantage of various organizations when they are solely dependent on volunteers, but if their crucibles or other portal processes are effective, they will successfully weed out those whose enthusiasms, legitimate and misplaced alike, may cause problems for the organization and those it serves in the years that follow. **Are there leadership principles to be found in crucible-centric elite organizations that can be applied, positively or negatively, to business, government, military, academic, or other less "extreme" contemporary organizations?** Yes, absolutely. We would again posit the rubrics cited above, anchored in historic examples, as an excellent baseline template for any organization to consider and deploy in creating or maintaining their portal processes, regardless of whether they rise to the levels of difficulty or extremity that might lead us to call them crucibles. No organization becomes better by opening its doors to all applicants for all roles, and portal processes are an effective point for charitably weeding out those whose desires may exceed their talents, which is a far better outcome than discovering such a situation after an employee or member has been in-boarded, and now requires a negative personnel action to address, suboptimally for and disappointing to everyone involved.

To close out this work with our final thoughts on how crucibles can, and maybe should, work, we return in the following epilogue to the second part of our own personal experiences at the United States Naval Academy, and how those experiences shaped our own perspectives in the decades since we passed through that crucible together. Because ultimately, the success or failure of a crucible model must hinge on the ways in which those who experienced it feel about it after the fact, how they deployed its lessons, and how they share their experiences both within the organizations they seek to join, and in the greater world outside of those cloistered organizational structures. A sound and solid crucible should, by definition, turn one thing into another thing, ideally a useful one, and as such, it should represent a permanent change of state, one made memorable by the experiences and, hopefully, the successes that follow it.

That was certainly the case for us, as we now return to the story of our Plebe Year at the Naval Academy for proof . . .

EPILOGUE

On Being a Plebe (Part 2), Annapolis, Maryland, Autumn 1982 through Spring 1983

"If well thou hast begun, go on; it is the end that crowns us, not the fight."
—Robert Herrick

"The better you tell an old story, the more you are talking about right now."
—John Crowley

(CONTINUED FROM THE PROLOGUE)

ON SATURDAY, AUGUST 21, 1982, the full Brigade of Midshipmen returned to the United States Naval Academy in Annapolis, Maryland, after a long summer spent in various training activities around the world. That day marked the end of the Plebe Summer training phase for Jim McNeal, J. Eric Smith, and their fellow Plebe members of the Class of 1986. While that transition did feel like an accomplishment of sorts for the Plebes, it did not take long for the green training cohort to realize that having more than three times as many upper-class midshipmen on the Yard than had been the case during Plebe Summer (when only a small cadre of midshipmen first class oversaw the Plebes' training) created something of a geometrically scaled increase in the opportunities for Plebes to offend or annoy their seniors, and to receive and endure various punishments for their affronts.

There was an established hierarchy defining the return-ing Brigade's relationships to the Plebes, with each class of the older midshipmen having both official and "that's the way it's

always been" roles to play. The midshipmen third class (soph-
omores in a "normal" college, "Youngsters" in Navy parlance)
were supposed to be the stern older brothers and sisters, having experienced the Plebes' travails most recently themselves,
and ostensibly still carrying some small modicum of sympathy
for the plights of those following them. Not friends or friendly
much at all, but also not usually actively and overtly hostile. The
midshipmen second class (juniors, or "Flamers" at Annapolis)
had apparently lost the ability to feel that sympathy, and were
semi-officially tasked with being the hardest of hardcore nem-
eses for the hapless Plebes. Midshipmen first class (seniors, or
"Firsties") held the organizational leadership ranks and responsibilities within the Brigade at large, and were nominally focused
more on their upcoming graduations and commencements than
on tormenting the Plebes once Plebe Summer ended, though
plenty of them held steadfastly and sadistically to the Flamers'
roles that they had clearly enjoyed enough to pursue for another
year, just because they could.

During Plebe Summer, each company was composed of
about forty Plebes, led by a cohort of about fifteen Firsties. Once
the Brigade returned, the Plebes were outnumbered by about a
three-to-one ratio on both a macro basis about the Yard and on
a micro basis within the squads that served as the smallest organizational units within the Brigade. Each squad (there were 324
of them) was typically composed of something like four Plebes,
three Youngsters, three Flamers, and three Firsties. Three squads
made a platoon, three platoons made a company, six companies
made a battalion, three battalions made a regiment, and two
regiments made the complete Brigade. Each of those units was
led by a Firstie, with their uniform insignia running from "MIR"
(midshipmen in ranks, wearing no insignia bar on the sleeves
of their uniforms, but only the "eagle anchor" insignia on their
uniform collars) up to midshipman captain (the Brigade commander, who wore six bars per sleeve and collar). The squad

and platoon units remained the same throughout the full first semester, and then were reshuffled within the company after the Christmas holiday, allowing the majority of the midshipmen first class to hold some leadership role(s) over the course of their final year in Annapolis.

The Plebes experienced an uneasy first five days with the Brigade back in town, lightly enjoying the cessation of a very small number of Plebe Summer requirements (the early morning PEP exercise sessions perhaps first and foremost), but realizing with dismay that the burden of pleasing thousands more upper-class midshipmen on a minute-by-minute basis might be more time-consuming and intellectually taxing than running and push-ups had been. Then, on Wednesday of that first week, the academic year began, and most of the Plebes quickly realized that, on a net basis, things had gotten worse, rather than better, with Plebe Summer behind them.

Jim had validated out of a couple of semesters of calculus during summer testing, and Eric had cleared out one English requirement, leading to slight variances in their academic schedules. Eric's first semester included Intro to Naval Engineering (two credit hours), Rhetoric and Introduction to Literature (three credit hours), Leadership I: Fundamentals (two credit hours), Western Society Since 1715 (three credit hours), Calculus and Analytical Geometry I (four credit hours), General Chemistry I (four credit hours), and Physical Education (no credit hours assigned, but mandatory, and involving a long once-per-week class block). Jim's first semester also featured Rhetoric and Introduction to Literature, Leadership I: Fundamentals, Western Society Since 1715, General Chemistry I, and Physical Education, along with Intro to Computing (two credit hours) and Analytical Geometry and Calculus III (four credit hours). Under normal college standards, that equated to eighteen credit hours for the semester, but normal colleges would have counted the mandatory Physical Education, making an apples-to-apples comparison more like twenty credit hours. And even that underrepresented the actual classroom hours because lab periods provided only a single credit for a two-hour block of time during the academic day.

That is a heavy load under any circumstances for a typical college freshman, but the structure of the days made it even more of an extreme lift. In addition to their classroom and self-study times, Plebes were required to offer "chow calls" before each of the day's mandatory meal formations, standing in the hallways of Bancroft Hall, shouting a prescribed litany of required rates ten and five minutes before each formation, including the menu for the forthcoming meal, duty officers of the day, location of the upcoming formation, and the uniform to be worn by the midshipmen. The second chow call ended with the urgent "Time, tide and formation wait for no one, I am now shoving off," after which the Plebes scampered to muster, in immaculate uniforms, in their designated company areas. Plebes also had to attend "come arounds" every day, typically before the evening meal chow calls, and typically with one or more of the Flamers in their squads. The Plebes were required to have memorized at least three front-page news items and one sports news item each day, and to know all upcoming events on the Yard, the number of days remaining until the Army–Navy football game, the winter break, the Second Class Ring Dance, and the First Class graduation, and any other items that the upperclassmen felt like pulling from the *Reef Points* training handbook.

All these information items could also be requested upon demand during meals, which were served in the immense King Hall, each squad seated at its own twelve-person table, the entire Brigade receiving fresh, plentiful food, served family style on trays to each table. The Plebes were responsible for grabbing the often extremely hot serving trays as they passed by their table on massive rolling carts, then for carving any unportioned items into the correct number of slices or chunks, then for passing the food up to the Firsties at one end of the table, then down to the Flamers at the other end, then across to the Youngsters, with the Plebes serving themselves last. Woe unto the unfortunate Plebe who made a carving mistake on the roast loin of beef and ended up with but a tiny sliver of meat, while some Firsties enjoyed hearty slabs. Plebes had to eat "square meals" at their squad tables, sitting with rigid backs, eyes straight forward unless addressed by an upper-class midshipman, fork raised from the plate vertically, then moved toward the mouth at a ninety-degree angle, then placed back upon the plate before the next bite could be processed.

Plebe movements throughout Bancroft Hall continued to adhere to the Plebe Summer paradigm of "pinging" down the center of corridors, eyes forward, turning only at silver plates embedded in the floors at junctions, shouting "Beat Army!" or similar spirit-related phrases at each turn. Outside of Bancroft Hall, the Plebes' movements about the Yard were restricted to straight pathways, the curved ones (typically the shortest routes) restricted to the upper-class midshipmen. Plebes could not use elevators and could not break from a ping into a run, no matter how late they were going to be for their next commitment. And the commitments just kept coming: in addition to the formations and the classroom blocks, Plebes were also required (as were all midshipmen) to participate in a sporting activity every afternoon (either varsity, junior varsity, club, or intramurals, depending on their skills), and there were regular platoon or company drill practices for the formal parades of the Brigade that were always a big hit with the tourists. The entire Brigade also marched together to all home football games, and the Plebes were required to rush the field and do as many push-ups as Navy had tallied points, each time the home team scored. High-scoring games were exciting, sure, but terribly exhausting for the Plebes.

The days were packed full, at bottom line, and yet they all had a hard end point that made the time crush feel even more formidable: lights went out for Plebes at 10 p.m., and any Plebe found up with lights on after that was subject to being "fried" (i.e., charged with a performance violation) under the Academy's robust disciplinary structure, which scaled offenses from minor 1000-level infractions up to potentially career-ending 6000-level infractions. And, of course, said Plebes' roommates would also be fried if one was caught up after hours, since those roommates should have enforced the rules themselves before any upper-classman had to get involved.

There were countless offenses, obvious and subtle, that could result in getting fried, and once convicted, Plebes could be assigned area tours (marching in circles with a drill rifle outside of Bancroft Hall) and restriction musters (having additional for-mations each day for mandatory uniform inspections). For their part, offending upper-class midshipmen could also be assigned restriction musters or room tours (i.e., sitting in an immacu-late room in a perfect uniform, with doors open and no music, studying diligently, for ninety minutes per tour). The nature of the punishments was such that they tended to build upon themselves, as it was (and is) virtually impossible to maintain an impeccable room and uniform hour after hour after hour. Severe offenses (of which we both had several) tended to be hard to work off accordingly, and chronic offenders could be subject to separation from the Academy via formal Conduct Boards.

Those Conduct Boards were but one of the many bodies convened to discipline or remove midshipmen from the Brigade. There were also Academic Boards for those struggling with their classroom work, Performance Boards that considered physical readiness and the ability to pass the required mile run, obsta-cle course, swimming, and applied strength (known colloquially as "applied struggle") tests if the mandatory "sub squad" train-ing after a failed test did not get the job done. Most fearsome were the Honor Boards, called in cases when a midshipman was charged with a violation of the Honor Code: "A Midshipman does not lie, cheat, or steal." The absolute nature of the code created frequent conundrums, as midshipmen were routinely asked about the whereabouts and activities of their roommates and classmates, and were honor-bound to answer truthfully, even if it meant that their friends and colleagues would suffer because of their words. While "cheating" and "stealing" seem clear-cut on the surface, there were ample opportunities to be charged under their terms for incidents that may not have seemed so clear-cut in the moment, such as taking additional food from King Hall after hours or overhearing a classmate talking about an examination that you had not yet taken yourself.

Beyond the formal rules and regulations (and the various punitive responses to them discussed above), there were also a wide range of informal approaches that upper-class midshipmen could, and did, deploy to make the lives of the Plebes even more miserable than they already were. Some were just absurd, such as the unwritten law that if more than four Plebes were found in a room together with their shoes on, then there must surely be a "mutiny" afloat, which dictated walking the plank—i.e., all the Plebes in the room had to get into a running shower, in whatever clothes or uniforms the Plebes happened to be wearing when the "mutiny" was discovered. Given the finite number of uniform items that Plebes possessed, this could often result in being late, or not having appropriately ship-shape garb for subsequent formations, which could then kick off the formal frying process. Upper-class midshipmen would also occasionally jam Plebes' room doors shut, usually right before some important inspection or formation, and when the Plebes finally freed themselves and were asked to account for their lateness, there was no allowable and legal response other than "No excuse, sir." Commence frying and area tours and restriction musters, then rinse, then repeat.

Other unofficial torments represented a more malignant and targeted form of psychological abuse, often for no clear and apparent reasons, other than because the upperclassmen so inclined could pursue them without fear of reprisal. As a personal example of that, Eric's father was deployed to Beirut throughout our entire Plebe Year, missing Eric's high school graduation, swearing in at Annapolis, and year-end activities discussed below. One first class midshipman in Eric's company was aware of this fact, and routinely responded to any perceived failings on Eric's part by describing how disappointed his father must be over Eric's awful performance, and what a failure Eric was compared to the clear accomplishments that his Marine Corps father had earned and was continuing to earn. (Eric finally snapped, cursed out, and threatened the offending upperclassman; no specific punishment ensued from that outburst, probably because the upper-class midshipman knew he was in the wrong, and because there were no witnesses to that act of insubordination, so he didn't have to save face with anybody. That particular angle of abuse did abate after that point, though, so mission accomplished, on some plane.)

As a general rule, most members of the Class of 1986 at the Naval Academy had, and still have, a sort of vague sense of unease and resentment toward the members of the Class of 1983 who made our Plebe Year so miserable, so much of the time. In another of his books (discussed below), Jim recounted the story of a member of the Class of 1983 who stood as a particular nemesis throughout our Plebe Year. Many years later, Jim was in an airport in Hawai'i when his former nemesis walked through the terminal, and he recounted an upwelling and strong feeling of fear and revulsion, even though they were nominally peers, post–Naval Academy, and there wasn't a thing in the world that the former first class midshipman could have done to inconvenience or annoy Jim in any fashion whatsoever. But those feelings of fear ran deep throughout our Plebe Year, and they linger with us and many of our classmates, all these years on. It was not unusual during our Plebe Year (and those that came before us, and those that came after) to see a hastily scribbled bit of graffiti reading "IHTFP" on various blackboards or walls or bulletin boards around Bancroft Hall. That acronym stood for "I Hate This Fucking Place," and those seeing the scrawls knew exactly what feelings produced them, and why. It was a futile and pointless act of rebellion, sure, but with so few other outlets for expressing outrage at our circumstances, we understood why people chose to share the sentiment that way.

Perhaps the most noxious unofficial hazing activities inflicted during our Plebe Year were directed toward the female members of the Class of 1986. We were still within the first decade in which women were admitted to the Naval Academy (and the other service academies), and they composed only about 10 percent of our class when we were sworn in. The language commonly used to describe them was often vile (e.g., one of our uniforms was called, at the time, "Working Uniform Blue: Alpha" or "WUBA" for short; that acronym was retrofitted to describe female midshipmen, alleging them to be "Women Used By All"), and they were forced to witness "guys being guys" in ways that were often inappropriate or actively abusive. For some of the upper-class midshipmen at the time, even that 10 percent female class composition was too much, and they often made it their openly stated mission to drive as many of the women out as they could. They would often justify their odious activities by claiming that they were undertaken to protect their male classmates from undue sea-time service after graduation, claiming that the women would be assigned to the more cushy and highly coveted shore-duty assignments at the men's expense, were they allowed to graduate. In Eric's 23rd Company, there were seven women on our Induction Day among forty members of the Class of 1986. Only one of those women graduated with us. The other six were all fine people, and would have made fine Naval or Marine Corps officers, so their attrition was a loss to the Academy and to the armed services, which would have benefited from their commissioning.

There were brief reprieves from both the formal and informal torments through that brutal first semester of our Plebe Year, with limited weekend liberty hours offered to the Plebes and opportunities to travel home (for those not local) over the Thanksgiving holiday. The entire Brigade traveled to Philadelphia in early December for the Army–Navy football game, and the excitement of that special annual event produced some sense of conviviality and inclusion directed by (some of) the upperclassmen toward (some of) the Plebes. Then came the Christmas break, the first extended trip away from Annapolis for the Plebes since they had arrived six months earlier.

The second semester period between the Christmas break and spring break was known on the Yard as the "Dark Ages," as the weather was dreary, and there were few opportunities for fun or exciting upcoming events to ponder. Jim and Eric each added an additional credit hour to their first semester academic loads, while moving forward in the ever-more-difficult multi-semester calculus, chemistry, and naval sciences curricula, tacking on some computing and (in Eric's case) political science classes to boot. Spring break offered a too-short time away before the final slog of Plebe Year rolled slowly by, leading up to "June Week" (which occurs in May), the series of huge ceremonial events that marked various rites of passage for various classes. The midshipmen second class had their Ring Dance, when they first donned the items of jewelry that give Naval Academy alumni the nickname "Ring Knockers" in the fleet, but only after their rings were baptized in the waters of the Seven Seas in a formal blessing ceremony. June Week, and the academic year, ended with the commencement ceremony at Navy's football stadium, where the outgoing midshipmen were awarded their diplomas and were commissioned as second lieutenants in the Marine Corps or ensigns in the Navy. The entire Brigade was in attendance.

But for Jim and Eric and the rest of the Class of 1986, those June Week events were minor ancillary activities compared to the one scheduled specifically for the Plebes: the Herndon Climb. The Herndon Monument is a nondescript-looking twenty-one-foot-tall obelisk at the heart of the Yard, erected to honor a nineteenth-century captain who went down with his ship, which is special and memorable, of course, though the Yard has many other monuments of greater visual grandeur, honoring equally admirable heroes. What separates Herndon from all the other iconic statues, buildings, relics, and markers about the Academy is the fact that each Plebe class since the early twentieth century has swarmed and climbed it every May (barring COVID time and a couple of other similarly anomalous years), formally marking the end of their physically, psychologically, and emotionally grueling first year in Annapolis. The task is greatly complicated by the fact that the monument is thoroughly, disgustingly greased with various unsavory unguents before the climb, top to bottom, and by the fact that the Plebes must remove a "Dixie cup" sailor's cap from its apex (which is typically glued and/or taped in place), and replace it with an officer's combination cover, while being hosed down by various upper-class midshipmen, ostensibly to cool the scrum, but not really.

It sounds absurd, doesn't it? Sure, it does. Most great traditions are. But it is truly an amazing thing to see, is a whole lot harder than it sounds, and serves as an unparalleled portal of transformation for those who experience it, "Plebes No More" once that combo cover rests upon Herndon's peak. The emotional heft associated with seeing any class collectively celebrating the end of a truly brutal year of insanely rigorous intellectual and physical training is infectious and intoxicating, a messy explosion of joy, relief, and gratitude unlike anything most folks are likely to see or experience elsewhere. It was thrilling for us to go through at the end of our own Plebe Year, of course, but also thrilling every year after that to watch subsequent classes tackle and achieve the long-awaited goal that linked them inexorably with those who had passed through the greasy crucible before

them. It is also popular with those who were never Plebes themselves, a truly unique spectator event that brings out locals and
travelers year after year to share in that magic, muddy moment
of transformation and release.

With Herndon behind us, we were no longer Plebes. And
with the story of our crucible year in Annapolis told in full, we
feel entitled to reflect on what followed, and what it all meant for
us. Our time at the Academy together was not over, of course,
as we had three more years of onerous academic work ahead of
us, just without the Plebe hazing aspects shaping and defining
the days. We graduated on May 21, 1986, and both of us went
on to the Naval Supply Corps School in Athens, Georgia, as we
had both suffered severe and chronic shoulder injuries that pre-
cluded us from other direct line activities in the Marine Corps
or Navy. (Neither of us were unhappy about that.) Jim married
one of our classmates, Peggy Mansfield, a few years after our
graduation. Peggy and Jim went to serve in the fleet in San Diego
after Jim and Eric's time in Athens was complete, while Eric was
selected to serve a five-year tour at Naval Reactors headquarters in Washington, DC. Soon after arriving at that post, Eric
met Marcia Brom, a fellow Supply Corps officer from Minnesota
who had finished her own time at Athens a year before Eric and
Jim did. Eric and Marcia married two years later.

After our initial service obligation times were completed
in the early 1990s, Eric left the Navy but stayed on with Naval
Reactors in a civilian capacity for another five years before
embarking on a career as a nonprofit executive and writer. Jim
transitioned into the Naval Reserves, and eventually retired
decades later as a rear admiral, one of the most senior members
of the Class of 1986. One of Jim's first big post-Navy projects
was researching, writing, and publishing the definitive account
of our Plebe Year's culmination, *The Herndon Climb: A History
of the United States Naval Academy's Greatest Tradition* (Naval
Institute Press, 2020), working with his longtime high school

friend in California, Scott Tomasheski. Then Jim and Eric (we kept in touch over the years) teamed up to coauthor and publish *Side by Side in Eternity: The Lives Behind Adjacent American Military Graves* (McFarland Books, 2022), followed soon after by the very book you are reading now.

Of the approximately 1,400 members of the Class of 1986 who took the Oath of Office during the summer of 1982, just over one thousand of us graduated, having successfully run the gauntlet of the various crucibles into which we had been stuffed over that four-year period. We would both absolutely be lying if we said that the four years in Annapolis between I-Day and graduation were not absurdly hard, and we would equally totally be lying if we said that we enjoyed the experience much at all on a day-to-day basis, as described in detail above. But, in the end, we got it done, and that is what matters, and that is what counts, and that is what is remembered, no matter how much we struggled along the way.

On the upside of things, both of us feel as though we formed some of the best friendships of our lives during those four years by the Severn River in Annapolis. Also, there is some question in both of our minds as to whether we would have finished college in four years without the controls and constraints imposed upon us by the Academy. Certainly, the lessons learned at Annapolis in how to take initiative, how to manage time, how to function under stress, how to work efficiently and effectively, how to direct teams, how to be directed as a team member, how to prioritize, and so many other aspects of leadership and management were truly transformative for us. Those lessons fundamentally shaped everything we have done throughout our personal and professional careers. We were not grateful while being taught those lessons, but we are forever grateful that we learned them.

We also learned during our crucible years at Annapolis just what we were physically capable of when pushed beyond the points of comfort and (sometimes) common sense. The enjoyment of that strange euphoric satisfaction that comes in the aftermath of brutal physical activity apparently has stuck with us both, as we've both long engaged in a variety of endurance-level swimming, running, hiking, and/or cycling events over the years, and continue to do so as we both eyeball our sixtieth birthdays, coming up sooner than we would have imagined possible. We certainly better understand what drove our old PEP instructor, the late (and truly much beloved among Navy alumni) Heinz Lenz, who demanded more than seemed demandable during our Plebe Summer all those years ago. That honestly stands as a surprise to both of us, reasonably fit old men that we are.

In another unexpected turn of events in the years that followed our graduation, and because Eric was a weird web nerd before too many other weird web nerds had emerged, he ended up building the platform for the Class of 1986's first online community presence in the early 1990s. After serving the class as "Web Drone" for some years, Eric then went on to serve as the scribe for '86's monthly column in *Shipmate*, the Naval Academy Alumni Association magazine. And then became the class secretary because of that. And then got heavily involved in reunion planning because of that. And then, somehow, Eric was elected '86's class president for a five-year term, culminating with our twenty-fifth class reunion in 2011. Following Eric's tenure as a class officer, Jim then stepped up and took leadership of the next major class reunion in 2016, and he is serving at the time of this writing as the vice president of the Class of 1986.

We both have received a lot of joy and satisfaction from these volunteer experiences, even though they were and are a lot of hard work. We also experienced a lot of sadness from those experiences, as we have lost many classmates along the way, some giving their lives in service to their nation, some who died as victims of terrorism on September 11, 2001, some who fell to illness, or perished in training accidents, or succumbed to the bodily travails that ail us as we get older. In our roles as class officers, we were often tasked with disseminating those sad news items among the class at large, and with planning and implementing various memorial services. As there were (and are) fewer and fewer of us, the links that bound and bind us seem to grow tighter, and to mean more, with each of those losses.

During our time in Annapolis, we never would have foreseen ourselves holding those later leadership roles. We also never would have expected that we would put in so much time and money and effort giving back to an institution that had seemed most determined to make us miserable while we were there. But that is sort of the beauty of the Naval Academy experience: it takes you as you come, it fires you hard through a challenging crucible, and it sends you out as you will be, and maybe, hopefully, as you *should* be. And like all great crucibles throughout history, the Naval Academy experience also inculcates in its alumni a desire to be a part of something bigger than ourselves, "links in the chain," bound together by history, by shared experience, and by a desire to see those who follow undergo the same transformations and build the same senses of community that we once experienced together, all those years, all those haircuts, all those miles, all those stories, and all those lives ago.

ACKNOWLEDGMENTS

FIRST, ALWAYS, AND FOREMOST, WE wish to thank our wives, Marcia Brom Smith, Esq., and Dr. Peggy Mansfield McNeal, for their support and belief throughout this project, and their bemused patience in dealing with our perhaps occasionally overenthusiastic pursuit of same. With further gratitude and respect, we thank the following "without whom" individuals whose time, wisdom, encouragement, and/or perspective made this book possible: Maj. Gen. Charles F. Bolden Jr., USMC (Ret.), Ying Compestine, John Cross, Yseult Digan (YZ), Mark Gottlieb (Trident Media Group), Dr. Marcus Hedahl, Sgt. Thierno Mamadu Jalloh, USMC, Dr. Eleanor Janega, Blake Kimzey (Writing Workshops), Kendall Linn, Brook Kapūkuniahi Parker, Lt. Gen. Lori Reynolds, USMC (Ret.), Geoff Schumacher, Doug Seibold (Agate Publishing), Katelin Smith, Linda Waters Smith, Nancy Tomasheski, Scott Tomasheski, and Dr. Todd L. Wagner, DO.

SOURCES AND
RECOMMENDED READING

NOTE: WE HAVE TRIED TO deploy new interviews and primary source documents as often as practical in telling the various stories contained in this book. In the bibliography that follows, we provide citations for a set of general references that cover or expand upon common aspects of our stories in broad terms, then we provide a chapter-by-chapter set of selected citations for key articles and pieces that either shaped our narrative or expand upon it in depths beyond what we chose to document in this omnibus introductory exploration of the concept of crucibles. The specific chapter citations represent the most significant ancillary resources in our research, but do not represent the totality of sources consulted. Publisher information reflects the book editions accessed in our research and are not necessarily original editions.

General References (Introduction and Conclusion)

Argyris, Chris. *Interpersonal Competence and Organizational Effectiveness.* Dorsey, 1962.

Argyris, Chris. *Personality and Organization: The Conflict Between System and the Individual.* Harper, 1957.

Block, Peter. *Community: The Structure of Belonging.* Berrett-Koehler, 2009.

Deal, Terrence W., and Allan A. Kennedy. *Corporate Cultures: The Rites and Rituals of Corporate Life.* Addison-Wesley, 1982.

French, Wendell L., and Cecil H. Bell Jr. *Organization Development: Behavioral Science Interventions for Organizational Improvement.* 6th ed. Prentice Hall, 1999.

Goldwag, Arthur. *Cults, Conspiracies, and Secret Societies: The Straight Scoop on Freemasons, the Illuminati, Skull and Bones, Black Helicopters, the New World Order, and many, many more.* Vintage Books, 2009.

Grimes, Ronald L. *Deeply into the Bone: Re-Inventing Rites of Passage.* University of California Press, 2000.

Hilton, Andy. *Anthropology and Mysticism in the Making of Initiation: A History of Discourse and Ideas for Today.* Wageningen Academic, 2019.

Huntington, Samuel P. *The Soldier and the State: The Theory and Politics of Civil-Military Relations.* Belknap, 1981.

Kahneman, Daniel. *Thinking, Fast and Slow.* Farrar, Straus and Giroux, 2011.

Lewin, Kurt. "Action Research and Minority Problems." *Journal of Sociology,* June 1946.

Lewis, Michael. *The Undoing Project: A Friendship That Changed Our Minds.* W. W. Norton, 2017.

Logan, Dana Wiggins. *Awkward Rituals: Sensations of Governance in Protestant America.* University of Chicago Press, 2022.

Magida, Arthur J. *Opening the Doors of Wonder: Reflections on Religious Rites of Passage.* University of California Press, 2006.

March, James G., and Herbert A. Simon. *Organizations.* 2nd ed. Wiley-Blackwell, 1993.

Maslow, Abraham. *Motivation and Personality.* Harper, 1954.

Morgan, Gareth. *Images of Organization.* Updated ed. Sage, 2006.

Philbin, Ann, and Sandra Mikush. *A Framework for Organizational Development: The Why, What, and How of OD Work—Perspectives from Participants in the Mary Reynolds Babcock Foundation's Organizational Development Program, 1995–1999.* The Mary Reynolds Babcock Foundation, 2000.

Redfern, Nicholas. *Secret Societies: The Complete Guide to Histories, Rites, and Rituals.* Visible Ink, 2017.

Reynolds, John Lawrence. *Secret Societies: Inside the World's Most Notorious Organizations.* Arcade, 2007.

Salinas, Cristóbal, and Michelle L. Boettcher. *Critical Perspectives on Hazing in Colleges and Universities: A Guide to Disrupting Hazing Culture.* Routledge, 2018.

Schein, Edgar H. *Organizational Culture and Leadership.* 4th ed. Jossey-Bass, 2010.

Senge, Peter M. *The Fifth Discipline: The Art and Practice of the Learning Organization.* Doubleday, 1990.

Sora, Stephen. *Secret Societies of America's Elite: From the Knights Templar to Skull and Bones.* Destiny, 2003.

Thomas, Robert J. *Crucibles of Leadership: How to Learn from Experience to Become a Great Leader.* Harvard Business Press, 2008.

Thompson, Oliver. *Hazing in the Military: Persistence, Policies, Recommendations.* Nova Science, 2016.

Van Gennep, Arnold, and Monika B. Vizedom (trans.). *The Rites of Passage.* 2nd ed. University of Chicago Press, 2019.

Wakin, Malham M. *War, Morality, and the Military Profession.* Westview, 1986.

Wilson, John P., Zev Harel, and Boaz Kahana. *Human Adaptation to Extreme Stress: From the Holocaust to Vietnam*. Plenum, 1988.

Yardley, Roland J., Dulani Woods, Cesse Ip, and Jerry M. Sollinger. *General Military Training: Standardization and Reduction Options*. RAND, 2012.

On Being a Plebe: United States Naval Academy (Prologue and Epilogue)

Disher, Sharon Hanley. *First Class: Women Join the Ranks at the Naval Academy*. U.S. Naval Institute Press, 1998.

Hubbard, Elbert. *A Message to Garcia*. Peter Pauper, 1982.

McNeal, James R., and Scott Tomasheski. *The Herndon Climb: A History of the United States Naval Academy's Greatest Tradition*. U.S. Naval Institute Press, 2020.

Prothro Arbuthnot, Nancy. *Guiding Lights: United States Naval Academy Monuments and Memorials*. U.S. Naval Institute Press, 2012.

Reef Points (1982–1983). U.S. Naval Institute Press, 1982.

Ross, Sue. *The Naval Academy Candidate Book: How to Prepare, How to Get In, How to Survive*. 4th ed. Silver Horn, 2014.

The U.S. Naval Institute on the U.S. Naval Academy: The Challenges. U.S. Naval Institute Press, 2016.

The U.S. Naval Institute on the U.S. Naval Academy: The History. U.S. Naval Institute Press, 2015.

United States Naval Academy. "The Blue and Gold Book." Accessed March 10, 2024. https://www.usna.edu/BlueAndGoldBook.

Webb, James. *A Sense of Honor*. Prentice-Hall, 1981.

We Make Marines: Boot Camp at MCRD Parris Island

Krulak, Victor H. *First to Fight: An Inside View of the U.S. Marine Corps*. U.S. Naval Institute Press, 1984.

Marine Corps Recruit Depot Parris Island. "History of Parris Island." Accessed March 10, 2024. https://www.mcrdpi.marines.mil/About/History-of-Parris-Island/.

Marine Corps University. "History of Marine Corps Recruit Training." Accessed March 10, 2024. https://www.usmcu.edu/Research/Marine-Corps-History-Division/Brief-Histories/History-of-Marine-Corps-Recruit-Training/.

Marine Corps University. "Key Events in the History of Port Royal/Parris Island." Accessed March 10, 2024. https://www.usmcu.edu/Research/Marine-Corps-History-Division/Brief-Histories/Key-Events-in-the-History-of-Port-Royal-Parris-Island/.

Novelly, Thomas. "Since 1949, SC's Parris Island Was the Only Place Women Trained to Be Marines. Until Now." *The Post and Courier*, December 20, 2020.

Parris Island Heritage Foundation. "Visit the Parris Island Museum and Learn
What It Means to Become a United States Marine." Accessed March 10,
2024. https://parrisislandmuseum.org/.

Salley, A. S. *Parris Island, the Site of the First Attempt at a Settlement of White
People Within the Bounds of What Is Now South Carolina.* Commission by
the State Co., 1919.

Stevens, John C. III. *Court-Martial at Parris Island: The Ribbon Creek Incident.*
G. K. Hall, 2000.

Today's Military. "Joining and Eligibility: Boot Camp." Accessed March 10,
2024. https://www.todaysmilitary.com/joining-eligibility/boot-camp.

U.S. Department of Defense: Military Installations. "MCRD Parris Island."
Accessed March 10, 2024. https://installations.militaryonesource.mil
/in-depth-overview/mcrd-parris-island.

Kung Fu and Koans: The Shaolin Monks

Draeger, Donn F., Chye Khim P'ng, and Alexander Bennett. *Shaolin Kung Fu:
The Original Training Techniques of the Shaolin Lohan Masters.* Tuttle, 2020.

Henning, Stanley E. "Academia Encounters the Chinese Martial Arts." *China
Review International* 6, no. 2 (Fall 1999).

Lau, Mimi. "The Decline and Fall of Chinese Buddhism: How Modern Politics
and Fast Money Corrupted an Ancient Religion." *South China Morning Post,*
September 21, 2018.

RZA, and Chris Norris. *The Tao of Wu.* Riverhead, 2010.

Sekida, Katsuki, trans. *Two Zen Classics: The Gateless Gate and the Blue Cliff
Records.* Shambhala, 2005.

Shahar, Meir. "Ming-Period Evidence of Shaolin Martial Practice." *Harvard
Journal of Asiatic Studies* 61, no. 2 (December 2001).

Shahar, Meir. *The Shaolin Monastery: History, Religion, and the Chinese
Martial Arts.* University of Hawai'i Press, 2008.

Shaolin Monk Corps. "About Shaolin Temple." Accessed March 10, 2024.
http://www.shaolin.org.cn/newsinfo/217/226/345/22757.html.

Stokes, Lisa, and Jean Odham, Michael Lukitsh, and Tyler Stokes. *Historical
Dictionary of Hong Kong Cinema.* Scarecrow, 2007.

Wong, Lok-to. "China's Ruling Party Hoists the Red Flag Over Henan's Shaolin
Temple." *Radio Free Asia,* August 29, 2018.

Space Is the Place: The U.S. Astronaut Program

Chaikin, Andrew. *A Man on the Moon: The Voyages of the Apollo Astronauts.*
Penguin, 2007.

Collins, Michael, and Scott Kelly. *Flying to the Moon: An Astronaut's Story.*
Farrar, Straus, and Giroux, 2019.

Court, Ben. "Here's Exactly What NASA Training Is Like for Astronauts." *Men's Health*, February 8, 2018.

Kranz, Gene. *Failure Is Not an Option*. Simon & Schuster, 2009.

Lovell, Jim, and Jeffrey Kluger. *Lost Moon: The Perilous Voyage of Apollo 13*. Houghton Mifflin, 1994.

National Aeronautics and Space Administration. "Astronaut Selection Program." Accessed March 10, 2024. https://www.nasa.gov/humans-in -space/astronauts/astronaut-selection-program/.

National Research Council. *Preparing for the High Frontier: The Role and Training of the NASA Astronauts in the Post–Space Shuttle Era*. National Academies Press, 2011.

Rosa-Aquino, Paolo. "Here's How NASA Determines Which Applicants Make It to Be Astronauts." Science Alert, November 25, 2022.

Sgobba, Tommaso, Barbara Kanki, Jean-François Clervoy, and Gro Mjeldheim Sandal, eds. *Space Safety and Human Performance*. Butterworth-Heinemann, 2018.

Wolfe, Tom. *The Right Stuff*. Picador, 2008.

Poor Fellow Soldiers of Christ: The Knights Templar

Baigent, Michael, Richard Leigh, and Henry Lincoln. *The Holy Blood and the Holy Grail*. Arrow, 2006.

Dawes, Christopher. *Rat Scabies and the Holy Grail*. Thunder's Mouth, 2005.

Demurger, Alain. *The Persecution of the Knights Templar: Scandal, Torture, Trial*. Pegasus, 2019.

Evans, G. R. *Bernard of Clairvaux*. Oxford University Press, 2000.

Hietala, Heikki. "The Knights Templar: Serving God with the Sword." *Renaissance Magazine*, 1996.

McGuire, Brian Patrick. *Bernard of Clairvaux: An Inner Life*. Cornell University Press, 2020.

Nicholson, Helen J. *The Everyday Life of the Templars: The Knights Templar at Home*. Fonthill, 2017.

Read, Piers Paul. *The Templars*. St. Martin's, 2000.

Scott, Walter. *Ivanhoe: A Romance*. Modern Library, 2001.

Tangredi, Sam J. "The Elusive Fleet of the Knights Templar." *Naval History Magazine*, April 2023.

Knives in the Mountains: The Gurkhas

BBC News. "Bravery Medal for Gurkha Who Fought Taliban." Accessed March 15, 2024. https://www.bbc.com/news/uk-13619825.

BBC News. "Who Are the Gurkhas?" Accessed March 15, 2024. https://www .bbc.com/news/uk-10782099.

Bellamy, Chris. *The Gurkhas: Special Force*. John Murray, 2011.

Gurung, Tim I. *Ayo Gorkhali: The True Story of the Gurkhas*. Blacksmith, 2021.

International Labour Organization. *Promoting Informed Policy Dialogue on Migration, Remittance, and Development in Nepal*. International Labour Organization, 2016.

Kaphle, Anup. "Nepali Men Have Been Fighting for Britain for 200 Years. One Photographer Shows What It Means to Be the Gurkhas." *Washington Post*, April 30, 2015.

King, Hannah, and Ros Moore. "Exclusive: Becoming a Gurkha." Accessed March 15, 2024. https://www.forces.net/services/gurkhas/exclusive -becoming-gurkha.

Manandhar, Asmita. "Who Wants to Be a Gurkha? Women." *Kathmandu Post*, February 18, 2019.

Sadler, John. *The Gurkha Way: A New History of the Gurkhas*. Pen & Sword Military, 2023.

Van Der Vat, Dan. "Lachhiman Gurung VC Obituary." *The Guardian*, December 22, 2010.

Our Mothers: The Dahomey Amazons

Alpern, Stanley B. *Amazons of Black Sparta: The Women Warriors of Dahomey*. 2nd ed. New York University Press, 2011.

Bamidele, Michael. "The Story of the Fearless Women Warriors of Dahomey." *The Guardian* (Nigeria), June 14, 2020.

Bay, Edna G. *Wives of the Leopard: Gender, Politics, and Culture in the Kingdom of Dahomey*. University of Virginia Press, 1998.

Bay, Edna G. *Women and Work in Africa*. Routledge, 2019.

Dash, Mike. "Dahomey's Women Warriors." *Smithsonian Magazine*, September 23, 2011.

Fraser, Louis, and Robin Law. *Journals and Correspondence of Louis Fraser: British Vice-Consul to the Kingdom of Dahomey, West Africa, 1851–1852*. Oxford University Press, 2012.

Macdonald, Fleur. "The Legend of Benin's Fearless Female Warriors." BBC. Accessed March 15, 2024. https://www.bbc.com/travel/article/20180826-the -legend-of-benins-fearless-female-warriors.

Superselected. "Art: French Street Artist YZ Pays Homage to the Warrior Women of Dahomey on the Walls of Senegal." Accessed March 15, 2024. https://www.superselected.com/art-french-street-artist-yz-pays-homage-to -the-warrior-women-of-dahomey-on-the-walls-of-senegal/.

UNESCO Women in African History. "The Women Soldiers of Dahomey." Accessed September 13, 2024. https://unesdoc.unesco.org/ark:/48223 /pf0000230934.

Widewalls. "YZ/Yseult Digan." Accessed March 15, 2024. https://www
.widewalls.ch/artists/yz.

Honor and Fidelity: The French Foreign Legion

Blanchard, Jean-Vincent. *At the Edge of the World: The Heroic Century of the French Foreign Legion*. Bloomsbury, 2017.

Doty, Bennett J. *The Legion of the Damned: The Adventures of Bennett J. Doty in the French Foreign Legion as Told by Himself.* Westholme, 2020.

Foreign Legion Info. Accessed March 15, 2024. https://foreignlegion.info/.

Langewiesche, William. "The Expendables." *Vanity Fair*, November 12, 2012.

Riding, Alan. "A Legionnaire, She Was Never Timid in Amour or War." *New York Times*, April 21, 2001.

Rockwell, Paul Ayers. *American Fighters in the Foreign Legion: 1914–1918*. Houghton Mifflin, 1930.

Sundberg, Mikaela. *A Sociology of the Total Organization: Atomistic Unity in the French Foreign Legion*. Routledge, 2016.

Tom, Steven T. *First to Fight: An American Volunteer in the French Foreign Legion and the Lafayette Escadrille in World War I*. Stackpole, 2019.

Travers, Susan. *Tomorrow to Be Brave*. Bantam, 2000.

Wren, P. C. *Beau Geste*. John Murray, 1924.

Crouching Dragons and Divine Wind: Japan's Special Attack Units

"Advice to Japanese Kamikaze Pilots During the Second World War." *The Guardian*, September 7, 2009.

Anderson, Michael. "Kamikazes: Understanding the Men Behind the Myths." *International Journal of Naval History*, December 30, 2020.

"Anti-Aircraft Action Summary: Suicide Attacks, April 1945." Accessed March 15, 2024. https://www.ibiblio.org/hyperwar/USN/rep/Kamikaze/AAA -Summary/AAA-Summary-2.html.

Axell, Albert, and Hideaki Kase. *Kamikaze: Japan's Suicide Gods*. Pearson, 2002.

Herder, Brian Lane. *East China Sea 1945: Climax of the Kamikaze*. Osprey, 2022.

Iredale, Will. *The Kamikaze Hunters: Fighting for the Pacific, 1945*. Pegasus, 2016.

Odachi, Kazuo. *Memoirs of a Kamikaze: A World War II Pilot's Inspiring Story of Survival, Honor, and Reconciliation*. 2020. Tuttle, 2020.

Ohnuki-Tierney, Emiko. *Kamikaze Diaries: Reflections of Japanese Student Soldiers*. University of Chicago Press, 2006.

Record, Jeffrey. *The War It Was Always Going to Lose: Why Japan Attacked America in 1941*. Potomac, 2011.

Wallace, Bruce. "They've Outlived the Stigma." *Los Angeles Times*, September 25, 2004.

An Offer You Can't Refuse: Mafia Made Men

DeStefano, Anthony M. *The Deadly Don: Vito Genovese, Mafia Boss*. Citadel, 2021.

Doherty, Thomas. *Hollywood's Censor: Joseph I. Breen and the Production Code Administration*. Columbia University Press, 2009.

Gasparini, Marco, and Brian Eskanazi, trans. *The Mafia: History and Legend*. Flammarion, 2011.

National Crime Syndicate. "How Do You Become a Made Man?" Accessed March 15, 2024. https://www.nationalcrimesyndicate.com/become-made-man/.

Lyman, Michael D., and Gary W. Potter. *Organized Crime*. 5th ed. Pearson Prentice Hall, 2011.

Nicaso, Antonio, and Marcel Danesi. *Made Men: Mafia Culture and the Powers of Symbols, Rituals, and Myth*. Rowman and Littlefield, 2013.

Robb, Brian J. *A Brief History of Gangsters*. Running, 2015.

Sullivan, Larry E. *Encyclopedia of Law Enforcement*. Sage, 2005.

Tano, Don. "The Sordid History of the Sicilian Mafia." We Are Palermo. Accessed March 15, 2024. https://wearepalermo.com/the-history-of-sicilian-mafia/.

Tyler, Adrienne. "Goodfellas: What Being a Made Man Means (And Why Henry Hill Can't Be One)." *ScreenRant*, July 27, 2020.

Great Tiger Sharks Swimming on Land: The Hawaiian Koa

Campbell, Sid. *Warrior Arts and Weapons of Ancient Hawai'i*. North Atlantic, 2006.

Gonschor, Lorenz. *A Power in the World: The Hawaiian Kingdom of Oceania*. University of Hawai'i Press, 2020.

Legends and Chronicles. "Hawaiian Warriors." Accessed March 15, 2024. https://www.legendsandchronicles.com/ancient-warriors/hawaiian-warriors/.

Hommon, Robert J. *The Ancient Hawaiian State: Origins of a Political Society*. Oxford University Press, 2013.

Kamakau, Samuel Manaiakalani. *Ruling Chiefs of Hawai'i*. Kamehameha, 1992.

KoaWood Ranch. "Koa Weapons of Ancient Hawai'i." Accessed March 15, 2024. https://koawoodranch.com/blogs/news/koa-weapons-of-choice.

Kona Historical Society. Accessed March 15, 2024. https://konahistorical.org/.

Paglinawan, Richard Kekumuikawaiokeola, Sally-Jo Keala-o-Ānuenue Bowman, and Tamara Leiokanoe Moan. *Lua: The Art of the Hawaiian Warrior*. Bishop Museum Press, 2006.

Parker, Brook Kapūkuniahi, and Joylynn Paman. *Our Ahupuaʻa: Sustainable Living in Traditional Hawaiian Culture*. Conservation Council for Hawaiʻi, 2010.

Wedlake, Lee. *The Kenpo Karate Compendium: The Forms and Sets of American Kenpo*. North Atlantic, 2015.

Fiercely and Faithfully: The Swiss Guard

Bauer, Conrad. *Protecting the Vatican: The Mysterious History of the Swiss Guard*. Maplewood, 2019.

Brockhaus, Hannah. "Six Things to Know About the Swiss Guard and Its Swearing-In Ceremony." Catholic News Agency, May 6, 2023.

Browne, Christian. *The Pearl of Great Price: Pius VI and the Sack of Rome*. Arouca, 2019.

Janin, Hunt, and Ursula Carlson. *Mercenaries in Medieval and Renaissance Europe*. McFarland, 2013.

Murphy, Francois, and Philip Pullella. "Vatican Swiss Guard's New Barracks Designed to Include Women, Newspaper Says." Reuters, September 12, 2021.

Royal, Robert. *The Pope's Army: 500 Years of the Papal Swiss Guard*. The Crossroad/Herder & Herder, 2006.

Shaw, Christine. *Julius II, The Warrior Pope*. Blackwell, 1993.

Stringer, Kevin D. *Swiss-Made Heroes: Profiles in Military Leadership*. Hellgate, 2012.

Villarrubia, Eleonore. "Five Hundred Years of Loyalty: The Gallantry of the Pope's Swiss Guard." Catholicism.org, December 29, 2008. https://catholicism.org/five-hundred-years-of-loyalty-the-gallantry-of-the-popes-swiss-guard.html.

Zubova, Xenia. "Welcome to the Swiss Guard: The World's Smallest Army." Forces News. Accessed March 10, 2024. https://www.forces.net/military-life/fun/welcome-swiss-guard-worlds-smallest-army.

Doctor, Doctor: The White Coat Ceremony and Beyond

American Medical Association. "The Meaning Behind Your White Coat." Accessed March 15, 2024. https://www.ama-assn.org/medical-students/medical-school-life/meaning-behind-your-white-coat.

Hochberg, Mark S. "The Doctor's White Coat: An Historical Perspective." *AMA Journal of Ethics* (April 2007). https://journalofethics.ama-assn.org/article/doctors-white-coat-historical-perspective/2007-04.

Huber, S. J. "The White Coat Ceremony: A Contemporary Medical Ritual." *Journal of Medical Ethics* 29, no. 6 (December 2003): 364–366.

Humphrey, Holly J. "White Coat Ceremonies: Then and Now." Josiah Macy Jr. Foundation. Accessed March 15, 2024. https://macyfoundation.org/news-and-commentary/white-coat-ceremonies-then-and-now.

Marino, Jacqueline. *White Coats: Three Journeys Through an American Medical School*. Kent State University Press, 2012.

Ross University School of Medicine. "White Coat Ceremony: First Steps on the Path to MD." Accessed March 15, 2024. https://medical.rossu.edu/about/blog/white-coat-ceremony-history-importance.

University of Arizona College of Medicine, Phoenix. "The Significance of the White Coat." Accessed March 15, 2024. https://phoenixmed.arizona.edu/about/news/significance-white-coat.

Uscher, Jen. "Celebrating 20 Years of the White Coat Ceremony." *Columbia Medicine Magazine*, Fall 2013.

Veatch, R. "White Coat Ceremonies: A Second Opinion." *Journal of Medical Ethics* 28, no. 1 (February 2002): 5–6.

Warren, Peter M. "For New Medical Students, White Coats Are a Warm-Up." *Los Angeles Times*, October 18, 1999.

The Poor Widow's Sons: American Freemasonry

Anderson, James A. M., and Benjamin Franklin. *The Constitutions of the Free-Masons (1734)*. Edited by Paul Royster. UNL Libraries. Accessed March 15, 2024. https://digitalcommons.unl.edu/cgi/viewcontent.cgi?article=1028&context=libraryscience.

Dumenil, Lynn. *Freemasonry and American Culture, 1880–1930*. Princeton University Press, 2014.

Harland-Jacobs, Jessica, Jan C. Jensen, and Elizabeth Mancke. *The Fraternal Atlantic, 1770–1930: Race, Revolution, and Transnationalism in the Worlds of Freemasonry*. Routledge, Taylor and Francis Group, 2021.

Kinney, Jay. *The Masonic Myth: Unlocking the Truth About the Symbols, the Secret Rites, and the History of Freemasonry*. HarperOne, 2009.

Lang, Ossian. *History of Freemasonry in the State of New York*. Hamilton Printing, 1922.

Lomas, Robert. *The Secret Science of Masonic Initiation*. Weiser, 2010.

Mackey, Albert Gallatin. *The Symbolism of Freemasonry*. Andrews UK, 2010.

McCarthy, Charles. *The Antimasonic Party: A Study of Political Anti-Masonry in the United States, 1827–1840*. Forgotten Books, 2018.

Morgan, William. *Exposition of Freemasonry*. Kessinger, 2003.

Vaughn, William Preston. *The Anti-Masonic Party in the United States: 1826–1843*. University Press of Kentucky, 2009.

INDEX

ABOUT THE AUTHORS

JAMES R. MCNEAL GRADUATED FROM the United States Naval Academy in 1986. After six years on active duty in the Supply Corps, he transitioned into the reserve component, retiring as a rear admiral in 2017. Rear Admiral McNeal is an accomplished entrepreneur and business executive with deep experience in staffing solutions, training, consulting, and coaching. He currently serves as an adjunct leadership professor at the Naval Academy, as well as the defensive and special teams coordinator for Navy's sprint football team. He is the coauthor (with Scott Tomasheski) of *The Herndon Climb: A History of the United States Naval Academy's Greatest Tradition* and (with J. Eric Smith) of *Side by Side in Eternity: The Lives Behind Adjacent American Military Graves.*

J. ERIC SMITH WAS REAR Admiral McNeal's classmate at the U.S. Naval Academy and at the Naval Supply Corps School. Following eleven years serving within the Naval Reactors headquarters directorate, Mr. Smith transitioned to the nonprofit sector, where he held four CEO positions and maintained a long-standing freelance writing career, earning hundreds of bylines in scores of print outlets. Mr. Smith was a digital-space pioneer, having launched a still-active personal website in 1995; over 1,200 archival articles remain available at jericsmith.com. In addition to *Side by Side in Eternity* (with Rear Admiral McNeal), he is the author of *Ubulembu and Other Stories*, winner of the 2023 Unleash Creatives Book Prize, and the novel *Eponymous.*